The Origin and Formation
of the Gospel

The Origin and Formation of the Gospel

Yoseop Ra

WIPF & STOCK · Eugene, Oregon

THE ORIGIN AND FORMATION OF THE GOSPEL

Copyright © 2015 Yoseop Ra. All rights reserved. Except for brief quotations in critical publications or reviews, no part of this book may be reproduced in any manner without prior written permission from the publisher. Write: Permissions. Wipf and Stock Publishers, 199 W. 8th Ave., Suite 3, Eugene, OR 97401.

Wipf and Stock
An Imprint of Wipf and Stock Publishers
199 W. 8th Ave., Suite 3
Eugene, OR 97401

www.wipfandstock.com

ISBN 13: 978-1-4982-0310-4

Manufactured in the U.S.A.   02/10/2015

Unless otherwise noted, Scripture quotations contained herein are from the HOLY BIBLE, NEW INTERNATIONAL VERSION® Copyright © 1973, 1978, 1984 by International Bible Society. Used by permission of Zondervan Publishing House. All rights reserved. The "NIV" and "New International Version" trademarks are registered in the United States Patent and Trademark Office by International Bible Society. Use of either trademark requires the permission of International Bible Society.

Dedicated to
Dr. Daniel SungYul Kim, DDS, and Mrs. Hooja Chon Kim
with thanks in Jesus Christ.

Contents

Preface | ix
Abbreviations | xi

Part I: Prologue
1 The Biblical Theological Approach | 3
2 The Formation of Christian Tradition | 8
3 The Concept of Gospel | 32

Part II: The First Gospel and its Development
4 According to the Scriptures | 43
5 The Death of Christ | 53
6 The Burial of Christ | 68
7 The Resurrection of Christ | 76
8 The Epiphany of Christ | 88

Part III: The Gospel of Q and its Development
9 The Edenic Kingdom of God | 99
10 The Ascension of Jesus | 116
11 The Second Advent of Jesus | 125

Part IV: The Pauline Gospel and its Development
12 The Adam Christology | 139
13 The Birth of Jesus Christ | 162
14 The Theology of Redemption | 179
15 The Lord's Supper | 192

Epilogue | 201
Bibliography | 205
Ancient Document Index | 211

Preface

MANY BIBLICAL SCHOLARS HAVE studied the origin and formation of the gospel, which generally refers to the instruction regarding Jesus Christ. Thus, I was doubtful whether there was a need to write another book about it. However, I reached the conclusion that there are still many things that can be discovered and written. Judging from a new perspective, there are still many instructions to be uncovered about the gospel.

I have approached the gospel of Christianity from a chronological point of view. In other words, I will trace how the traditions developed from Jesus to the writers of the Christian Scripture. First of all, I have paid attention to Q, which is presumed to have been written about Jesus and completed by the twelve apostles or under their supervision. At the same time, I looked at some contemporaneous Jews who lived in the Diaspora and interpreted the Christ prophesied about in the Bible. They left teachings about the death, burial, resurrection, and epiphany of Christ. Having received revelation about the Son of God at Damascus, Paul later understood this revelation to be of the Christ, whom he learned about from the Diaspora Jews. He went to Jerusalem and met Cephas Peter, then learned about Jesus on the basis of Q. During that meeting, Paul came to the conclusion that Jesus was also to be identified with the Christ, the Son of God. He then began proclaiming the gospel in the Gentile regions, and many Gentiles responded to his gospel. Later, however, after his meeting with the apostles in Jerusalem and the conflict at Antioch, Cephas and the other apostles of the Jerusalem Church turned their backs on Paul. When Paul's gospel and authority were seriously challenged by the Gentile Christians sponsored by the Jerusalem apostles, he began to assert his own gospel, which put forth the cross of Jesus Christ as the means of redemption and salvation. Along with this, Paul taught many things about him that were further developed through the books of Gospel. The development of the core gospel believed by Christians today is covered in this book.

I will show that the Christian gospel is composed of both historical fact and theological interpretations. These two elements are interwoven with regard to various subjects that constitute the content of the gospel: the hermeneutic principle of "according to the Scriptures," the birth, death, burial, resurrection, epiphany, ascension, and second coming of Jesus Christ, the Edenic kingdom of God, the Adam Christology, the theology of redemption, and the Lord's Supper. Each subject will be studied from a chronological perspective; in other words, how each subject was formed and developed through Q, the earliest Christian gospel, the Pauline epistles, the Gospels, or other Christian documents. These studies will contribute to the argument that Paul's foundational work on behalf of Christianity was in response to the challenge from Gentile Christians sponsored by the Jerusalem apostles after the conflict with Cephas Peter at Antioch. If my study could present a new interpretation to the academic world of the Christian Scripture, I would be pleased. For this reason, I will avoid mentioning scholars and refer to them through footnotes only when necessary.

I have been helped by many people in publishing this book. First, I would like to thank Dr. Dennis R. MacDonald at Iliff School of Theology (now at Claremont School of Theology), from whom I received tremendous academic support. While studying there, he provided generous critiques and encouragement. I would also like to thank Dr. F. Rachel Joy Magdalene and Rev. Aaron Seney, who helped me improve my writing in English. Above all, I would like to show my gratitude to Dr. Daniel SungYul Kim, DDS, and Mrs. Hooja Chon Kim, who have encouraged me and helped this book be published in English, and to whom it is dedicated. Finally, I would like to thank Mr. Jim Tedrick, Managing Editor of Wipf and Stock Publishers, for allowing my manuscript published.

Yoseop Ra

August 15, 2014

Abbreviations

AB	Anchor Bible
BETL	Bibliotheca Ephemeridum Theologicarum Lovaniensium
CBQ	*Catholic Biblical Quarterly*
EKK	Evangelische–Katholischer Kommentar zum Neuen Testamentum
ETL	*Ephemerides Theologicae Lovanienses*
HTKNT	Herders Theologischer Kommentar zum Neuen Testamentum
HTR	*Harvard Theological Review*
KNTS	*Korean New Testament Studies*
NovT	*Novum Testamentum*
NTS	*New Testament Studies*
RGG	Religion in Geschichte und Gegenwart
SBLSP	*Society of Biblical Literature Seminar Paper*
SNTSMS	Society for New Testament Studies. Monograph Series
VoxEv	*Vox Evangelica*
WBC	Word Biblical Commentary

PART I

Prologue

THE FOLLOWING PROLOGUE WILL help readers understand the context of this book. The appropriateness of the biblical theological approach, the sequence of the writings of the Christian Scripture, and the process of how the concept of gospel has changed over time will be studied in the prologue. This will help the reader gain a broader perspective on the common doctrinal positions they have learned to date and also to notice the historical facts as well as the theological interpretations of those facts. Through this process, readers will learn that the Christians of the first century CE lived vividly, helping them to form and develop their faith in Jesus Christ from different perspectives. As a result, this prologue will show that the content of the gospel went through a process of change and development over a short period of time. With this, the prologue will help build a foundation upon which readers can notice and understand the differences in the Christian Scripture.

1

The Biblical Theological Approach

EVERYONE HAS CERTAIN PRESUPPOSITIONS about their life and surroundings. For those who read and study the Bible, this is no less the case. Many such presuppositions about the Bible, however, were developed and taught for doctrinal purposes over a long period of time. These doctrinal positions are created so as to connect the various writings of the Bible thematically. As a result, content that goes against the prescribed doctrines is often overlooked or misinterpreted. In response to this doctrinal approach to understanding the Bible, biblical theology began to come into favor approximately 250 years ago. The intent of biblical theology is to look at each individual book and author so as to understand the intent without having to compare it to the larger canon. In this sense, biblical theology takes primarily a historical and literary approach. This is the process of uncovering what God has revealed to each writer through the Spirit and then tracing this special revelation given to each person in their different situations. Using the biblical theological approach, it becomes clear that people have confessed their faith by adding new interpretations to what had been passed down through tradition. Each writer left his or her own theological interpretation about Jesus Christ, and this collection is the Christian Scripture.

A. The Nature of Faith

A common presupposition that many Christians share is that something can be believed only if it can be proven historically true. They can believe what is written in the Bible because it is historically true. Conversely, they refuse to accept something that is not historically true. Of course, this does not mean that the historicity of the events written in the Bible should be denied. As it turns out, however, many Christians believe a lot of things written in the Bible that are not necessarily historical. Faith involves not only believing historical facts but also the theological interpretations of certain events and words. This is the nature of the faith the Bible teaches.

The Christian Scripture itself tells people about the nature of faith. For example, 1 Cor 15:3 conveys a historical fact as well as a theological interpretation. In this verse, the death of Christ is presented as a historical fact. However, saying that Christ died "for our sins according to the Scriptures" is a subjective theological interpretation. While there are those who accept this, many do not. The former are Christians, and the latter are not. Christians are those who believe the historical fact "Christ died" as well as the theological interpretation "for our sins according to the Scriptures." In this way, faith is composed of two elements: one is the historical fact, and the other is its theological interpretations. Therefore, Christians are able to believe something more than the historical facts alone.

The Hebrew Bible shows the nature of faith as well. A fairly typical case is the account of Abram's emigration (Gen 12:1–5). Many people are inspired by the thought that Abram immediately obeyed God when he was told to go to the land to be shown to him. In order to have a proper understanding, however, people must read between the lines. In fact, the person who wished to go to Canaan was Abram's father, Terah, but he died when he came to Haran after leaving his hometown, Ur (Gen 11:31–32). At that time, Abram had to make a decision among three possible choices: he could have gone back to his hometown, settled at Haran, or gone to Canaan as his father had wished. Abram decided to go to Canaan according to the will of his father, Terah. He would have told this story to his children later, and they would have passed the story on to their descendants. This is a historical fact. However, after a long period of time, that information was left out of the historical fact as it went through the process of theological interpretation. The author of Genesis wrote that Abram left for Canaan because the Lord had told him to go from his country and take his people to the land the Lord would show him, had given him a promise about his children, and had told him that he would be a blessing. Such writing is the result of the author's theological interpretation about the historical event that happened to Abram long ago. Today's Christians believe that such content is the Word of God. As mentioned above, faith involves believing theological interpretations as well as historical facts. In this sense, Christians necessarily believe in things that extend beyond the realm of provable historical fact.

Faith is a two-sided coin, with historical fact on one side and theological interpretation on the other. As people get to know the essence of faith, they come to accept the theological interpretation as well as the historical fact. If a person only accepts one side, that person is not a true Christian. However, embracing and obeying both sides is not easy. This is only possible when people are guided by the Spirit of God. Therefore, Christians are those who reflect themselves in Jesus Christ as the Spirit guides them and continually renews their theological interpretations.

B. The Formation of Christian Writings

Another common presupposition that many Christians have regards the sequence in which the Christian writings were composed. It is often presumed that the Christian Scripture was written in the order it is listed today—that the four Gospels, including Matthew, were written first, then the Pauline epistles were written later. They think that Paul learned about Jesus Christ from the four Gospels and wrote his letters according to their teachings. It is more probable, however, that the Pauline epistles were written before the four Gospels and that there was an early written document used as the source for the Synoptic Gospels.

Paul is understood to have left the most writings in the Christian Scripture. Although tradition holds that he is the author of thirteen letters, critical scholars conclude that only seven of them are from Paul's own hand. These include Romans, 1 Corinthians, 2 Corinthians, Galatians, 1 Thessalonians, Philippians, and Philemon, which were written between the late forties and the early sixties CE. The rest include Ephesians, Colossians, 2 Thessalonians, 1 Timothy, 2 Timothy, and Titus, which are believed to have been written by the disciples of Paul between the eighties and the first decade of the second century CE.[1] This is due to the fact that the Deuteropauline epistles show different styles of writing, theology, historical context, and other factors compared to those presumed to be genuine. In addition, while Paul's genuine epistles reflect the situation of the time of writing, the Deuteropauline epistles are more obsessed with doctrine and ecclesiastical issues. Therefore, when looking at the letters according to the chronological order, we can see how Paul and his disciples' perspective of the gospel changed and developed.

Four Gospels describe the life of Jesus Christ in the Christian Scripture. It is believed that Mark was written first in Galilee around 70 CE, and then Matthew in Galilee between 85 and 95. John is presumed to be an

---

1. Brown, *Introduction*, 5–7, 585–680.

edited work written in the border area of Syria around 90 to 110. Finally, Luke is believed to have been written at Ephesus in Asia Minor between 100 and 120, and it was followed shortly by Acts, written by the same author. From a chronological perspective, it is not difficult to accept that the Gospel authors acknowledged Paul's genuine epistles and reflected his theology either positively or negatively in their Gospels. Written in different times and places, the four Gospels show their own understanding and theology of Jesus Christ. Acts was written specifically to resolve the conflict between the Jerusalem Church of Cephas Peter and the Gentile churches of Paul to describe their unity. This shows that there were different perspectives on Jesus Christ in the late first century CE.

The rest of the documents in the Christian Scripture must be taken under consideration as well. It is probable that Hebrews, 1 Peter, 2 Peter, and Revelation were written for those who were under the persecution of the Roman Empire in the Gentile area around 95 CE. They aimed to encourage contemporary Christians to keep their faith in Christ. In addition, the Johannine epistles are likely to have been sent to the local churches by the leader between 100 and 110. The epistles therefore reflect the relationships between them, and theologically they follow the Gospel of John. Finally, James and Jude show different theological tracks.

There is also a piece of writing that was not included in the Christian Scripture. This document is called "Q" and includes the first writings about Jesus. Its final form was probably redacted. Unfortunately, Q is not left to us in the form of a written document; therefore, biblical scholars have attempted to extract its final form on the basis of the common texts between Matthew and Luke that do not appear in Mark. Its scope and content are still under investigation by scholars. Nevertheless, it is difficult to deny its existence at one time in document form.[2] Although Paul knew about Q, he only reflected a small part of it in his writings.[3] In addition, as a number of biblical scholars recently concluded, Mark wrote about Jesus Christ while reflecting Q.[4] Interestingly, Mark also reflected the Pauline theology, especially the theology of redemption. Later, Matthew and Luke wrote their theology based on Q and Mark, reflecting Paul's theology positively or negatively. Therefore, examining the sequence in which the Scripture was written can help clarify the origin, formation, and development of the gospel in the Christian tradition during the first century CE.

---

2. Ibid., 116–22; and Crossan, *Cross That Spoke*, xii. "Q" originated from the German word *Quelle*, which means "source."

3. Allison, *Jesus Tradition*, 54–60, 111–19.

4. Cf. Lambrecht, "John the Baptist," 357–84; and Fledderman, "Mark's Use of Q," 17–33. Against this opinion, see Neirynck, "First Synoptic Pericope," 41–74.

C. Conclusion

The biblical theological approach appeared in order to overcome presuppositions created for doctrinal purposes and to understand the Hebrew Bible and the Christian Scripture in a more fundamental sense. This is the way of interpreting them according to the situation of the time of writing and revealing their original meaning. As people follow the chronological order in which the books were written, they will be able to see how gospel has formed, changed, and developed. The fact that each writer succeeded previous traditions and added his or her own sources and interpretations to write a new document will eventually be revealed. Each author conveys his or her own theological interpretation about Jesus Christ through the revelation the Spirit of God sent individually.

2

The Formation of Christian Tradition

THE GOSPEL RELATED TO Jesus Christ began with some very simple traditions. In fact, there is not much tangible historical information left about Jesus. What remains are the theological interpretations that have been added to his words and actions. Later, these were developed into the Gospels. In order to know the origin and formation of the gospel, people must take a chronological approach. This approach begins with Q and then the first gospel contemporaneous Jewish Christians conveyed to Paul. Next, it is necessary to see the genuine Pauline epistles, Mark, Matthew, John, and Luke, which were written afterwards. In addition, Hebrews, 1 Peter, Revelation, the Deuteropauline epistles, and the Johannine epistles should also be considered. Using this chronological approach to the writings, people can see that the content of the gospel has formed, changed, and developed along with its theological interpretations in order to solve the problems that resulted from contemporary circumstances.

A. Q, the First Writing about Jesus

Q is supposed to be the first document that recorded the words and actions of Jesus and John the Baptist. Q is believed to have been written much earlier than it is commonly known; its final form was probably completed by the twelve apostles or under their supervision. It must be admitted, however, that Q is a hypothetical document and does not exist today as a separate text. Nevertheless, Q is an indispensable document for studying the development of the gospel.

Q is a well-structured document. It begins with the appearance of John in the wilderness and ends with the apocalyptic promises of Jesus. To be more specific, Q includes the ministry of John and Jesus at the beginning, then the disciples of Jesus and their mission in the middle, and the Son of Man and the kingdom of God at the end. To my judgment, there is reason to accept the Q hypothesis because of its clear literary structure and prominent logic.[1] Scholars have studied the redaction of Q in various ways,[2] but I propose Q was redacted four times as follows.[3] The superscript represents the layer of redaction to which the designated text belongs.

I. John and Jesus

A. The Ministry of John

Q^1 3:2–4 (Luke 3:2–4 / Matt 3:1–3, 5–6)
Q^1 3:7–8a (Luke 3:7–8a / Matt 3:7–9a)
Q^4 3:8bc (Luke 3:8bc / Matt 3:9bc)
Q^1 3:9 (Luke 3:9 / Matt 3:10)
Q^3 3:16–17 (Luke 3:16–17 / Matt 3:11–12)
Q^3 3:21–22 (Luke 3:21–22 / Matt 3:16–17)

B. The Ministry of Jesus

1. The Temptation

   Q^4 4:1–13 (Luke 4:1–13 / Matt 4:1–11)

2. The Twelve Apostles

   Q^4 6:12–16 (Luke 6:12–16 / Matt 5:1a; 10:2–4)

3. The Sermon

   Q^4 6:20a (Luke 6:20a / Matt 5:1b)
   Q^1 6:20b (Luke 6:20b / Matt 5:2b–3)
   Q^2 6:21 (Luke 6:21 / Matt 5:4, 6)
   Q^3 6:22–23b (Luke 6:22–23b / Matt 5:11–12b)
   Q^4 6:23c (Luke 6:23c / Matt 5:12c)
   Q^1 6:27–38 (Luke 6:27–38 / Matt 5:44, 39–40, 42, 7:12; 5:45–48; 7:1–2)

---

1. Cf. Allison, *Jesus Tradition*, 8–40; and Arnal, *Jesus*, 168.
2. For the opinion of single redaction of Q, see Lührmann, *Redaktion*. For the study of double redaction, see Schultz, *Q*. For the study of triple redaction, see Kloppenborg, *Formation*; Sato, *Q*; Jacobson, *First Gospel*; and Allison, *Jesus Tradition*. For the history of Q research, see Robinson et al., *Critical Edition*, xix–lxxi.
3. Ra, *Q*, 43–314.

Q^3 6:39–42 (Luke 6:39–42 / Matt 15:14; 10:24–25; 7:3–5)
Q^3 6:43–45 (Luke 6:43–45 / Matt 7:16, 18; 12:33–35)
Q^3 6:46–49 (Luke 6:46–49 / Matt 7:21, 24–27)

4. The Activity

Q^3 7:1–10 (Luke 7:1–10 / Matt 8:5–10, 13)
Q^3 17:6 (Luke 17:6 / Matt 17:20)

C. Jesus and John

Q^3 7:18–27 (Luke 7:18–27 / Matt 11:2–10)
Q^4 7:28 (Luke 7:28 / Matt 11:11)
Q^4 16:16 (Luke 16:16 / Matt 11:12–13)
Q^1 7:29–30 (Luke 7:29–30 / Matt 21:31–32)
Q^3 7:31–34 (Luke 7:31–34 / Matt 11:16–19a)
Q^4 7:35 (Luke 7:35 / Matt 11:19c)

II. Jesus' Disciples and Their Missions

A. The Disciples of Jesus

Q^2 9:57–58 (Luke 9:57–58 / Matt 8:19–20)
Q^4 9:59–60 (Luke 9:59–60 / Matt 8:21–22)

B. The Mission of Disciples

Q^3 10:2 (Luke 10:2 / Matt 9:37–38)
Q^4 10:3 (Luke 10:3 / Matt 10:16a)
Q^2 10:4–12 (Luke 10:4–12 / Matt 10:7–15 [11:24])
Q^3 10:13–16 (Luke 10:13–16 / Matt 11:21–23; 10:40)

C. The Lord's Prayer and Its Application

1. Jesus the Mediator

   Q^3 10:21–24 (Luke 10:21–24 / Matt 11:25–27; 13:16–17)

2. The Lord's Prayer

   Q^2 11:2–4 (Luke 11:2–4 / Matt 6:9–13)

3. The Confidence in the Prayer

   Q^2 11:9–10 (Luke 11:9–10 / Matt 7:7–8)

4. The Faith in the Father: The Vocative of God

   Q^2 11:11–13 (Luke 11:11–13 / Matt 7:9–11)

5. The Kingdom of God: The Second Petition

   Q^2 11:14–15, 17–20 (Luke 11:14–15, 17–20 / Matt 12:22–28)
   Q^3 11:21–23 (Luke 11:21–23 / Matt 12:29–30)
   Q^4 11:24–26 (Luke 11:24–26 / Matt 12:43–45)

6. The Temptation: The Fifth Petition

Q^2 11:16, 29–30 (Luke 11:16, 29–30 / Matt 12:38–40)
Q^3 11:31–32 (Luke 11:31–32 / Matt 12:41–42)
Q^3 11:33–35 (Luke 11:33–35 / Matt 5:15; 6:22–23)
Q^3 11:39–46 (Luke 11:39–46 / Matt 23:25–26, 23, 6–7, 27–28, 4)
Q^4 11:47–51 (Luke 11:47–51 / Matt 23:29–31, 34–36)
Q^3 11:52 (Luke 11:52 / Matt 23:13)
Q^3 12:2–3 (Luke 12:2–3 / Matt 10:26–27)

7. The Fear of the Lord: The First Petition

Q^4 12:4–5 (Luke 12:4–5 / Matt 10:28)
Q^2 12:6–7 (Luke 12:6–7 / Matt 10:29–31)
Q^3 12:8–9 (Luke 12:8–9 / Matt 10:32–33)
Q^4 12:10–12 (Luke 12:10–12 / Matt 12:32; 10:18–19)

8. The Daily Bread: The Third Petition

Q^2 12:22–31 (Luke 12:22–31 / Matt 6:25–33)
Q^3 12:33–34 (Luke 12:33–34 / Matt 6:19–21)
Q^4 16:13 (Luke 16:13 / Matt 6:24)

9. The Forgiveness: The Forth Petition

Q^2 17:3–4 (Luke 17:3–4 / Matt 18:15, 21–22)

D. The Discipleship

Q^4 14:26–27 (Luke 14:26–27 / Matt 10:37–38)
Q^4 17:33 (Luke 17:33 / Matt 10:39)

III. The Son of Man and the Kingdom of God

A. Preparation for the Son of Man

Q^3 12:39–40 (Luke 12:39–40 / Matt 24:43–44)
Q^3 12:42–46 (Luke 12:42–46 / Matt 24:45–51)
Q^4 12:49, 51–53 (Luke 12:49, 51–53 / Matt 10:34–36)
Q^4 12:54–56 (Luke 12:54–56 / Matt 16:2–3)
Q^4 12:58–59 (Luke 12:58–59 / Matt 5:25–26)

B. The Kingdom of God

Q^3 13:18–21 (Luke 13:18–21 / Matt 13:31–33)
Q^3 13:24–27 (Luke 13:24–27 / Matt 7:13–14; 25:10–12; 7:22–23)
Q^4 13:28–30 (Luke 13:28–30 / Matt 8:11–12; 20:16)
Q^4 13:34–35 (Luke 13:34–35 / Matt 23:37–39)
Q^4 14:8, 11 (Luke 14:8, 11 / Matt 23:6, 12)
Q^4 14:16–24 (Luke 14:16–24 / Matt 22:1–10)
Q^4 14:34–35 (Luke 14:34–35 / Matt 5:13)
Q^4 15:4–7 (Luke 15:4–7 / Matt 18:12–14)

Q⁴ 17:1–2 (Luke 17:1–2 / Matt 18:6–7)

C. Coming of the Son of Man

Q³ 17:23–24 (Luke 17:23–24 / Matt 24:26–27)
Q³ 17:26–27, 30 (Luke 17:26–27, 30 / Matt 24:37–39)
Q³ 17:34–35 (Luke 17:34–35 / Matt 24:40–41)
Q⁴ 17:37c (Luke 17:37c / Matt 24:28)
Q⁴ 19:12–26 (Luke 19:12–26 / Matt 25:14–30)
Q⁴ 22:30 (Luke 22:30 / Matt 19:28)

IV. Other Related Verses[4]

Q⁴ 14:5 (Luke 14:5 / Matt 12:11–12)
Q⁴ 16:17–18 (Luke 16:17–18 / Matt 5:18, 32)

As the above shows, Q is organized according to theme. Its literary structure shows that it was possibly written by a well-trained author or authors. Moreover, it was written according to a specific purpose through editing.

Although it seems that Q was composed through a highly complex process, its composition was accomplished quite simply through a series of supplements. The first redactor listed the sources he collected, which became the main texts of the first redaction regarding the ministry of John and Jesus. The second redactor interpolated a couple of sentences into the main texts of the first redaction and attached his or her own sources—that is, the main texts of the second redaction regarding the disciples of Jesus and their mission (the manual for missionary journey, the Lord's Prayer, and its applications). Thereafter, it was followed by the third redactor, who inserted his or her own sources into some parts of the main texts of the previous two redactions and attached the main texts of the third redaction regarding the Son of Man and the kingdom of God. Finally, the fourth redactor added parts he or she wanted to convey in between the texts of previous three redactions. The following is a diagram to help understand the process of redaction.

1. The First Redaction ①①①
2. The Second Redaction ①②①① ②②②
3. The Third Redaction ①②③①③① ②③②③② ③③③
4. The Fourth Redaction ①②③④①③④① ②③④②③②④ ③③④③④

---

4. Other Related Verses deals with Q 14:5 and 16:17–18 that are fragmentary. It is difficult to restore their original location in Q because they did not leave any clue. Considering that Q 16:17–18 is about the commandments of the Law, it is possible that it follows Q 16:16 in terms of the same theme of "the commandment." However, they do not fit well in terms of context.

The redactors of Q seemed to follow the Jewish tradition of supplementary editions as used for the Pentateuch and the book of Isaiah.[5]

People must recognize some important factors about Q. First, this document does not introduce Jesus as savior, as it does not use the title "Christ." Instead, Q introduces him as a Jewish wisdom teacher and prophet. Such content does not describe main Christian doctrines such as redemption through the death of Jesus Christ. For this reason, it is difficult to regard Q as a Christian Gospel.

Second, Q is believed to have been finally written by the twelve apostles or under their supervision. The disciples of Jesus formed at the rural area of Galilee around the late twenties or early thirties CE; later, they collected his words and activities, probably after he had died. Then they moved to Capernaum, where they probably completed the third redaction of Q. Finally, they entered Jerusalem and built a small community. They selected twelve leaders and made them the apostles at the final stage of redaction (Q^4 6:13–16; 1 Cor 15:5).[6] Q seems to have been finally edited around 41 CE while resisting the Roman Emperor Gaius Caligula, who attempted to establish his statue in the temple (Q^4 4:1–13).[7]

Third, the contents of Q are very different from what today's Christians think and believe. Above all, it does not say a single word about the birth, suffering, death, resurrection, or epiphany of Jesus.[8] In this sense, Q cannot be used as historical evidence for the resurrection and epiphany. In addition, having faced the event of the Roman Emperor Gaius Caligula, the fourth redactor emphasized observing the Law in spite of persecution and martyrdom (Q^4 4:1–13; 14:5; 16:16–18). The people who made this document seem to have kept their faith in God based on the teaching of Jesus within Judaism. The twelve apostles seemed to have emphasized the observance of the Law in the forties and fifties CE.

---

5. Critical scholars conclude that the Pentateuch is composed of the so-called J, E, D, and P documents. The documentary hypothesis of the Pentateuch was put forth by Karl Heinrich Graf and Julius Welhausen. The book of Isaiah underwent triple redaction among chs. 1–39, 40–55, and 56–66, as argued by Johann Gottfried Eichhorn. Psalms and Proverbs also went through a process of supplementary editions, as shown by the fact that they are composed of five parts.

6. It is noteworthy that the twelve apostles appear for the first time in the fourth redaction of Q. It seems that they represented the descendants of Abraham mentioned in Q^4 3:8bc and are elected as the leaders of Q community at the final redaction. It is, therefore, not certain that the historical Jesus had twelve disciples during his earthly ministry.

7. Theissen, *Gospels in Context*, 205–209. Cf. Arnal, *Jesus*, 167, 172; and Allison, *Jesus Tradition*, 49–54, 60.

8. Cf. Mack, *Lost Gospel*, 4–5; and Kloppenborg, *Q*, 75–84.

Fourth, Q is the first stepping-stone to understanding Jesus. Q helps readers take a closer approach than any other document at the historical Jesus. However, this does not mean that every single teaching and action of Jesus written in this document actually happened. It seems that the third and fourth redactors imposed theological meanings to Jesus. For example, in the third redaction, Jesus is identified as the Son of God using the background of Psalms 2:7 and Isaiah 42:1 (Q^3 3:21–22; 10:21–22) and the eschatological Son of Man using the background of Daniel 7:13–14 (Q^3 12:8–9, 40; 17:24, 30). These steps also appear on the final redaction; for example, Jesus is typologically compared with Moses (Q^4 4:1–13; 6:13–16; 22:30, etc.). It can be said that the texts of the third and fourth redactions reflect their contemporary social situation and reveal their theological interpretation applied to Jesus. It seems that the addition of theological interpretations about Jesus started in the late thirties CE. To my judgment, texts that belong to the first and second redactions convey the words and actions of the historical Jesus, while texts of the third and fourth redactions include theological interpretations of the redactors about Jesus.[9] Thus, Q is composed of both historical facts and theological interpretations about Jesus.

B. The First Christian Gospel

Apart from the twelve apostles, there was another group of people who taught about Christ. They are probably the first group of people who formed faith in Christ and handed down the gospel about him to Paul. The Christ of this gospel appears to be different from the Jesus in Q.

The gospel the first group of people conveyed to Paul is reflected in his letter to the Corinthians (1 Cor 15:1–8). Paul clearly says that he communicated what had been passed on to him from them. His statement gives his readers two kinds of information. First, there were those who formed faith in Christ before Paul. In this respect, they could be called "the First Christians." However, not much is known about their identities. Second, the tradition they conveyed to Paul is about the death, burial, resurrection, and epiphany of Christ. In this respect, this should be considered "the first Christian gospel."

The identities of the First Christians are difficult to uncover, though Paul did leave some clues. They seem to be members of the Greek-speaking Jewish-Christian community because the tradition reflected in 1 Cor 15:3–5

---

9. Compare my analysis with Allison's regarding the reliable sources for the historical Jesus in Q: Cf. Allison, *Jesus Tradition*, 60–62.

echoes the Septuagint (LXX).[10] In this respect, they probably lived in the Diaspora—that is, Gentile areas outside of Israel. It is also probable that Paul met them at Damascus, as it is reflected in the expression that he returned to Damascus after he had received the revelation about the Son of God and had gone to Arabia (Gal 1:15–17).[11] In other words, having received the revelation, Paul did not consult his former associates; rather, he went into Arabia and then returned to Damascus. The location of the Arabia Paul mentioned is still under dispute among biblical scholars, and there is still no consensus; however, I believe it should be identified with the place related with the Law because Paul himself connected it with the Mount Sinai from a negative perspective (4:25). Therefore, it seems that Paul tried to explain the Son of God in the context of the Law; however, it only resulted in an unsatisfactory conclusion. Having returned from Arabia, Paul probably met the First Christians at Damascus. At this time they gave Paul the tradition about Christ, and he identified Christ with the Son of God he had received through revelation. Later, when the governors under King Aretas tried to arrest Paul at Damascus, it most likely was the First Christians who helped him escape through the window in the wall (2 Cor 11:32–33; Acts 9:23–25). This can be induced from Paul's autobiographical descriptions. The First Christians inherited many of the Pharisaic traditions. This is detected through the fact that they had faith in resurrection. In this respect, Paul could have fellowship with them because he was also a Pharisee. In addition, they had their own way of training in interpreting the Scriptures of the Bible. The First Christians show these characteristics as Pharisees using the hermeneutic principle of "according to the Scriptures." They created new faith in Christ by interpreting the Scriptures based on their training as Pharisees. In this sense, the First Christians were theologically trained and spiritually exceptional. However, there are no further sources to disclose their identities.

The First Christians handed over their gospel to Paul. He reflects this tradition in 1 Cor 15:3–8, from which the original can yet be distinguished. First of all, 1 Cor 15:8 does not originally belong to the tradition because Paul talked about himself. While some biblical scholars examine 1 Cor 15:3b–7 as the tradition, others see 1 Cor 15:3b–5, which consists of Cephas

10. Conzelmann, *I Corinthians*, 252.

11. Although Acts does not always describe the event with historical accuracy, it provides a hint that Paul had met the First Christians at Damascus. According to Acts, having heard the heavenly voice of Jesus of Nazareth on the way to Damascus, Paul had fellowship with the disciples there. He immediately proclaimed that Jesus was the Son of God and Christ (Acts 9:20–22). It seems to reflect the historical event that happened to Paul at Damascus. In this respect, Acts supports the possibility that Paul met the First Christians at Damascus and learned about Christ from them there.

Peter and "the twelve," as the tradition.[12] On the contrary, I would argue for a shorter form that 1 Cor 15:3b–5a belongs to the original tradition for two reasons. First, a balanced structure of parallelisms is found between the death and resurrection of Christ using the phrase "according to the Scriptures" and between the burial and epiphany, which simply narrate facts. Second, Cephas and "the twelve" were not a part of the prepauline tradition from a chronological point of view. Paul had received the tradition from the First Christians between 35 and 38 CE at Damascus (Gal 1:15–17) before he met Cephas at Jerusalem in 38 (1:18–19) and the fourth redactor of Q introduced the twelve apostles in 41 (Q^4 6:13–16).[13] In other words, the First Christians were not able to know the twelve apostles in Q beforehand. In addition, the fact that Paul met no other apostles except Cephas and James, the Lord's brother, at Jerusalem implies that the title "apostle" was used even though the identities of the twelve apostles were not beginning to be decided upon until around 38 (Gal 1:18–19) and this was not completed until 41. It is therefore possible that Paul added Cephas and the Twelve to the tradition about the epiphany of Christ when 1 Corinthians was written, probably in the early or mid-fifties CE. Paul seemed to attach a long list of witnesses starting from Cephas because he wanted to include himself in it in order to strengthen his apostolic authority at the time of writing 1 Corinthians.

The prepauline tradition probably did not include the phrase "for our sins." A certain number of scholars have pointed out that Paul added this phrase to the previous tradition when writing 1 Corinthians.[14] This is supported by the fact that Paul did not connect the death of Christ with the sins of people in his first letter, 1 Thessalonians, which was probably written before 1 Corinthians. In other words, the First Christians did not impose a redemptive meaning to the death of Christ; on the contrary, Paul added

---

12. For more detailed study of 1 Cor 15:3–5, see Conzelmann, "On the Analysis," 15–25; and ibid., *I Corinthians*, 251–57. He concludes that the tradition ends at 1 Cor 15:5. There is, however, another opinion that 15:4 is the end of tradition that the First Christians handed down to Paul. See Jeremias, *Eucharistic Words*, 101.

13. Paul used the phrases "then after three years" and "fourteen years later" before the Apostolic Meeting held at the Jerusalem Church, probably around 49 CE (Gal 1:15–18; 2:1–10; Acts 15:1–21). Then the time when Paul received the revelation is decided. It depends upon how these numbers should be counted. It could have happened in 35 CE, that is, fourteen years before the Apostolic Meeting, or in 32 CE, seventeen years before it. However, I would like to conclude that Paul received the revelation about the Son of God in 35 CE, fourteen years before the meeting, because the phrases indicate the chronological sequence.

14. Following Hooker, Barrett argues that the phrase "our sins" was added by Paul to the primitive tradition (Barrett, *Commentary*, 339. Cf. Hooker, *Jesus and the Servant*, 119).

it later in 1 Corinthians. In this respect, the tradition the First Christians handed over to Paul was concise, as follows:

> Christ died according to the Scriptures,
> was buried,
> was raised on the third day according to the Scriptures,
> and appeared (1 Cor 15:3–5).

This is the summary of the gospel that the First Christians handed over to Paul, probably at Damascus between 35 and 38 CE. He did not leave any further details about the gospel and the First Christians.

The gospel the First Christians gave to Paul was formed by focusing on Christ. As is commonly known, the Greek word "Christ," Χριστός, is a translation of the Hebrew word "Messiah," משיח, meaning "God's anointed servant." The statement of death, burial, resurrection, and epiphany according to the Scriptures can refer to any servant of God who has fulfilled such work. It is, however, not clear whether Christ as presented by the First Christians is the Jesus presented in Q. Although the First Christians did not reveal the identity of Christ, they created faith in Christ the Messiah in their own way on the basis of the Bible.

The First Christians introduced five theological elements in regards to the interpretation of Christ. First of all, they understood Christ primarily from a theological perspective. As the hermeneutic principle of "according to the Scriptures" shows, the death and resurrection of Christ must be understood in the light of the prophecy written in the Bible. Second, the First Christians mentioned the death of Christ according to the Scriptures. It is clear that they attempted to interpret his death in the context of the Scriptures; however, it does not mention which verse of the Bible predicted it. Third, the First Christians mentioned the burial of Christ. A person is buried by others when he or she dies, but this does not seem like the ultimate reason the First Christians mentioned Christ's burial. Although they did not evince the reason, the mention of the burial of Christ makes it important. Fourth, the First Christians wrote about the resurrection of Christ. The phrase "he was raised on the third day according to the Scriptures" means that there is a prophecy in the Bible about it. However, they did not give a clue as to which prophecy of the Bible predicts the resurrection of Christ. Fifth, the First Christians conveyed the tradition about the epiphany of Christ. They proclaimed that Christ appeared after his death and resurrection. As such, the epiphany of Christ indeed appears to be one of their interpretations. The first Christian gospel has many differences from Q in terms of content. While the twelve apostles wrote about the actions and words of Jesus in Q, the First Christians left the gospel about the Christ of faith according to the Scriptures. In this sense, the First Christians created faith in Christ. Focusing on these differences, people can see that the First Christians took an entirely different theological line from the twelve apostles. With this in mind, there were two different traditions in the late thirties and early forties CE relating to Jesus and Christ.

C. The Pauline Epistles

Paul holds a key post in the origin and formation of the gospel. He probably knew about Q as well as the first Christian gospel. Based on the two traditions, Paul defined the Son of God as Jesus Christ. The formation and development of Paul's gospel can be detected in his letters, and this will be found when his genuine epistles are examined in chronological order.

There are some important factors that must be considered when understanding the theological interpretations of Paul. First, the Pauline epistles are the earliest documents written among the Christian writings, having been composed between the late forties and the early sixties CE. They must be dealt with when studying the origin and formation of the gospel.

Second, Paul inherited the traditions about Jesus Christ in various ways. Above all, Paul received the revelation about the Son of God around Damascus in 35 CE (Gal 1:15-16). Next, Paul went to Arabia and then returned to Damascus, where he probably learned the traditions about Christ from the First Christians (Gal 1:17; 1 Cor 15:3b-5a). In this sense, they are the religious precedents to Paul. Moreover, three years later in 38 CE, Paul went up to Jerusalem and met Cephas and James, the Lord's brother, when he possibly learned about Jesus on the basis of Q (Gal 1:18-19). Furthermore, Paul received traditions about the Supper from the Lord (1 Cor 11:23-26).[15] However, it does not seem that Paul inherited this from Jesus himself, since he does not explain in detail how he got the tradition about the Lord's Supper. As a result, it is undeniable that Paul received tradition about Jesus and Christ in various ways and developed them further. For instance, Paul developed the gospel about Jesus Christ, the Son of God, based on the traditions. Some clues can be deduced about the identity of the Son of God using Paul's own descriptions of his travels. It seems that Paul, a Pharisee, persecuted the disciples of Jesus who had constituted the churches in Judea, undoubtedly including Jerusalem (Gal 1:13, 22-23; Phil 3:5-6; 1 Thess 2:14). In the middle of his persecution, Paul received the revelation

---

15. As for the way of transmission in the first century CE, refer to Barrett, *Commentary*, 265-66.

about the Son of God on his way to Damascus and then went to Arabia and back to Damascus (Gal 1:15-17; Acts 9:1-9). It is likely that, having heard the tradition about Christ from the First Christians there, Paul could identify the Son of God with the Christ, the Messiah, according to the Jewish tradition.[16] In addition, Paul accepted the hermeneutic principle "according to the Scriptures" from the First Christians. Then Paul probably got a chance to find clues to identify the Christ the Son of God with Jesus, whose disciples he had persecuted. Thus, in 38 CE the third year after receiving the revelation about the Son of God, Paul went up to Jerusalem and learned about Jesus from Cephas and James, the Lord's brother (Gal 1:18-19). At that time, the third redaction of Q was probably complete. It reflects the historical situation that they proclaimed Jesus as the Son of God (Q^3 3:21-22; 10:21-22), were hated and insulted by their fellow Jews on account of him (6:22-23b), were already rejected in several cities such as Capernaum, Korazin, and Bethsaida (10:13-16), and were in conflict with the Pharisees (11:39-46, 52). Paul was probably one of the Pharisees who persecuted the followers of Jesus, as it was reflected in the third redaction of Q. This shows that the disciples of Jesus advanced to the region of Judea, including Jerusalem, from Galilee before Paul had received the revelation about the Son of God in 35 CE. As a result, having learned about Jesus from Cephas and James, Paul could relate the Son of God with Jesus, whom they also defined as the Son of God. This is supported by the fact that he connected the tradition about the death and resurrection of Christ with the Son of God and Jesus later in his first letter, 1 Thessalonians (1 Thess 1:10). This is how Paul identified the Son of God with Christ and then Jesus based on the traditions that he received. Thus, he could use the name Jesus with the titles Christ and the Son of God in his later letters. Therefore, it is important to trace how each element of the gospel developed from a chronological perspective.

Third, Paul creatively developed the gospel he inherited from the First Christians. For instance, he inherited the tradition about the death of Christ according to the Scriptures. Later, however, Paul interpreted that Christ died "for us" from a sacrificial perspective (1 Thess 5:10). Then he connected the death of Christ with the cross of Jesus (1 Cor 1:18–2:9) and insisted that Christ died "for our sins" from a redemptive perspective (1 Cor 15:3).

---

16. Dunn lists the concept of the Son of God in the Jewish tradition as follows: angels or angelic beings, Israelites as individuals or on the whole, a king, a righteous person, and the eschatological Davidic Messiah in the context of 2 Sam 7:11-14 and Ps 2:7 (Dunn, *Christology*, 12-22). In particular, among Dunn's list, the last one attracts our attention as reflected in 4QFlor. 1.10-11; 4QpsDan A. On the basis of the Jewish tradition, Paul could connect the Son of God with Christ and then Jesus as the Davidic Messiah later.

For this interpretation, it seems that Paul found its theological basis from the Suffering Servant of YHWH, who played the role of the guilt offering (Isa 52:13–53:12).[17] Finally, Paul connected the death of Christ on the cross with redemption under the light of Deut 21:23 (Gal 1:4; 3:13). As a result, Paul did the theological work of connecting the death of Jesus on the cross with the prophecies of the Bible about redemption. The creative theological interpretations would have been possible because he was a Pharisee used to developing former biblical traditions.

Fourth, it is necessary to see how Paul's genuine epistles are composed in order to see the development of his thought relating to the gospel. They often show that the flow of content is not consistent in many places, revealing that some of the letters are actually compilations of several shorter letters.[18] Then, it is necessary to separate the short letters from each epistle. Therefore, it is important to list them in chronological order to take a look at how Paul changed and developed his thoughts and theology in response to the changing environments during his missionary journey.

First of all, 1 Thessalonians is supposed to have been written first, but is composed of two short letters.[19] A clue to this is found in the sudden change of content occurring from 1:1—2:16 to 2:17—3:13. While the former concentrates on the relationship between Paul and the Thessalonians in the past, the latter suddenly deals with his intention to visit the church on account of turmoil caused by the outsiders. Another clue is detected in the fact that using the term "finally" in 4:1, the following text is too long to be considered the ending part of the letter. This means that 4:1–28 is composed of texts that belong to at least two separate letters. In addition, 1 Thessalonians shows inconsistency of content in many places. For example, when 1:1—2:16 is connected with 4:1–8, they naturally flow. These phenomena inform the reader of the possibility that 1 Thessalonians is composed of two short letters. There are texts that reflect good relationship between Paul and the Thessalonians (1 Thess 1:1—2:16; 4:1–8); therefore, this could be the first letter termed 1Thess(1) focusing on "being holy." The rest, however, describes tension

---

17. Cullmann, *Christologie*, 75–76, 79. Of course, some scholars refuse to accept that the interpretation of 1 Corinthians 15:3 alludes to Isaiah 52:13–53:12. Following Hooker, Barrett says, "It may well be that the general allusion to the Scriptures was made before specific passages were alleged in support of it" (Barrett, *Commentary*, 339. Cf. Hooker, *Jesus and the Servant*, 117–20; and Hahn, *Christologische*, 56–61, 197–213).

18. For more detailed analysis, see Ra, *Paul*, 99–182.

19. Brown says, "That two letters have been combined to make up 1Thess has been suggested by a small number of respected scholars (e.g., W. Schmithals), but unity is overwhelmingly asserted" (Brown, *Introduction*, 457). However, he does not discuss this matter in any further detail. Nevertheless, it is important to see that there are many scholars who have argued for the fragmentary theory of 1 Thessalonians.

initiated from within and without among the Thessalonians and Paul's joy over their means of coping with it. In addition, it includes his answer to their questions (2:17—3:13; 4:9—5:28). Therefore, this could be the second letter 1Thess(2). Each letter reveals its own coherency of content. This makes it possible that 1 Thessalonians is composed of two short letters.

Philippians also appears to be composed of two short letters.[20] With regard to the letters, a clue is detected in the fact that Philippians uses the term "finally" two times, indicating the ending of the letter (Phil 3:1a; 4:8).[21] In addition, Philippians shows two different groups of recipients (1:1; 4:3). This implies that Philippians is at least composed of two short letters. Moreover, Philippians also shows inconsistency of content in many places. In particular, an inconsistency is found in 3:1b—4:3 because Paul suddenly mentions his opponents. On the other hand, there are some that reveal Paul's thanks to and his joy over the financial support (2:25—3:1a; 4:4–7). Interestingly, the natural flow of content from 3:1a to 4:4 implies that 3:1b—4:3 is an interpolated text of another letter. While some texts reflect a tension and conflict among the Philippians and Paul's joy of their restoration (3:1b—4:3, 8–9), they could be named as the first letter Phil(1). Other texts reveal Paul's thanks for their financial support while he was in prison (1:1—3:1a; 4:4-7, 10-23) and can be named as the second letter Phil(2). In this, Philippians seems to be composed of two short letters.

From a compositional perspective, 1 Corinthians and 2 Corinthians need to be examined more carefully. Their composition is complicated by the fact that Paul seemed to send six short letters to the Corinthian Church.[22] However, the person that collected these letters may have edited them into two parts, 1 Corinthians and 2 Corinthians, by compiling three letters for

---

20. Brown says, "That two or three letters have been combined to make up Philippians is widely suggested, but a respectable case can be made for unity" (Brown, *Introduction*, 484, 497–98). There are many scholars who argue for the unity of Philippians. Cf. Garland, "Composition and Unity," 141–73; Schnelle, *History and Theology*, 135–37; and Standhartinger, "Join in Imitating Me," 418–26. However, as for the scholarly opinion that Philippians is composed of short letters, see Reuman, *Philippians*; and Osiek, *Philippians, Philemon*.

21. Many scholars recognize that Paul implied a previous letter by saying, "To write the same things to you is no trouble to me" in 3:1b; then, this means that the text that includes 3:1b belongs to the second letter. Cf. Brown, *Introduction*, 497. However, it could also be argued that Paul was not hesitant to write again what he had told the Philippians in his previous visit.

22. Hurd lists the opinions of scholars how 1 Corinthians is composed of three short letters (Hurd, *Origin*, 45). His study is based on the studies of scholars such as Johannes Weiss, Alfred Loisy, Paul Louis Couchoud, Maurice Goguel, Johannes Zwaan, Walter Schmithals, and Erich Dinkler.

each book.[23] This can be seen by the fact that the context of 1 and 2 Corinthians is not consistent in many places. For instance, in 1 Corinthians, a clue to this is detected among chapters 12 through 14 with regard to inconsistence of content. First Corinthians 12:31b—14:1a talks about "love"; on the other hand, the surrounding texts deal with various spiritual gifts. This informs us that 12:31b—14:1a was interpolated into the present place. Another clue is found with regard to the role of tongues, which is one of the spiritual gifts. While Paul introduced it as a sign for the unbeliever in 14:20-22, he then took an opposite perspective on it in 14:23-25. This shows his contradictory interpretation regarding the role of tongues, showing that they belong to two different letters with each other. In other words, Paul changed his perspective on tongues as the situation changed. A sudden change of content is also detected between 15:1-11 and 15:12-28, which includes the theme of resurrection; while the former concentrates on Paul's defense of apostleship, the latter deals with the resurrection of the saints. This implies that they also indicate two different letters. In addition, in the case of 2 Corinthians, critical scholars have acknowledged that the content flows naturally from 2:13 to 7:5; therefore, the text of 2:14—7:4 is also an interpolation. Moreover, an abrupt change of content is found in Paul's radical instruction about the religious principle in 6:14—7:1 because the surrounding texts speak about Paul's request for welcoming (6:11-13; 7:2-4). Thus, it can be concluded that 6:14—7:1 was interpolated in between 6:11-13 and 7:2-4. Furthermore, Paul revealed a different perspective on the collection between chapters 8 and 9. While the economic equality between the contributor and the receiver is the primary reason for the collection in 8:13, an effort to collect more is detected in 9:6. It seems that chapter 8 was a part of letter written earlier than that including chapter 9, because Paul pushed the Corinthians to participate in collection harder in the latter than in the former. Chapter 8 was added by chapter 9 later in terms of common theme—that is, collection by the compiler. Finally, as critical scholars have pointed out, the different tone is found between chapters 1 through 9 and 10 through 13. It seems they belong to different letters with each other. There are too many cases like this to deal with in both epistles.

It seems that 1 Corinthians is composed of three short letters. Paul clearly sent a letter before he visited the church a second time. This seems to be the first letter 1Cor(1), written in an authoritative manner with the main theme of "being holy" (1 Cor 1:1-9; 3:16-17; 2 Cor 6:14—7:1; 1 Cor

---

23. Brown says that some scholars recognized two or more separate letters interwoven in 1 Corinthians but that the majority of scholars favored its unity. As for 2 Corinthians, Brown acknowledges that two or more letters are combined (Brown, *Introduction*, 512, 542. Cf. Furnish, *II Corinthians*, 30–48).

6:12–20; 10:1–22; 11:2–16; 12:2–3, 12:31b—14:1a; 14:20–22, 33b–38; 16:5–6, 10–11, 13–14). This implies that 1Cor(1) was written during a similar time as 1Thess(1) based on its common theme of "being holy." After receiving 1Cor(1), the Corinthians sent the people of Chloe to Paul in order to ask some questions and report the situation of their church. In response, Paul sent another letter, 1Cor(2), with the theme of edifying for virtue (1 Cor 1:10–17; 5:1–5, 9–13; 6:1–11; 7:1–17, 25–40; 8:1–13; 10:23—11:1; 11:17–29, 33–34; 12:1, 4–12, 14–31a; 14:1b–19, 23–33a, 39–40; 15:12–28, 35–49; 16:1–4, 12, 15–18). It is noteworthy that Paul mentioned Cephas, who had visited the Corinthian Church and baptized some of them (1:10–17).[24] His visit and baptism resulted only in division and conflict among the Corinthians. When Paul visited the Corinthian Church thereafter, some members denied his gospel and challenged his authority. Offended by such actions, Paul rebuked them and returned to Ephesus of Asia Minor, where he sent the third letter, 1Cor(3). This consists of Paul demonstrating his gospel and apostleship (1 Cor 1:18—3:15; 3:18–23; 4:1–21; 5:6–8; 7:18–24; 9:1–27; 11:30–32; 12:13; 15:1–11, 29–34, 50–58; 16:7–9, 19–24). Defending his authority as an apostle, Paul revealed the conflict with the apostles of the Jerusalem Church by mentioning Cephas' marriage and salary (9:4–7). It seems that 1Cor(3) may be the so-called "Letter of Tears" (2 Cor 2:4; 7:8).

It seems that 2 Corinthians is also composed of three short letters. After hearing Titus' optimistic report when he returned from delivering 1Cor(3), Paul sent the fourth letter, 2Cor(1). This consists of Paul admitting his mistake and his consolation (2 Cor 1:1—2:13; 7:5–16; 8:1–24; 13:11–13). His effort to restore the relationship is clearly shown in this letter. However, when the Corinthians did not respond as he had expected, Paul sent the fifth letter, 2Cor(2), which focuses on the reconciliation between Paul and the Corinthians (2:14—6:13; 7:2–4; 9:1–15). He revealed his strong wish to restore the relationship. When the Corinthians still did not respond, Paul sent the sixth letter, 2Cor(3), prior to his third visit to Corinth (10:1—13:10). Strongly criticizing the apostles of the Jerusalem Church (11:12–15, 21–27), Paul also gave the Corinthians a warning not to neglect his instruction.

In conclusion, the literary and thematic analysis above shows that Paul sent six letters to the Corinthians. It seems that Paul made theological interpretations according to changes in situation. As a result, the six letters show how his thought changed and developed in response to the Corinthians. However, it is to be admitted that although the above analysis is not entirely

---

24. Vielhauer, "Paul and the Cephas," 129–42. See especially ibid., 133. He argues for the hypothesis of Cephas' ministry in Corinth.

conclusive, it still demonstrates the complexity of 1 Corinthians and 2 Corinthians with regard to their literary composition.

Paul also sent several letters to the Roman Church.[25] Like the epistles mentioned above, Romans shows an inconsistent flow of content. A clue to this is found in the change of thematic emphasis occurring among Rom 1:1–17; 1:18—3:31; 4:1—5:11; 5:12—8:30; 8:31–39 and 9:1—12:2. This leads to the conclusion that Romans is also composed of several short letters. Paul tried to visit the Roman Church and wished to get financial support so that he could be sent as a missionary to Spain. For this purpose, Paul sent a letter that is possibly composed of texts such as 1:1–17; 4:1—5:11; 8:31–39; 12:3–13; 14:1—16:16; 16:21–27. This is the first letter to the Romans, Rom(1). It seems, however, that the Romans would not accept Paul's intention and raised a question about his perspective on the Law because he had insisted on righteousness by faith in Christ (4:13-15). They probably heard about his negative perspective on the Law from the Corinthians and the Galatians who had challenged him. Thus, Paul had to respond to the Romans by writing a letter probably composed of texts such as 1:18—3:31; 12:14—13:7. This is the second letter, Rom(2). Nevertheless, they were not satisfied with his response and raised another question about the Law. This made him write another letter focused on the relationship of the Law with sin and flesh. This includes texts such as 5:12—8:30; 13:8–14, to be named as Rom(3). In spite of his previous letters, the Romans did not agree with him, and they asked for his opinion about the relationship between the Jews and the Gentiles. Responding to their question, Paul wrote the fourth letter, composed of texts such as 9:1—12:2; 16:17–20, to be named as Rom(4). The above analysis shows how Paul changed and developed his perspective on the Law in response to the Romans' questions. It is unknown whether Paul was ever able to go to Spain. Although the above analysis is not entirely satisfactory enough, it can be concluded that Romans is composed of four short letters. These four letters to the Romans do not reflect the conflict between Paul and the Jerusalem apostles, since he did not establish it and they did not send representatives to the church in Rome.

Paul sent letters to the Galatian Church and to Philemon as well. In their case, however, they stand as complete units insofar as they show consistency of content. Galatians reflects the situation that some of the Galatians challenged Paul and refuted his gospel and authority. Responding to their challenge, Paul tried to persuade them to stay in his gospel. Galatians is a very important

---

25. Brown says, "A very small minority posits the joining of two separate letters; a larger minority maintains that chap. 16 was added later" (Brown, *Introduction*, 560). See also ibid, 575–76. However, he does not discuss how two letters are joined in Romans. It is likely that he is referring to the opinion that Rom 9–11 were added.

letter in the fact that it shows the contemporary situation of his missionary work. On the other hand, Philemon is a personal letter in which Paul asked for the forgiveness of Onesimus; however, due to the personal nature of the letter, it delivers little of the aspects of the particular theology of Paul.

The Pauline epistles reflect the historical context of the time each was written. This is especially evident in the conflict between Paul and the Gentile Christians sponsored by the apostles of the Jerusalem Church. What should be considered primarily are the events of the apostolic meeting at Jerusalem and the conflict between Paul and Cephas at Antioch (Gal 2:1–14). Later, having been sponsored by the Jewish apostles who emphasized the observance of the Law as reflected in the fourth redaction of Q, some people were sent to the churches in Thessalonica, Philippi, Corinth, and Galatia. Especially, Cephas visited the Corinthian Church and baptized some people during his short stay and ministry. At any rate, the Jerusalem Church caused the Gentile Christians to doubt Paul's gospel and challenge his authority, probably between 51 and 53 CE. This situation is reflected in 1Cor(2), 1Thess(2), Phil(1), 1Cor(3), Galatians, and 2Cor(3); and a stronger challenge and opposition is reflected in the books according to this order. While the Thessalonians and the Philippians rejected those sent by the Jerusalem apostles, the Corinthians and the Galatians accepted them and backed away from Paul's teaching by observing the Law and circumcision. Therefore, Paul had to respond to the situation, and accordingly started emphasizing the cross of Christ as a means of redemption in 1Cor(3) (1 Cor 1:18—2:16; 15:3) and Galatians (Gal 3:1, 13), thus demonstrating his gospel and apostleship. As a result, Paul delivered his own theological alternative on the basis of the cross and, consequentially, founded Christianity. In this way, the Pauline epistles show how Paul responded theologically to the changing situation of the Gentile churches.

It has been shown that the Pauline epistles reflect their occasion for writing and display how his theology developed. Thus, it is necessary to examine them in chronological order as follows: 1Thess(1), 1Cor(1), 1Cor(2), 1Thess(2), Phil(1), 1Cor(3), Galatians, 2Cor(1), 2Cor(2), 2Cor(3), Rom(1), Rom(2), Rom(3), Rom(4), Phil(2), and Philemon. Although the above analysis is not entirely conclusive, it still demonstrates the complexity of the Pauline epistles. When the chronological order is considered in studying the Pauline letters, it is clear how Paul developed the Christian tradition.

D. Mark

Mark is the first written Gospel aside from Q. It was most likely penned in Galilee around the time the Romans took Jerusalem around 70 CE. Therefore, Mark has an older tradition about Jesus Christ than any of the other Gospels. In spite of this, it cannot be assumed that all of the Markan traditions are historically accurate about the life of Jesus. Like the Pauline epistles, Mark delivers its own theological interpretation about Jesus.

Although Mark seems to have been aware of Q, it does not directly use Q as a whole. There are, however, several texts that Mark adopted from Q: the role of John (Mark 1:2–5, 7–8; Q^1 3:2b–4, 7–9; Q^3 3:16–17; 7:27), the baptism of Jesus (Mark 1:9–11; Q^3 3:21–22), the temptation (Mark 1:12–13; Q^4 4:1–13), the list of the twelve disciples (Mark 3:16–19; Q^4 6:13–16), the Beelzebul controversy (Mark 3:22–29: Q^2 11:14–15, 17–20), the parable of the Lamp (Mark 4:21–22; Q^3 11:33; 12:2–3), the parable of the Mustard Seed (Mark 4:30–32; Q^3 13:18–19), the sermon for missionary journey (Mark 6:7–11; Q^2 10:4–11), the demand for a sign (Mark 8:11–12; Q^2 11:16, 29–30), and the discipleship (Mark 8:34–35; Q^4 14:26–27; 17:33). More texts can be found in Mark from Q according to the reader's theological perspective. Mark cited the parts of Q he needed for his purpose and did not use the other parts. Without doubt, Mark considered Q as a source for composing the account of the life of Jesus.

Mark also seems to have known about the Pauline epistles and theology. It is not clear if the author of Mark is the Mark that followed Paul (Acts 15:36–41; 2 Tim 4:11); however, the fact that there is some relation between the two is undeniable. Even if he was not the man who followed Paul, it would not have been difficult to learn about the Pauline epistles later on. Thus, at the very beginning of the Gospel Mark defined Jesus as the Christ the Son of God, reflecting the Pauline understanding (Mark 1:1; 1 Thess 1:10). In addition, Mark paid attention to the tradition that originated with the First Christians and was developed by Paul regarding the death of Jesus Christ. For this, Mark reflects the Pauline theology that Christ died "for our sins according to the Scriptures" in the description of the redemptive role of Jesus (Mark 10:45; 1 Cor 15:3; Gal 1:4).[26] Mark indirectly cited Isa 53:10 and conveyed it as the words of Jesus. In this way, a theological meaning was imposed to his death. Moreover, Mark created the Passion Narrative that includes the suffering, death, burial, and resurrection of Christ, and attached it to the description of the life of Jesus based on the texts from Q.[27] The life

---

26. Cf. ibid., 534.

27. Crossan suggests his own hypothesis that there was a document called "the Cross Gospel" used for the intracanonical Gospels (Crossan, *Cross That Spoke*, xiii,

of Jesus is understood to be modeled after the Suffering Servant of YHWH when Mark wrote about the process of his suffering, death, and burial by alluding to those of Isa 52:13—53:12. Jesus is the person fulfilling the role of the guilt offering that is the key to the Suffering Servant of YHWH. In other words, Mark focused on the historical description of the redemptive death of Jesus on the cross. In this way, Mark made Paul's theological statement into a historical narrative. In the meantime, Mark applied Paul's theology of redemption attributed to Christ to the Passion Narrative. Through these descriptions, Mark completed a biographical narrative about Jesus Christ based on Isaiah's prophecy of the Suffering Servant of YHWH. In this way, Mark created a literary genre of "Gospel" written about the life of Jesus from the perspective of redemption.

Mark also added many of his own sources in order to describe Jesus Christ. For example, there is the calling of the four disciples (Mark 1:16-20), the healing of a paralytic (2:1-12), controversy over the Sabbath (2:23—3:6), the parable of the Sower (4:1-20), the prayer at Gethsemane (14:32-42), the interrogation before the Sanhedrin at night (14:53-65), the competition with Barabbas (15:6-16), the crucifixion (15:21-32), and the empty tomb (16:1-8), to name a few. It could also be argued that all the texts, excluding those from Q, were original to Mark. Mark related many accounts that remind the reader of Elijah and Elisha; for example, the revitalization of the daughter of Jairus (Mark 5:22-24, 35-43; 1 Kgs 17:17-24; 2 Kgs 4:17-37), the feeding miracle (Mark 6:35-44; 8:1-10; 1 Kgs 17:8-16; 2 Kgs 4:1-7, 42-44), and the transfiguration (Mark 9:2-13). There are still other bundles of stories that identify Jesus as a miraculous servant of God.

E. Other Gospels

Matthew and Luke used both Q and Mark as sources when they composed their accounts of the life of Jesus Christ. On account of the similarities between them, the three Gospels became known as the Synoptic Gospels. Matthew and Luke, however, wrote about Jesus from a different perspective than Mark while adding sources to what each writer had collected. As a result, Matthew and Luke, though similar to Mark, are revealed to be different when examined closely. Each Gospel demonstrates how it used the previous tradition to describe Jesus according to each subsequent author's theological interpretations.

16-20, 404–408). However, Crossan does not pay attention to the relationship between "the Cross Gospel" and the Pauline tradition inherited from the First Christians (1 Cor 15:3–5).

Matthew and Luke used the data from Q and Mark for their own purposes. By doing so, they show what they tried to emphasize. For instance, in their description of the order of temptation, while Matthew described that the temptation went on from the wilderness to the Jerusalem temple, then on to the very high mountain (Matt 4:1–11), Luke changed the order to the wilderness, a high place, and Jerusalem (Luke 4:1–13). Each Gospel puts an emphasis on the last place, showing each author's theological interest. Moreover, while Matthew conveyed the Sermon on the Mount (Matt 5:1–7:27), Luke described the sermon on a level place (Luke 6:20–49). Matthew puts an emphasis on the mountain, which reminds the reader of Moses. In this way, each Gospel delivers a different theological perspective using the previous tradition.

Matthew and Luke also wrote about Jesus using data of their own not based on Q or Mark, which was collected at different times and different places. For example, in the description of the birth of Jesus, Matthew used data about King Herod and the Magi (Matt 2:1–12), while Luke used data about Caesar Augustus and the shepherds (Luke 2:1–21). It is to be noted, however, that at least ten or twelve years' difference is found between the descriptions about the birth of Jesus. This implies that each author wrote according his own theological rather than historical purpose. Furthermore, while Matthew reported that Jesus appeared on a mountain in Galilee after the resurrection (Matt 28:16–20), Luke wrote that he appeared on the road to Emmaus (Luke 24:13–35). Matthew and Luke described Jesus according to the way they theologically desired, and their descriptions are not necessarily historical.

Matthew and Luke also present different interpretations about Jesus Christ, especially in regard to the theology of redemption that Mark inherited from Paul. The theology of redemption is the belief that Christ died on the cross for the sins of people. In connection to this belief, Matthew emphasized the interpretation of Mark in which he claimed Jesus to be the Suffering Servant of YHWH, while Luke weakened this position. This is shown in the reference to Mark 10:45 (Isa 53:10), which Matthew used (Matt 20:28) and Luke did not. While Matthew further cited prophecies connected with the Suffering Servant of YHWH (Matt 8:17; 12:18–21; Isa 42:1–4; 53:4), Luke participated in quoting a prophecy about him (Luke 22:37; Isa 53:12) but refrained from mentioning the role of redemption. The author of the Lucan documents described in Acts that Philip did not explicitly say Jesus was the sacrificial offering according to the writing of Isaiah in the account of the Ethiopian Eunuch (Acts 8:32–33). This also shows that the Lucan documents weakened the redemptive role of Jesus. As a result, Matthew and Luke displayed different perspectives on Jesus Christ.

Matthew and Luke wrote about the Jesus Christ they wanted to convey in other ways as well. Matthew described him as the savior of his people from their sins by comparing him with Moses, who saved the people of God from bondage in Egypt (Matt 1:21; Exod 3:10). This is shown by the fact that the events surrounding Jesus described in Matthew run parallel with the events that occurred to Moses in many ways. It has been acknowledged by biblical scholars that Jesus' escape to and return from Egypt, his baptism and temptation, the Sermon on the Mount, the ten miracles, the calling of the twelve disciples, the transfiguration, and the Great Commission remind the reader of what Moses did on the way of Exodus to Canaan (Matt 2:13–23; 3:13–17; 4:1–11; 5:1—7:27; 8:1—9:34; 10:2–4; 17:1–8; 28:16–20). In addition, the five sermons in Matthew remind the reader of the Pentateuch presumed to have been written by Moses (chapters 5–7, 10, 13, 18, 23–25). It is thus well known to biblical scholars that Matthew used the Moses/Exodus typology to describe Jesus. Moreover, Matthew also connected Jesus to Adam using the typology. Luke, on the other hand, wrote about the life of Jesus while comparing him to the prophets. As a result, Luke described many more miracles, compared with the other Gospels, as Elijah and Elisha worked many miracles in the Bible. It is also written that when Jesus was ostracized after he gave the sermon citing Isaiah as he started his public life, Luke demonstrated this by mentioning the widow of Sarepta and Naaman, who lived contemporaneously with Elijah and Elisha (Luke 4:16–30). Hereupon, Luke described Jesus as "a great prophet" (7:16). In this way, Luke theologically described Jesus based on the prophetic tradition. This shows that Matthew and Luke have also developed the tradition of faith from a different perspective.

John, on the other hand, took a different path from the Synoptic Gospels. This causes the reader to see a different track of tradition emerging at the end of the first century CE.[28] This is shown in various ways through the use of sources, the literary characteristics, and theological aspects of John. First, for example, in John's use of sources, the perspective on the cleansing of the temple is different. While the Synoptic Gospels wrote of this event at the last part of the public ministry of Jesus when he entered Jerusalem to die (Mark 11:15–18; Matt 21:12–17; Luke 19:45–48), John wrote of it at the beginning of his public ministry (John 2:13–22). John's use of sources is also unique. Content that is treated as important in the Synoptic Gospels is omitted in John, and vice versa. For instance, John seems to have been

---

28. Brown recognizes several layers of redaction in John (Brown, *Introduction*, 334). It is believed by scholars that chapter 21 of the Gospel of John was attached first at the ending, then the prologue was added to the beginning (John 1:1–18), and finally the story about the adulterous woman was interpolated much later (John 8:2–11).

opposed to ceremonies by the fact that John neither mentioned anything about the baptized Jesus with the Spirit of God nor described the Lord's Supper held on the first day of the Unleavened Feast. In addition, John did not write about the temptation of Christ. John also does not mention the list of the twelve disciples. The eschatological sermon was replaced with the last sermon. The prayer at Gethsemane, which is treated importantly in the Synoptic Gospels, is also omitted in John.

Second, there are differences in regard to literary aspects. While the Synoptic Gospels were written in prose form, John uses verse form in the prologue (John 1:1–18). From a theological perspective, John identified Jesus Christ with the Word while defining him as God from the beginning. The High Christology implies that John includes a more advanced theological statement than the Synoptic Gospels. In this respect, it seems that the prose form of Christology was developed later.

Third, John took a different path from the Synoptic Gospels in the sense of theology. For example, Jesus plays the role of the Lamb of God who takes away the sin of the world (John 1:29). Although the Suffering Servant of YHWH is compared to a lamb (Isa 53:7), John's reference to the Lamb of God conveys a limited image of the servant compared to that in the Synoptic Gospels. In addition, while the Synoptic Gospels mentioned the love of neighbors, John emphasized that people must love each other in emulating the love of God (John 13:34–35). This emphasis on loving each other shows the love within a sect that was a closed community. Moreover, John introduced the "I am" sayings in seven instances that do not appear in the Synoptic Gospels (6:35; 8:12; 10:9, 11; 11:25; 14:6; 15:1). They were probably created by John for his own specific purposes. Other differences between John and the Synoptics show that he developed his own interpretations in regard to the status and role of Jesus Christ.

F. Conclusion

It is important to know when each book of the Christian Scripture was written in order to learn the origin and formation of the gospel. This is due to the fact that at the time of the first century CE, the gospel gradually developed into enhanced theological comprehensions and interpretations as the writers confessed Jesus as Christ. Traditions about Jesus Christ are largely based on two different tracks. First, traditions about Jesus started by some followers in Galilee and were finally edited in the form of Q, probably by the twelve apostles or under their supervision at Jerusalem. Second, the First Christians, presumed to be Pharisees among the Jews of the

Diaspora, possibly at Damascus, made interpretations based on the Bible and formed faith in Christ. After receiving the revelation of the Son of God, Paul confessed him as Christ and then identified him with Jesus based on these traditions. Responding to the changing situations in his relationship with the apostles of the Jerusalem Church and the Gentile Christians, Paul wrote his epistles and introduced the redemptive death of Christ for the first time. Later, Mark wrote about the life of Jesus based on the sources from Q and the Pauline tradition about Christ. Applying the Pauline theology of redemption to the account of Jesus became a new literary genre termed "Gospel." Matthew, John, and Luke interpreted Jesus Christ from different points of view. Each writer of the four Gospels made their own theological interpretations about Jesus Christ.

Besides the documents of the Christian Scripture dealt with above, others will not be studied any further here. More space is necessary for their study, but only yeilds a small amount of fruit in regard to the origin and development of the gospel. This does not mean that they are of no use for the study of development of Christian tradition. Nonetheless, what is important is the fact that they also kept interpreting Jesus Christ theologically and developing the Christian tradition. This is how the gospel of Christianity was formed and developed in the first century CE.

3

The Concept of Gospel

THE TERM "GOSPEL" ORIGINALLY refers to the good news sent from God. However, gospel in the Bible conveys different meanings according to the one using the word. Each writer understood the gospel differently. As a result, it is important to observe the process of how the concept of gospel changed and developed as time passed at the beginning of Christianity. The way the gospel was understood by the author of Q, Paul, the four Gospels, and the rest of the Christian Scripture will be discussed in this chapter. This is necessary because it provides a key to acknowledging how each author developed the instructions of Christianity according to his or her understanding of the gospel. At first, the gospel was understood to have been an announcement of blessing that was sent to the prophets by God. Later, as time passed, it became more focused on Jesus Christ.

A. Q

The term "gospel" is used only once in Q. Consequently, it is not easy to infer its meaning from Q alone. However, the specific context allows the presumption that Q defined it from a prophetic perspective. The third and fourth redactors regarded themselves as the prophets who proclaimed the gospel of God.

Q uses the word "gospel" only once in the third redaction. For this, the third redactor described that Jesus had talked about John by alluding to Isa 29:18–19; 35:5–6 and 61:1 (Q^3 7:22):[1] the blind receive sight, the lame walk,

---

1. Tuckett, Q, 126.

those who have leprosy are cleansed, the deaf hear, the dead are raised, and the good news is proclaimed to the poor. At this point, Q uses the Greek verb εὐαγγελίζομαι ("proclaim good news"). The gospel is the good news and the joyful sounds that God conveyed through the prophets. The most beautiful and joyful words for the poor would be those that tell them how to solve their economic problems. The gospel explains the specific ways to free the people of God from their financial hardships and social bondage. In this respect, the gospel held a practical aspect for those who heard it.

The gospel is indirectly related to the kingdom of God in Q. Proclaiming the gospel as good news for the poor, Jesus already announced that the kingdom of God belonged to them according to the first redactor (Q^1 6:20b). Then, the phrase "the poor" becomes the medium that connects the gospel and the kingdom of God when the third redaction was completed. Thus, the gospel is a message of God through prophets that allows the poor have hope for freedom from economic difficulties and to possess the kingdom of God.

Q describes the prophets as those who proclaimed the gospel. The third redactor described Jesus as a prophet who proclaimed the gospel like Isaiah in Q^3 7:22. Then, the redactor mentioned that the people went out to the wilderness in order to see a prophet and that John is the one who is more than a prophet (7:24–26). This means that John was also a prophet sent by God, just as God had sent the prophet Isaiah to proclaim good news to the poor. Then, the third redactor indirectly identified the disciples of Jesus with those who were more than the prophets because the former had seen and heard what the latter would have liked to but could not (10:24). Finally, the redactor defined Jesus as the one greater than Jonah the prophet (11:32). In this way, Jesus, his disciples, and John were considered by the third redactor to be prophets who proclaimed the gospel. Later, the fourth redactor further developed the status of the disciples with regard to the prophets. After pointing out the ancestors' persecution of the prophets (Q^4 6:23c), the redactor mentioned that the contemporary Jews built the tombs for the prophets (11:47). This implies that the Jews consistently persecuted the prophets even though they claimed to respect them. Then the redactor described the death of the prophets in Jerusalem (13:34). They were none other than the disciples of Jesus who were regarded as the prophets. In this respect, it is highly probable that the fourth redactor considered him or herself to be one of the prophets as the disciple of Jesus. In addition, in creating the words of Jesus, the redactor believed that he or she had proclaimed the gospel of God. In this way, the fourth redactor seemed to have self-understanding that he or she was a prophet as a disciple of Jesus who proclaimed the gospel. In conclusion, the third redactor formed the concept of the gospel and the fourth redactor developed it in Q.

B. The Pauline Epistles

Paul also used the word "gospel" in various places. It seems that while he learned about the word "gospel" from the Jewish tradition, he might have been familiar with its use in Q and the first Christian gospel. Moreover, Paul is the first person who defined the gospel in his own way with regard to the prophecy about Jesus Christ.

Paul explained the gospel in connection with Jesus Christ. Written as "the gospel of God" or "the gospel of Christ," he defined the gospel in Rom(1): "he [God] promised beforehand through his prophets in the Holy Scriptures regarding his Son" (Rom 1:2–3). Paul saw the gospel as the prophecy about Jesus Christ the Son of God in the Bible. In this respect, Paul was the first person who defined the gospel in the Christian writings. The fact that Romans was written near the end of his life shows that it took some time for him to fully develop his understanding of the gospel.

Paul's gospel included his own opinions while also reflecting previous traditions. Though Paul acknowledged Q's concept of the gospel as the good news of the prophets, he himself uncovered other prophecies about Jesus and included them in the gospel. For this, Paul considered the perspective of the First Christians, who interpreted the death and resurrection of Christ while applying the hermeneutic principle "according to the Scriptures." He adopted this tradition and defined every prophecy about Jesus Christ in the Bible as the gospel. In this sense, Paul's definition of the gospel was on a larger scale than that of the First Christians, who understood the instruction about the death, burial, resurrection, and epiphany of Christ to be the gospel, but on a smaller scale than that of Q, which regarded the proclamation of prophets sent by God as the gospel.

Paul added to the depth and extent of the gospel. He accepted the verses he believed to be prophecies about Jesus Christ as gospel. A typical example would be Gal 3:8. Paul interpreted the prophecy that the Gentiles would be blessed through Abraham as the gospel (Gen 12:3). This is because Paul believed that the prophecy had been fulfilled by Jesus, who was the descendant of Abraham. In addition, Paul clearly kept the content of the Bible in mind when he used the word "gospel." For instance, Paul would have believed the event when Moses brought water out of a rock by striking it in the wilderness to be gospel since he interpreted that rock as Christ (1 Cor 10:4; Num 20:10–13). Thus, every prophecy or verse in the Bible that can be connected to Jesus is gospel in Paul's view. Paul included as many biblical allusions in his gospel as possible. In its midst, the allusion to the redemptive death of the Suffering Servant of YHWH is located (1 Cor 15:3; Isa 53:10). In this sense, Paul made his own theological interpretations about Jesus Christ in connection with the gospel. This kind of description reveals Paul's discovery and interpretation of the gospel beyond the tradition he inherited from the First Christians. This shows how the gospel was formed and developed by Paul in the mid-first century CE.

C. Mark

Mark received the concept of the gospel from Q and Paul. Depending upon them, he defined the gospel from the very beginning. This is unique in the fact that Mark applied it to the whole life of Jesus Christ.

Mark effectively defined the gospel. This is shown at the beginning of the book, where Mark prominently used the phrase "the gospel about Jesus Christ the Son of God" (Mark 1:1). Reflecting Paul's definition, "gospel" and "the Son of God" also appear in Mark. In addition, Mark defined "gospel" as the meaning of Jesus' teachings and actions during his life, which fulfilled the prophecies. This is why Mark described it generally taking after the Suffering Servant of YHWH and using lots of quotations from the Bible. Such perspectives are the result of Mark inheriting the ideas of Paul and applying them to the life of Jesus as the gospel itself.

Mark put Jesus Christ in parallel with the gospel to his understanding of discipleship. Narrating that Jesus announced the coming of the kingdom of God and proclaimed the need to repent and believe the gospel (Mark 1:14–15), Mark then put the gospel in close relationship with Jesus Christ. In other words, believing in the gospel is accepting the proclamation of Jesus Christ. Mark then related that Jesus taught his disciples to lose their life, family, and even material possessions for him and for the gospel (8:35; 10:29). Putting the gospel in parallel with Jesus Christ, Mark supported the concept that Jesus himself is the gospel. In this respect, the gospel and Jesus are interchangeable in Mark as the objects for which one should give one's life and material possessions. This interpretation can be supported by the account of the woman who poured expensive perfume on Jesus' head (14:3–9). Afterwards, Jesus explains that she had done this in preparation for his burial and that from that moment on, as the gospel is preached throughout the world, what she has done will also be told. Because the woman used all of her material possessions for the preparation of his death and burial, she was a real disciple who believed in the gospel. In this respect, Mark once again stated that the gospel is Jesus Christ himself and that it is closely related with the discipleship.

Mark described the death of Jesus Christ as a part of the gospel, reflecting Paul's perspective on the gospel. Having composed the life of Jesus, Mark described the suffering and death of Jesus as the events that fulfilled the prophecies; according to Paul, the prophecies about Jesus Christ are the gospel. To be more precise, Paul confessed his belief in redemption by saying that Christ "died for our sins according to the Scriptures"; however, he only left hints about a sacrificial and guilt offering without revealing which Bible verses were being referenced. Following Paul's perspective on the gospel, Mark applied to Jesus the image of the Suffering Servant of YHWH who died for our sins. In order to do this, Mark clarified that Jesus gave his life as a guilt offering for many people while alluding to the prophecy written in Isa 53:10 (Mark 10:45). Mark also developed this description and indicated that Jesus Christ will be sacrificed for many by declaring that the wine cup at the Lord's Supper is the blood he shed (14:24). Later, though Jesus wanted to avoid the cup of death at Gethsemane (14:36), he obeyed God and died on the cross for many people (15:21–41). However, Mark did not mention the people's sins in connection with the death of Jesus directly. Mark thus implicitly applied the theology of redemption to the death of Jesus as he inherited it from Paul. In this respect, with the redemptive death of Jesus being the highlight of the gospel itself, it is apparent that the gospel was formed and developed from Paul to Mark in the second half of the first century CE.

In conclusion, Mark defined the gospel as the instruction that came from the life of Jesus Christ. For this, he added new sources to the transmitted tradition; while some of these sources were probably collected, the rest were created by Mark. Imposing the Pauline theology of redemption to the biography of Jesus Christ he composed, Mark put Jesus in parallel with the gospel. As a result, Mark believed that he was delivering the gospel. In this respect, Mark was a creative writer from a theological perspective.

D. Matthew and Luke

Matthew and Luke have nearly the same perspectives on the gospel. These two Gospels see the proclamations of Jesus Christ about the kingdom of God as gospel. However, having used the previous traditions, they defined "the gospel" a little differently.

Matthew and Luke defined gospel as the good news that solves problems by providing for people in need. For this, Matthew and Luke took the text from Q³ 7:22 and use it in the context of revealing the role of Jesus (Matt 11:5; Luke 7:22). Matthew and Luke defined gospel as the teachings of Jesus to enjoy the things available in their actual life. In this respect, they followed Q's definition of gospel than that of Paul and Mark.

Matthew and Luke also seem to have changed their perspectives about the subject of the gospel. While Q saw the gospel as the good news the prophets sent by God have conveyed, Matthew and Luke think of the gospel as the good news Jesus Christ spoke about the kingdom of God (Matt 4:23; 9:35; 24:14; Luke 4:43; 8:1; 16:16). It seems that Matthew and Luke made the relationship between the gospel and the kingdom of God even closer and stronger than Q did. On the other hand, while Paul saw the gospel as the prophecies about Jesus through the prophets, Matthew and Luke think of the gospel as the teachings of Jesus Christ alone. While Mark saw the gospel as the meaning conveyed through the life of Jesus, Matthew and Luke thought of the gospel as the lessons from Jesus about the kingdom of God. In this way, Matthew and Luke changed the subject of the gospel from God to Jesus Christ.

Matthew and Luke reflected the perspective of Paul and Mark on the gospel. According to Matthew, Jesus Christ is the one who fulfilled prophecies (Matt 1:22; 2:15, 17–18, 23; 4:14; 8:17; 12:17–21; 13:35; 21:4; 27:9). Among this content, there are many that notify the fulfillment of prophecies. Of course, Matthew did not define these prophecies as gospel, but he applied the perspective of Paul on the gospel in order to confirm that Jesus had fulfilled the prophecies of the Bible. Moreover, Matthew wrote about Jesus as one who fulfilled prophecies many times in his life while applying Mark's view on the gospel. In this respect, Matthew wrote about Jesus Christ using previous traditions about the gospel. Luke also defined Jesus as the Christ who fulfilled the prophecies of the Bible. For example, Jesus Christ authoritatively said, "Today this Scripture is fulfilled in your hearing" (Luke 4:21). Jesus, risen from the dead, told his disciples everything that had happened to him was to fulfill what was written in the Psalms and the writings of every prophet and Moses (24:26–27, 44–45). Along with this, in Acts, the author stated that God foretold the suffering of Christ through all the prophets (Acts 3:18). Finally, Jesus is defined as the Christ through this process, citing the prophecies of Moses and Samuel (3:20–26). With this kind of writing, the Lucan documents describe the life of Jesus as the one fulfilling the prophecies of the Bible. It could be said that Luke's description of Jesus also reflects the perspective of Paul and that of Mark on the gospel. However, Luke did not consider the prophecies to be the gospel about Jesus Christ.

E. Other Documents

The other documents exclusive of the Pauline epistles and the Synoptic Gospels do not mention much about the gospel. Of course, the reader must take a look at the perspective of each writer on the gospel, since it is impossible to explain it as a whole. It is, however, to be noted that the gospel was becoming more closely related with Christ at the end of the first century CE.

The Deuteropauline epistles also defined the gospel. According to Ephesians, "gospel" is the word of truth that leads people to salvation (Eph 1:13). It seems that Christ is the one who gives the word of truth—that is, the gospel—because people heard about it in Christ. Through the gospel, the Gentiles will also be the people of God with Christ as an expression of salvation (3:6–7). In this respect, the gospel was becoming more closely related with Christ at the turn from the first to the second century CE.

Hebrews used the term "gospel" two times in the form of the participle (Heb 4:2, 6). It connected the gospel with the term "the word" and defined "gospel" as the promise about the rest that the people of God would receive (4:1). This means the teaching on how to receive rest from heaven. In this sense, the gospel is the instruction about the peace that would be enjoyed at the place of eschatological rest. This is written in the sense similar to Matthew and Luke, which presented the gospel as the teaching on how to get into the kingdom of God. The reason Hebrews conveyed the gospel as eschatological rest seems to be because the recipients were under persecution from the Roman Empire. As such, the gospel was defined according to the situation of the time.

First Peter defines the gospel more concretely. The gospel must be preached to people by the power of the Holy Spirit (1 Pet 1:12). This is the word of the Lord (1:25), and it has the transcendental power that can be preached to those who are dead as well as those who are alive (4:6). In this sense, the gospel is described as an existing form that has been given spiritual power. Of course, it is clear that the gospel is given by God (4:17). This is written in the similar sense as Q, which describes the gospel as the good news God sent through the prophets. This perspective was developed into the teaching of Jesus about the kingdom of God in Matthew and Luke. Then 1 Peter also seems to have defined the gospel as the word of the Lord in connection with this perspective.

Revelation does not mention much about the gospel. The gospel is, however, defined as what God conveyed through the prophets, and among this is the content detailing how the mystery of God will be accomplished (Rev 10:7). This presents the judgment through catastrophe at the end as the fulfillment of the gospel conveyed by the prophets, which shows the apocalyptic aspects of Revelation. Of course, the gospel is eternal (14:6). In this sense, Revelation seems to have seen the gospel as the general perspective of the Jews at that time—that is, what God conveyed through the prophets, following the traditions of Q. This shows how the definition of the gospel has changed and developed at the end of the first century CE.

F. Conclusion

In general, the gospel means the instruction regarding Jesus Christ. The concept of gospel, however, has changed over time according to the writer. First, as the Jews at that time generally thought, Q defined the gospel as the good news God conveyed to his people through the prophets. In this sense, Jesus as a prophet conveyed the gospel. In fact, the third and fourth redactors of Q had self-understanding that they had delivered the gospel as the prophets of God through the lips of Jesus. Unlike this, the First Christians interpreted the death, burial, resurrection, and epiphany of Christ according to the Scriptures as the content of gospel. In this, the Bible is at least related to the gospel. Paul, who had inherited this tradition, defined the prophecies about Jesus as gospel. Giving shape to Paul's concept, Mark defined the gospel as the words, actions, and life of Jesus Christ, through which he fulfilled the prophecies. Later, Matthew and Luke defined the gospel as the teachings of Jesus about the kingdom of God. This changed the concept of Q, which said the gospel was the good news God conveyed through the prophets, into Jesus Christ conveying the good news about the kingdom of God. Following this, 1 Peter generalized the concept of the gospel while defining it as the words of the Lord that have power. In this way, the concept of the gospel has gradually changed over time in at least four different variations. The origin, formation, and development of the gospel can be uncovered as these changes are identified.

PART II

The First Gospel and Its Development

THE FIRST CHRISTIAN GOSPEL refers to the content, summarized in 1 Cor 15:3b–5a, which the First Christians conveyed to Paul. This deals with death, burial, resurrection, and epiphany of Christ. Each element of this written text is essential to the core of the Christian gospel. This is due to the phrase "according to the Scriptures," which is used in connection with the death and resurrection of Christ. Such events could be historical; however, the theological interpretations are more important. Not only did Paul inherit this content, but the authors of the Gospels and the other books in the Christian Scripture did as well. Christ is described as the one who fulfilled the prophecies of the Scriptures. The content of the first Christian gospel was developed through the transmission of tradition. In this section, each element of the first Christian gospel will be studied on the basis of the discussion in the prologue regarding the nature of faith, the chronological order of writings, and the concept of the gospel.

4

According to the Scriptures

THE BIBLE CAN BE seen as a background for explaining the status and role of Jesus Christ. The First Christians stated that Christ died and rose according to the Scriptures. They used the hermeneutic principle of "according to the Scriptures," and Paul, who inherited this principle, cited many verses from the Bible in order to explain about Jesus Christ. Paul, the first to apply this principle to Jesus, was then followed by Mark, Matthew, John, and Luke, as well as the writers of the other documents in the Christian Scripture. While doing so, they explained Jesus as the one who fulfilled the prophecies in the Bible. This was the way of interpreting Jesus' status and role and forming the gospel about him in early Christianity.

A. Q

Q quoted verses of the Bible while writing about specific characters. What is interesting is that Bible verses were cited to define the status and role of John rather than Jesus. Typology, on the other hand, was used in order to explain about Jesus.

Q applied the Bible verses to John. The first redactor cited Isa 40:3 and introduced John as the man calling in the wilderness (Q^1 3:4). He was the man shouting to prepare and straighten the way of God the Lord. The third redactor also cited Exod 23:20 and/or Mal 3:1 in order to again explain the role of John (Q^3 7:27). For this, the quotation formula "as it is written [γέγραπται]" was used for the first time. While the first quotation is the interpretation of the first redactor, the second is of the third redactor through the lips of Jesus. The second citation appears while Jesus himself was evaluating John. It is, however, noteworthy that Q did not quote the Bible verses for Jesus at all.

The fourth redactor cited the Bible in connection with Jesus. He responded to the test of the devil by quoting Deut 6:13, 16; 8:3 (Q^4 4:4, 8, 12; cf. Matt 4:7). Here the quotation formula "as it is written" is used again. According to the redactor, Jesus acknowledged the Bible as the word of God and used it as a weapon to defeat the devil. Although these verses are not intended to explain the status or role of Jesus, they do show him as a man with the capacity to defeat the devil with the words of God. However, it does not apply the principle "according to the Scriptures" to define Jesus' status and role.

Q causes readers to think about the characters or events of the Bible through specific texts. For this purpose, the baptism, temptation, the calling of the disciples, the intercessory prayer, and the eschatological promise should be introduced (Q^3 3:21–22; 10:21–22; Q^4 4:1–13; 6:13–16; 22:30). These are connected to the fact that Moses established the twelve tribes, interceded on their behalf at Mount Sinai after crossing the Red Sea, and was tempted in the wilderness while leading the people of Israel to the land of Canaan. Q explains the status and role of Jesus by comparing him to Moses.[1] This is a way of writing commonly used among Jews now known as Moses/Exodus typology. It was frequently used when they looked at their leaders theologically. Jewish characteristics are shown in Q when considering the literary methods of the Jews applied to Jesus. However, it is not written yet in Q that Jesus is the one fulfilling the prophecies according to the Scriptures.

B. The First Christian Gospel

The First Christians understood Christ in the light of the Bible. They applied the hermeneutic principle "according to the Scriptures" to the death and resurrection of Christ. They are most likely to have been Pharisees, since the interpretations they made about his death and resurrection based on the Bible reveal their characteristics in adding new interpretation to the previous traditions.

The First Christians were those who pioneered the understanding of Christ according to the Scriptures. They identified him with the one who fulfilled the prophecies of the Bible. This is similar to Q in that it describes John by quoting verses from the Bible. While Q directly applied the cited

---

1. Allison, *Intertextual Jesus*, 68–73.

verses from the Bible to John, the First Christians did not apply the verses directly to Christ. However, this does not mean that they learned from Q how to apply Bible verses to John and followed the example in terms of Christ. On the contrary, while Q directly quoted Bible verses to describe the role of John and applied typology to the public life of Jesus, the First Christians only applied the hermeneutic principle of "according to the Scriptures" to Christ. The First Christians were from the Jewish Diaspora, and they only applied the means of interpretation they had previously inherited from Jewish thinking.

The First Christians should be credited with a significant achievement regarding the hermeneutic principle. They interpreted the death and resurrection of Christ from the perspective of "according to the Scriptures." However, they did not mention to which verse of the Bible they were referring. It is not clear whether the death and resurrection of Christ is a historical event, or if it is just a theological interpretation based on the Bible. The First Christians probably meant the latter, since Christ was interpreted as the servant of God who lived according to the Scriptures. Their interpretation simply reflects that they used the previous Jewish tradition to connect a certain servant of God to the Messiah—that is, Christ.

The relationship between Jesus and Christ is to be investigated at least. It is not clear whether the Christ mentioned by the First Christians referred to the historical Jesus described in Q. This is because Q does not speak about Jesus' death and resurrection according to the Scriptures at all. In my view, it is illogical to identify the Christ with the historical Jesus because the First Christians of Diaspora, probably Damascus in Syria, were unable to know about him living in the rural area of Galilee. In addition, they had no relationship with the twelve apostles of the Jerusalem Church at that time. Thus, they seemed to have someone in mind with their own criterion.

C. The Pauline Epistles

Paul inherited the hermeneutic principle "according to the Scriptures" from the First Christians that was applied to Christ. In addition, he knew that a couple of the biblical verses were applied to John in Q. Thus, it seems that Paul creatively used both traditions to describe the status and role of Jesus Christ. In this way, Paul formed the gospel that is the prophecy about Jesus Christ.

Paul used various patterns to cite the Bible verses. However, Paul did not quote many in the early days of his missionary work. First, 1 Thessalonians contains no quotation from the Scriptures. Paul used quotation formula "as it is written [γέγραπται]" in 1Cor(1) (1 Cor 10:7; 14:21) and 1Cor(2) (1 Cor 15:45). As mentioned beforehand, this quotation formula was already used in Q for the first time. Therefore, it is possible to conclude that Paul inherited it from Q. While it was used to define the role of John in Q, Paul applied it to describe the status and role of Christ following the hermeneutic principle "according to the Scriptures" inherited from the First Christians. Then he used the quotation formula "as it is written" more frequently in 1Cor(3) (1 Cor 1:19, 31; 2:9; 3:19; 9:9), Galatians (Gal 3:10, 13; 4:22, 27), 2Cor(1) (2 Cor 8:15), 2Cor(2) (9:9), Rom(1) (Rom 1:17; 4:17; 8:36; 14:11; 15:3, 9, 21), Rom(2) (2:24; 3:4, 10; 12:19), and Rom(4) (9:13, 33; 10:15; 11:8, 26). Paul included the words "it was written," "written," and "wrote" in various places as well (1 Cor 9:10; 15:54; 2 Cor 4:13; Rom 4:23; 10:5). In addition, he used the expression "it is fulfilled," "say," "it is proclaimed," and "it is prophesied" as substitutes for the phrase "according to the Scriptures" (1 Cor 6:16; Gal 5:14; 2 Cor 6:2, 16–18; Rom 4:6–8, 18; 9:15, 25–26, 27–28, 29; 10:19, 20; 11:9; 15:10, 12). Moreover, "What does the Scripture say?" is used (Rom 4:3), and "as the Scripture says" appears (10:11). Paul also quoted various verses directly and indirectly from the Bible without any formula. Through these words, Paul showed that Jesus was a man who lived according to the Scriptures and that his teaching was to be understood as much as possible under the light of the Scriptures. This is most likely because he needed the Bible in order to explain Jesus or defend his own missionary work. In other words, certain circumstances came up that made him cite more and more verses from the Scriptures.

Paul increased the frequency of citations from the Bible after his gospel and authority had been challenged. Most citations were made when the Gentile Christians turned their back on him after the event at Antioch. Among the verses cited above, only a few citations are found in 1Cor(1) and 1Cor(2), which had been sent before he faced the serious challenge. At any rate, it is clear that Paul sought to deliver his teaching under the light of the Bible when he was seriously challenged by the Corinthians and the Galatians. The stronger the challenge against him grew, the more frequently Paul cited the words of the Bible to describe the status and role of Jesus and defend his gospel and authority. In this manner, Paul used more Bible verses as the prophecies about Jesus Christ—that is, the gospel.

Paul also conveyed his theological interpretations while comparing Jesus to biblical events. For this purpose he used typological approaches. For instance, in 1Cor(1) Paul connected baptism with the crossing of the Red Sea (1 Cor 10:1–2; Ex 14:21–25) and compared the miracle of water in the wilderness with Christ in order to explain him as a rock (1 Cor 10:4; Num 20:10–13). In addition, in 2Cor(1) he compared Christ with Moses when he put a veil over his face in order to explain Christ as the worker of the new covenant (2 Cor 3:2–18; Exod 34:29–35). All of these events occurred during or shortly after the Israelites' escape from Egypt. Such Moses/Exodus typology was already applied to Jesus by the third and fourth redactors in Q. Paul seemed to have adopted this from Q and applied it to Jesus Christ. Moreover, Paul also compared Christ to Adam (1 Cor 15:21–22, 45; Rom 5:14), and in this, he is the first in the Christian writings. Such typology is also the result of applying the principle "according to the Scriptures." The Bible verses that were quoted in this part were prophecies that were fulfilled by Jesus, and they became the gospel to Paul. In conclusion, Paul extended the scope of the gospel by applying the hermeneutic principle of "according to the Scriptures" to Jesus Christ.

D. The Four Gospels

The hermeneutic principle "according to the Scriptures" was utilized by the Gospel writers as well. They gave theological meaning to Jesus Christ by citing Bible verses. However, their way of doing so was different from the authors of other documents. Thus, the four Gospels made theological interpretations that Jesus did God's work in this world according to the Scriptures.

Mark described that Jesus lived his life according to the Scriptures. The author cited the Bible in various ways to prove this. First, he used quotation formula such as "as it is written [γέγραπται]" (Mark 1:2; 7:6; 11:17; 14:27). Such quotation formula was conveyed through Q and the Pauline epistles. Mark also directly cited Bible verses in order to describe the status and role of Jesus (12:10–11, 36). Moreover, he attempted to cite verses indirectly (4:12; 7:10; 10:4, 19; 12:19, 26, 29–31; 14:27). In other places he simply alluded to the Bible (15:24, 31, 34, etc.). These quotations show that Jesus lived and taught according to the Scriptures. In this manner, Mark strengthened the instruction that the life of Jesus, namely the gospel, fulfilled the Bible prophecies (14:49). Inheriting the hermeneutic principle of "according to the Scriptures" from Paul, Mark quoted the Bible prophecies as much as possible in order to describe the status and role of Jesus Christ. This is how Mark showed his theological understanding of the gospel, namely the instructions from the life of Jesus Christ.

Mark wrote about the suffering, death, and burial of Jesus Christ based on the prophecies of the Bible. It is well known that in the Passion Narrative, Jesus is described as the one who fulfilled the role of the Suffering Servant of YHWH (Mark 11:1–15:47; Isa 52:13–53:12). For this purpose, Mark applied the principle "according to the Scriptures" by alluding to some aspects of the Suffering Servant of YHWH; thus, Jesus Christ was without any response to the chief priests and the Roman Governor Pilate, was dragged to the place of crucifixion, and was buried in the tomb of rich Joseph of Arimathea (Mark 14:60; 15:4, 20, 46; Isa 53:7–9). While the First Christians interpreted the death of Christ simply according to the Scriptures, and while Paul inherited this tradition and confessed the death of Christ for the sins of the people in 1Cor(3), Mark wrote in narrative form that Jesus Christ died as a guilt offering for many people. Paul's declaratory description of the death of Christ was mixed with the historical descriptions of Mark. For this purpose, Mark used the prophecies of Isaiah as a theological basis to describe the status and role of Jesus in the Passion Narrative. As a result, Mark conveyed that the life of Jesus fulfilled the prophecy of Isaiah according to the Scriptures. While Q applied the Moses/Exodus typology to Jesus, Mark applied the Suffering-Servant-of-YHWH typology to Christ following the Pauline theology of redemption.

Finally, Mark developed the hermeneutic principle of "according to the Scriptures" for his own theological purpose. To do so, he described Jesus as a man who fulfilled prophecies on his own. These prophecies are connected to the first Christian gospel. While the First Christians and Paul told about the death, burial, resurrection, and epiphany of Christ, Mark wrote that Jesus fulfilled the prophecies that he had foretold about his suffering, death, and resurrection three times (Mark 8:31; 9:31; 10:33–34). Mark also included prophecies made by Jesus foretelling the disciples' abandonment and Peter's denial, showing that they had been fulfilled as well (14:27–31, 50, 66–72). Such patterns of fulfilling prophecies are the result of Mark developing and applying the perspectives of the First Christians and Paul on the gospel. Paul accepted the prophecies about the Son of God as gospel, and Mark inherited this perspective and described Jesus as a man who fulfilled even his own prophecies. Through this, Mark showed the process of how the hermeneutic principle "according to the Scriptures" was developed to describe the gospel that is the instruction of the words and actions of Jesus Christ the Son of God. Mark should be credited with a unique achievement in the description that Jesus fulfilled his own prophecies.

Matthew described Jesus Christ as one who lived "according to the Scriptures." The author cited the Bible in various ways for this purpose. First, Matthew used the quotation formula "as it is written [γέγραπται]" in various places (Matt 2:5; 4:4, 6, 7, 10; 11:10; 21:13; 26:31). Such quotation formula was conveyed through Q, the Pauline epistles, and Mark. Second, Matthew cited Bible verses while using the pattern of fulfilling prophecies. For this purpose, he used the pattern "to fulfill what was spoken" through the prophet and "came to pass" (1:22–23; 2:15, 17–18, 23; 4:14–16; 8:17–18; 12:17–21; 13:14–15, 35; 21:4–5; 27:9). With these formulas, Matthew asserted that Jesus had fulfilled the prophecies of the prophets with regard to his status and role. As a result, Matthew concretely applied the perspective of Paul, who thought the prophecies about Christ were gospel. Third, he used the comparative pattern "you have heard that it was said to the people long ago" (Matt 5:21, 27, 31, 33, 38, 43). This pattern was used to convey the status and role of Jesus, who was greater than Moses. In this way, Matthew applied the hermeneutic principle of "according to the Scriptures" to the life of Jesus. Fourth, Matthew directly quoted verses from the Bible with no discernible pattern (3:3; 9:13; 12:7; 15:4, 8–9; 19:5, 7, 18–19; 21:16, 42; 22:24, 32, 37, 39, 44; 24:15; 27:46, etc.). Many of these are used to describe that the status and role of Jesus was composed according to the Scriptures (26:54). This is how Matthew made theological interpretations about Jesus based on previous tradition. It is, however, noteworthy that Matthew did not regard these verses from the Bible as the gospel itself.

Following Mark, Matthew also described Jesus Christ as the one who had fulfilled the role of the Suffering Servant of YHWH. Matthew not only understood Jesus to be the guilt offering by indirectly citing Isa 53:10 (Matt 20:28; Mark 10:45) but also described the suffering, death, and burial of Jesus Christ (Matt 21:1–27:66). In addition, Matthew strengthened the role of Jesus as the one who had fulfilled the role of the Suffering Servant of YHWH by citing Isa 53:4 (Matt 8:17). In this, following the previous tradition, Matthew attempted to establish that Jesus was the one who had worked according to the Scriptures. However, Matthew rarely related the Bible verses with the gospel that is the instruction of Jesus Christ about the kingdom of God or heaven.

Matthew also applied the Moses/Exodus typology to Jesus Christ. As Moses provided freedom to the Israelites by leading them out of Egypt, Jesus is the one who saved his people from their sins (Matt 1:21; Exod 3:10). For this purpose, Matthew wrote comparisons of the life of Jesus to that of Moses. Examples of this include baby Jesus entering and exiting Egypt, the baptism, the temptation, the Sermon on the Mount, the ten miracles, the calling of the twelve disciples, the event of transfiguration, and the Great Commission (Matt 2:13–23; 3:16–17; 4:1–11; 5:1—7:27; 8:1—9:34; 10:2–4; 17:1–8; 28:16–20, etc.). The Moses/Exodus typology was already used in Q and the Pauline epistles, and Matthew developed it further and applied it to the whole life of Jesus. As a result, Matthew progressively used the hermeneutic principle of "according to the Scriptures."

John cited the Bible extensively in order to explain the status and role of Jesus Christ. While doing so, the author claimed that Jesus fulfilled what was written in the Bible (John 2:17; 6:45; 12:15, 38, 40; 13:18; 15:25; 19:24, 28, 36, 37). John also cited the Bible in order to explain the situation of John the Baptist (1:23; 6:31). On the other hand, the enemies of Christ also used it in order to refute him (7:42; cf. 8:2). Patterns of fulfilling prophecies are shown (12:38; 13:18; 15:25; 17:12; 19:24, 28, 36), and these patterns are similar to those used by Matthew. Particularly, John made a statement that the Scriptures testified about Jesus (5:39). This seems to be the author's theological conclusion announced through the mouth of Jesus. John developed the tradition that the status and role of Jesus was "according to the Scriptures" as it was passed down from the First Christians to Paul and the writers of the Gospels.

Biblical quotations also appear throughout the Lucan documents. Luke used both direct and indirect quotations to describe the status and role of Jesus Christ. He inherited the quotation formula "as it is written [γέγραπται]" from Q and used it in various places, citing the Bible verses (Luke 2:23; 3:4; 4:4, 8, 10; 7:27; 19:46). In addition, Luke adopted a modified phrase, "which is written [γεγραμμένον]" in several places (4:17; 20:17; 22:37). Of course, Luke quoted some verses from the Bible with an introductory phrase (2:24; 4:12; 20:28, 37, 42). There are other verses cited without any formula (6:3; 10:27; 18:20). However, unlike Matthew and John, the Lucan documents do not often use the pattern of fulfilling prophecies (Luke 4:21; 18:31; Acts 1:16; 13:27, 29). Nevertheless, Luke wrote that Jesus is the one who fulfilled the Law of Moses, the Prophets, and the Psalms (Luke 24:27, 44–45). Acts also introduces Jesus as the man who fulfilled the prophecies of Moses and Samuel and who represents many prophets (Acts 3:18–26, especially 24). Ultimately, Jesus is a man who lived according to the Scriptures. However, Luke did not quote the Bible verses much compared with Mark and Matthew. In addition, Luke did not use the Bible verses in order to explain the kingdom of God that is the core content of the gospel according to this perspective.

E. Other Documents

Most documents of the Christian Scripture show the interpretation according to the Scriptures about Jesus Christ. Thus, they quote the Bible for this purpose. For the sake of space, however, I would like to limit my comments to Hebrews since it cited many verses.

Hebrews is the most prolific Christian Scripture in its use of the Bible, and many of the included quotations are direct. The author cited the Bible in order to support what he was trying to convey. He cited the Bible using transitions such as "as has just been said" (Heb 3:15), "just as God has said"

(4:3; 8:8; 10:8), "spoke through David, as in the passage already quoted" (4:7), and "testifies to us" (10:15). The writer also used other verses or direct quotations from the Bible (1:5–14; 2:6–8, 12–13; 3:7–11; 4:4–5; 5:5–6; 6:14; 7:17, 21; 8:5; 9:20; 10:5–7, 30, 37–38; 12:5–6, 20–21; 13:5–6). Some of these were quoted in order to explain the status and role of Jesus. Along with direct quotations, the author used many descriptions that remind readers of specific Bible verses. The purpose of quoting many verses from the Bible and alluding to others was to show that the character and ministry of Jesus was "according to the Scriptures."

Hebrews made many theological interpretations about Jesus Christ while citing Bible verses. He is the high priest in heaven who is the greatest of all (Heb 1:2–4; 3:1, etc.), and he went to heaven in order to be where he originally belongs. The typology describing the status and role of Jesus based on a different figure was used in Q, the Pauline epistles, Mark, and Matthew. Similar to this, Hebrews sought to demonstrate the fact that Jesus is the Christ as high priest. The author was able to use quotations since he was already familiar with other Christian Scriptures that had been written ahead of Hebrews. In this sense, he made theological interpretations that Jesus was a man who did the work of God according to the Scriptures. Hebrews should be credited with a unique achievement in the fact that Jesus was depicted as the high priest in heaven.

Hebrew quotes many Bible verses from the beginning. It would be difficult to find another book in the Christian Scripture that cited the Bible verses as much as Hebrews; however, the author did not use the pattern of fulfilling prophecies as Matthew and John did. This seems to be the case since Hebrews delivered the instruction in the form of declaration rather than in the form of narrative used in the Gospels and Acts. Nevertheless, the hermeneutic principle of "according to the Scriptures" was still maintained in the fact that Hebrews attempted to connect Jesus with various figures of the Bible, especially the high priest. However, the author did not use it to explain the gospel that is the teaching on how to receive rest from heaven. In this manner, the way of describing the status and role of Jesus according to the Scriptures changed and developed at the end of the first century CE.

F. Conclusion

Most of the documents in the Christian Scripture quoted verses from the Bible in order to explain the fact that Jesus Christ lived according to the Scriptures. This began when the First Christians applied this method to Christ in order to explain the gospel. After that, Paul cited prophecies from the Bible and wrote that they were fulfilled by Jesus Christ. They are the gospel according to Paul. Mark followed this tradition and wrote that Jesus fulfilled the prophecies written in the Bible while writing about his life as the gospel. As a result, he adopted ways of quoting the Bible and reminding readers of the Suffering Servant of YHWH. Matthew, who inherited this, emphasized that the life of Jesus was composed according to the Scriptures while using patterns of fulfilling prophecies. However, Matthew did not use the hermeneutic principle of "according to the Scriptures" to directly convey the concept of the gospel. This was succeeded by John and was adopted by most of the documents that were written at the end of the first century CE.

The Bible verses were quoted for various purposes. This shows the process of how the hermeneutic principle "according to the Scriptures," a primary element of the first Christian gospel, was formed and developed in connection with the gospel. Quoting Bible verses is not a way to accurately explain the life of Jesus. Rather, it is the way to theologically interpret the gospel and give meaning to the life of Jesus Christ. In detail, each writer interpreted and conveyed the image of Jesus he believed in and confessed under the light of the Bible. This shows that more theological interpretations were added at that point, demonstrating that the gospel includes the theological interpretation added to the historical fact of Jesus.

5
The Death of Christ

THE ACCOUNT OF THE death of Jesus Christ developed in connection with gospel. The First Christians gave meaning to the death of Christ according to the Scriptures for the first time, though they did not mention how Christ died. This is similar to Q, which does not include an account of Jesus' death. Paul was the first to write about Jesus Christ's death on the cross from a redemptive perspective. Later, in Mark's narrative description of the life of Jesus Christ, his redemptive death on the cross is the climax. Other Gospels followed this narrative form in describing the crucifixion of Jesus, though each writer prioritized the concept differently. Among the General Epistles, Hebrews and 1 Peter are particularly interesting in their description of the crucifixion from a redemptive perspective as the result of interpretations stemming from their theological perspectives.

A. Q

Q does not mention anything about the death of Jesus. As a result, there is no reference to his death on the cross. This means that Q gives no particular meaning to his death. However, it is worth examining, since Q does mention the cross once for the discipleship.

The passage under consideration occurs as the fourth redaction discusses the conduct of a disciple of Jesus. This is the only instance in which the word "cross" is used in Q (Q^4 14:26–27). A person who wants to become a disciple must bear the cross given to him or to her and follow Jesus. However, this is simply a description of the requirements of discipleship and does not necessarily refer to Jesus' death in any specific way yet. If Jesus taught this knowing that he would die on the cross, he would have been a prophet who could see the future. Then, the people who wrote Q probably knew that Jesus died on the cross, but they did not mention the crucifixion at all. They probably believed that Jesus had been killed like the martyrs of prior ages. However, it is noteworthy that this saying does not evince the crucifixion of Jesus. On the other hand, if his disciples created this teaching after he died on the cross as if it had come from Jesus, it is a prophecy after the fact. However, this does not provide any theological meaning to his crucifixion, either. Jesus seemed to have been killed, but Q does not tell us how he actually died. As a result, no theological meaning was given to the death of Jesus in Q.

Q's connection between the cross and discipleship seems to reflect historical facts. If the temptation story was written by the fourth redactor when the Roman Emperor Gaius Caligula attempted to establish his statue in Jerusalem around 41 CE (Q^4 4:1–13), the instruction about the discipleship to carry his or her own cross to follow Jesus also ought to be interpreted in the same historical context. In other words, those who resisted the Roman Emperor were considered the traitors and sentenced to death on the cross. Then the discipleship should be interpreted in connection with crucifixion. This means that those who would follow Jesus and keep the Law had to be ready for the execution on the cross. This instruction is accordant with that of other texts that belong to the fourth redaction because it describes the persecution and martyrdom of disciples from the Deuteronomistic historical perspective (Q^4 6:23c; 11:47–51; 13:34–35).[1] In addition, when considering the instruction that Jesus came to the world so as to give a sword rather than peace (12:49–53), this means that the disciples had to rise up against the Roman Empire and cross swords. They had to run the risk of persecution and martyrdom, as the instruction about death dominates the fourth redaction (4:9–12; 9:59–60; 10:3; 12:4–5; 17:33; 17:1–2; 17:37). This is why the fourth redactor taught the disciples to carry their cross and follow Jesus. In this respect, the redactor paid more attention to the theological instruction in order to cope with the contemporary circumstances rather than the historical fact of the age.

In conclusion, Q did not impose any theological meaning on the death of Jesus. In addition, it did not describe how Jesus died. On the other hand, the fourth redactor described the persecution and martyrdom of disciples from the Deuteronomistic historical perspective. The cross was

---

1. Cf. Steck, *Israel und das gewaltsame Geschick*, 20–26, 257–60; Kloppenborg, *Formation*, 173, 190; and Jacobson, *First Gospel*, 72, 100–101.

mentioned in order to teach the disciples of Jesus how to respond to the situation that the Roman Emperor threatened the Jews with by erecting his statue in Jerusalem.

B. The First Christian Gospel

The First Christians expressed the view that Christ died according to the Scriptures. Along with Q, however, they did not mention how Christ died. Nevertheless, this interpretation demonstrates further theological progress than that found in Q, since they interpreted his death with the background of the Scriptures.

The First Christians imposed a theological meaning on the death of Christ. Even though they did not explain much about it, they interpreted his death based on the principle of "according to the Scriptures." The First Christians probably believed that Christ had been martyred like the prophets of the Bible. There are many verses that could be related with the death of the anointed servant of God in the Bible. However, they did not mention which verses prophesied it. At any rate, the First Christians are the first who theologically interpreted the death of the anointed servant of God, Christ.

The First Christians did not mention how Christ died. It is not clear whether they connected the death of Christ to the cross; probably they did not even know about it. The Bible does not provide any text that alludes to the crucifixion of Christ at all. In this sense, their descriptions about the death of Christ do not seem to have been written with the historical Jesus of Q in mind. Their confessions were about the death of Christ, the Lord's Anointed Messiah.

In conclusion, the First Christians seemed to create the instruction about the death of Christ. Even though they did not concretely describe the status of Christ, it is important that the First Christians formed theology about his death according to their interpretations of the Bible. In this way, the core teaching of Christianity began to be formed.

C. The Pauline Epistles

Paul inherited the traditions of Q and the First Christians, and Paul theologically interpreted the death of Jesus Christ in various ways. The death of Christ on the cross was most likely emphasized after the conflict at Antioch, when the apostles of the Jerusalem Church sent some people to the Gentile churches and challenged Paul's authority and gospel. Acknowledging that the Gentile Christians had accepted their teaching, Paul began to preach the death of Christ on the cross.

Paul referred to the death of Jesus Christ from the beginning of his missionary life. He stated that God had raised his Son from the dead in his first letter, 1Thess(1). This means that the Son of God actually died or was killed (1 Thess 1:10). It is, however, noteworthy that the Son of God is the one Paul got to know through revelation on the way to Damascus. Of course, Paul immediately identified the resurrected Son of God from the dead with Jesus. Then Paul mentioned that the Lord Jesus and the prophets were killed by the Jews (2:15). This is the first text that mentions Jesus being killed. It is, however, not known how Paul heard about the death of the Lord Jesus and whether he died on the cross. Thus, it is important to notice the enforced death of Jesus. In addition, it is also important to observe that the term "prophets" appears after Jesus. It seems that the prophets are the disciples of Jesus, not the prophets of the Bible. Then, it can be said that Paul also identified Jesus as one of the prophets. As shown beforehand, the third and fourth redactors of Q already identified Jesus and his disciples as the prophets. Especially from the Deuteronomistic historical perspective, the fourth redactor described their persecution and martyrdom by contemporaneous Jews. Thus, it can be surmised that Paul heard about the death of Jesus from Cephas when he visited Jerusalem around 38 CE. Inheriting the traditions of Q and the First Christians, Paul was probably able to define Jesus and his disciples as martyred prophets when he wrote 1Thess(1).[2]

Paul once again assumed the death of Christ in 1Cor(1). He mentioned that God had raised the Lord in connection with Christ (1 Cor 6:14–15). Paul presumed the death of Christ as the prior stage of his resurrection. It seems that Paul considered the death of Christ less significant than the resurrection. Like the First Christians, Paul did not mention the Scripture verses that provide the background for the theological interpretation of the death of Christ. There is no hint about how he died either. It is difficult to conclude that Paul took a look at the death of Jesus from a theological perspective. This implies that Paul did not yet need to think of the theological meaning of the death of Christ at the time of writing 1Cor(1).

The first occurrence of the imposition of meaning to the death of Christ is in 1Cor(2). When there was a conflict within the Corinthian Church concerning baptism, Paul mentioned the cross of Christ for the first time (1 Cor 1:10–17). The conflict occurred because while there were those who were baptized by Paul, others were baptized by Apollos or Cephas. It

---

2. As for the possibility that 1 Thess 2:14–16 reflects Q 11:47–51, see Allison, *Jesus Tradition*, 57–60.

seems that the Corinthians believed the person who baptized them was the most significant minister. As a result, they quarreled and were divided. When this dispute occurred, Paul rebuked the Corinthians through a series of rhetorical questions in regard to who was crucified for them. Then he asked the Corinthians not to nullify the power of Christ's cross. These descriptions inform the reader of how Paul understood Christ's death on the cross. First, Paul and the Corinthians knew about the cross. They knew it was a method of execution used by the Roman Empire to kill traitors. Second, the Corinthians knew that Christ died on the cross. This is known by the fact that the implied answer to Paul's rhetorical question was no one other than Christ and that the Corinthians were told not to nullify the cross of Christ. If they had not known about it, Paul would not have been able to speak in this way. This implies that Paul went one step further than the First Christians regarding the theological interpretation of the death of Christ. Third, Paul used the cross as a symbol of reconciliation, harmony, and unity, when the Corinthians were divided. He asserted that Christ should not have died in vain by emphasizing the need for unity among them. In conclusion, Paul imposed a meaning of reconciliation to the cross of Christ when he wrote 1Cor(2).

Paul imposed another meaning of sacrifice to the death of Christ in 1Cor(2). He announced that Christ died for the weak brothers and sisters (1 Cor 8:11). At this moment, the voluntary death of Christ was substituted for the enforced death of Jesus. In this way, Paul attributed a sacrificial meaning to the death of Christ. Paul went one step further by applying his death to the life of the weak, which had once been used to solve the quarrel and dispute. Then, Paul once again introduced the sacrificial death in connection with the supper held at the night of arrest (11:23–26). Paul described that whenever the Corinthians eat the bread given "for you" and take the cup of the new covenant, they must proclaim the death of the Lord until he comes again. Compared to the bread given for the Corinthians, his death was defined as a sacrifice for them. However, Paul did not talk about the way the Lord died or was killed. Paul went one step further in describing that the beneficiaries of the sacrificial death of the Lord Jesus were the participants in the Lord's Supper. The more Paul advanced writing 1Cor(2), the more he emphasized the sacrificial aspect of the death of Christ for the Corinthians. In this respect, Paul developed his theological understanding of the death of the Lord Jesus Christ.

When the church was in turmoil, Paul had the opportunity to pay attention to how Jesus Christ died. For instance, in 1Thess(2), hearing that the Thessalonians had recovered from being shaken, Paul dealt with the death of Jesus. Using the active verb ἀπέθανεν, Paul mentioned a second time that Jesus died (1 Thess 4:14). This is somewhat different from his previous expression in 1Thess(1) that Jesus was killed by the Jews. And then he used the expression "Jesus Christ died 'for us'" without talking about how he died (5:9–10). Once again Paul emphasized the voluntary and sacrificial death in a more direct way when he used the phrase "for us" here than compared to "for you" in 1Cor(2). The sequence between 1Cor(2) and 1Thess(2) is supported by the fact that both letters show Paul's interest in the sacrificial death of Jesus Christ.

Paul began to focus on the death of Christ on the cross when the Gentile Christians were shaken by the outsiders in Phil(1). Despite the turmoil they were in, he heard that they rejected the instruction of outsiders who were probably from the Jerusalem Church (Phil 3:1b–6). At this moment, Paul expressed his wish to become like Jesus Christ in his death (3:10). This means that Paul wanted to follow Jesus even to death. Then he defined the people who did not accept his instruction as enemies of cross of Christ (3:18). This is a strong critique against those who refused the gospel of Paul and followed the people from outside. It is important to notice that he began to emphasize the death of Christ on the cross as the core of his instruction. This is Paul's second mention after he mentioned the cross of Christ in connection with reconciliation in 1Cor(2). It seems that Paul imposed a theological meaning of salvation to the cross of Christ when he drew a contrast between the destruction and the Savior from heaven in the following texts (Phil 3:19–20). In this respect, as time passed, Paul developed his theological idea beyond the reconciliation in regard to the cross of Christ.

Paul added another meaning to the death of Jesus Christ on the cross in a continuing critical situation. Responding to the rebuke and rejection, Paul introduced a new interpretation about Jesus' death on the cross in 1Cor(3). For instance, Paul strongly commanded the Corinthians to return to the path that leads to salvation when he introduced the way of the cross (1 Cor 1:18—2:16). This is the third time that the cross of Christ is mentioned since its first use in 1Cor(2). Paul even proclaimed that he knew nothing other than the crucified Christ. He then defined the way of the cross as the wisdom of God that had been hidden, and only those of the Spirit could recognize the will of God embedded in the cross. In this respect, Paul suggested that the cross is the way of salvation a second time following the first suggestion in Phil(1). Paul then finally introduced the belief that Christ died "for our sins" (1 Cor 15:3). Thus, the redemptive role was attributed to the death of Christ for the first time. For this, Paul adopted the active verb once again in order to emphasize Christ's voluntary and sacrificial death as it was used in 1Cor(2) and 1Thess(2). At last, the death of Christ on the cross was related with people's redemption from sin in 1Cor(3). Paul made a breakthrough as he proclaimed the cross of Jesus Christ as the means of redemption and salvation at the very moment his authority was seriously challenged and the gospel was doubted. The executed Jesus was exalted as the crucified Christ, who voluntarily died for all humanity according to the Scriptures.

Paul also emphasized the death of Christ on the cross when he was seriously challenged by the Galatians. He pointed out that Jesus Christ died for the redemption of people (Gal 1:1, 4). Then he said that the Galatians knew about the crucified Jesus Christ (2:20; 3:1). In addition, Paul described the death of Christ on the tree as an event for the redemption of people according to the Scriptures (3:13). Without doubt, the tree refers to his cross. While doing so, Paul proclaimed that he could do nothing but emphasize the cross, even under persecution (5:11, 24; 6:12). Finally, Paul confessed that he would never boast in anything except the cross of Jesus Christ (6:14). Galatians reveals more intensified instruction than 1Cor(3) regarding the death of Christ on the cross. In this respect, Paul proclaimed the gospel of the cross as best as he could, preaching that Jesus Christ died on the cross for the redemption of people. Paul presented the cross of Jesus Christ as the uncompromising core of the gospel after he faced the challenge from the Galatians, which was probably sponsored by the apostles of the Jerusalem Church.

Later, Paul once again mentioned the death of Christ on the cross in 2Cor(3). On account of the consistent challenge of the Corinthians, Paul severely criticized the apostles of the Jerusalem Church who were behind them (2 Cor 11:5, 13–15). Paul argued that he was as strong as them, but immediately admitted his weakness, just as Jesus Christ had admitted weakness. He then stated, "Christ was crucified in weakness, yet he lives by God's power" (13:4). It means that the cross of Christ is the unique way leading the Christian life. It is, however, noteworthy that no particular meaning was assigned to his death here. It was written at the time when the instruction about the death of Christ was losing its influence over the Corinthians, reflecting the situation that they were straying away from Paul's gospel. Nevertheless, Paul did his best to keep the death of Christ on the cross as the core of gospel.

Paul kept emphasizing the death of Jesus Christ and the cross even after the challenge diminished. He referenced the death of Jesus Christ several places in Rom(1). Paul once again emphasized the historicity of Jesus' death by using the phrase "Jesus our Lord" (Rom 1:4; 4:24). Then, from a redemptive perspective, Paul clearly announced that Jesus Christ died for the people when they were sinners (5:6–10). In this way, Jesus' voluntary death is connected to the redemption of sinners. Paul continued mentioning the death of Christ to the end (14:7, 9, 15). Then in Rom(3), the redemptive role is once again assigned to the death of Jesus (6:3–11), which is the way to move from sin to righteousness (6:6–7). Thus, Paul articulated his idea that the Spirit made people understand the death of Christ as the means of delivering them from the death under the Law that lead them to sin (7:4–6). Then Paul simply mentioned the death of Jesus (8:11, 34). Paul continued mentioning the death of Christ in Rom(4). It is inevitably related to the salvation of people (10:7–9). However, Paul paid less attention to it at the end of his letters to the Romans. Nevertheless, it is important to observe that Paul kept delivering the theology of redemption in connection with the death of Jesus on the cross, even to the Roman Church, which he had not established and thus had not been shaken by the representatives of the Jerusalem apostles.

Paul mentioned the death of Jesus Christ on the cross from a christological point of view in Phil(2). He introduced it through a hymn (Phil 2:5–11).[3] Christ's death on the cross is interpreted as the result of his complete obedience to God; thus, the cross plays the key role of Christ's turning point from humbleness to exaltation. The more letters Paul wrote to the Gentile Christians, the more he developed his interpretation regarding the death of Jesus Christ.[4] In Phil(2), Paul connected Jesus' death on the cross with the will of God. Paul seemed to mention it in connection with Christians' attitude toward God. When considering that Phil(2) was written in Rome while Paul was in prison, Paul showed his understanding of his suffering under the light of Jesus Christ's complete obedience to the will of God. However, Paul did not need to deal with the cross of Christ much in Phil(2) because the Philippians stayed firmly in what he had taught. This indicates that he kept the death of Jesus Christ on the cross in his mind to the very end of his missionary journey as the core of his gospel.

In conclusion, Paul's theological perspective on the death of Christ changed according to the contemporary situation. From a chronological point of view, first Paul implied the death of Jesus by saying that God raised him from the dead in 1Thess(1) and 1Cor(1). Then Paul suggested the cross of Christ as a symbol of reconciliation and unity among the divided Corinthians and as an emblem of sacrifice by using the phrase "for you"

---

3. Most critical scholars have agreed that Phil 2:5–11 was an independent text. There are, however, various opinions about the date of its composition from the thirties to the end of the first century CE. For those who support the authorship of Paul, refer to Hofius, *Der Christushymnus*, 3–17; and Kim, *Origin of Paul's Gospel*, 147–49. On the contrary, for those who argue that Paul used the previous hymn sung in the early church, refer to Beare, *Commentary*, 77; and Hawthorne, *Philippians*, 103–104, 134.

4. For example, he had written that Jesus Christ died for the weak members of the Corinthian Church and the participants of the Lord's Supper in 1Cor(2) (1 Cor 8:11; 11:24–26), then for the Gentile Christians in general in 1Thess(2) (1 Thess 5:9–10), and finally for Paul himself, whom Jesus Christ loved in Galatians (Gal 2:20).

in 1Cor(2). When Paul faced the challenge of the Gentile Christians sponsored by the Jerusalem Church, he began to emphasize the sacrificial death of Jesus Christ by using the phrase "for us" in 1Thess(2). In addition, the cross of Christ was introduced as the unique means of salvation in Phil(1) and 1Cor(3). Finally, Paul considered the cross of Christ as the means of redemption in 1Cor(3), Galatians, Rom(1), and Rom(3). As time passed, Paul attributed more theological meaning to the death of Christ on the cross in response to the circumstances he faced during his missionary journey.

In exploring the historical background, we can explain why Paul articulated and renewed his thoughts on the cross of Jesus Christ. After the dispute between Paul and Cephas at Antioch around 50 CE, it seems that the apostles of Jerusalem thought Paul was overreacting. They began to criticize Paul and convinced the Gentile Christians to accept their instruction. They sent people to the Gentile churches to tell them to deny the authority and gospel of Paul, keep the Law, and be circumcised. This is supported by the fact that the Law was emphasized in the fourth redaction of Q, which was written by the Jerusalem apostles or under their supervision around 41 CE. While doing so, they received consent from the Corinthians and Galatians. When this happened, many people began to follow the apostles instead of Paul since they were the disciples of Jesus. Paul nearly lost the churches he founded among the Gentiles when his relationship with the apostles became estranged. This annoyed Paul and caused him to gain a new theological perspective based on the redemptive death of Jesus Christ on the cross. He proclaimed that there was no other gospel than his, and he cursed those who conveyed other teachings in Galatians. This is closely related to the fact that before Paul faced the challenge from the Gentiles, he had kept a positive view on the Law as revealed in 1Cor(1) (1 Cor 11:2; 14:21, 34). However, after the challenge of the Gentile Christians, Paul denied the role of the Law for righteousness in Phil(1) (Phil 3:9). He then took a neutral attitude toward the Law momentarily to support his argument in 1Cor(3) (1 Cor 9:8–9, 20–21) and then immediately showed his negative perspective on the Law, as reflected in 1Cor(3) (15:56), Galatians (Gal 2:18–19; 3:10, 19; 4:21; 5:3; 6:13), Rom(1) (Rom 4:13–15), Rom(2) (2:17–29), Rom(3) (5:20; 7:4–6; 8:3, etc.), and Rom(4) (9:31). In this respect, the Law was substituted with the cross of Christ for the redemption and salvation of the Gentiles.

There was a theological reason that Paul strongly emphasized the death of Jesus Christ on the cross when challenged at the Gentile churches. It was because only the people who received the Spirit of God could understand it (1 Cor 2:6–16). Such assertions were made according to Paul's own theological logic. It seems that the Corinthians and Galatians had experienced the Spirit of God (1 Cor 12:1–3; Gal 3:1–5), which is why Paul appealed to their experience of the Spirit. This was an alternative for the Gentiles that could surpass the mark pursued by the Jews and the wisdom pursued by the Greeks (1 Cor 1:18–25). Then, the Gentiles no longer had to keep the Law or be circumcised, as the apostles of Jerusalem demanded. This not only added mystery to the spiritual aspect, but also lowered the religious burden of keeping the Law, the physical burden of being circumcised, and the social burden of pursuing wisdom in the practical sense. In this way, Paul introduced a new level of faith to the Gentiles as he pointed out their experience of the Spirit of God. In conclusion, Paul insisted that the death of Christ on the cross, understood in the Spirit of God, surpassed the Law in terms of the salvation and redemption of the Gentiles.

D. Mark

Mark treated the death of Jesus Christ as a significant part of the gospel. For this purpose, he changed the theological statements of Paul into historical descriptions. Mark described the death of Christ on the cross as an incident of redemption and salvation, fulfilling the prophecies according to the Scriptures, and reflecting the perspective of Paul on the gospel.

In Mark, the death of Jesus Christ is the acme of his life—that is, of the gospel itself. As the story of Jesus advanced, Mark reached the culmination in the description of his crucifixion. Scholars have noted that Mark related the gospel with Christians' readiness to give their lives and material possessions for Jesus (Mark 8:35; 10:29–30; 14:8–9). This kind of discipleship was delivered in the context of the sacrificial death of Jesus on the cross. Moreover, according to Mark, Jesus frequently alluded to or talked about his death, and he finally fulfilled it on the cross (8:31; 9:31; 10:33–34, 38–39, 45; 14:24, 36; 15:21–39). In this respect, the death of Jesus on the cross takes the place of climax in Mark from a literary point of view.

According to Mark, the death of Jesus on the cross is revealed as a part of the gospel that fulfilled the prophecies in the Bible. For this purpose, Mark described many situations using the Bible as a background. For example, the description that the clothes of Jesus were divided based on casting lots reminds the reader of Ps 22:18 (Mark 15:24). The image of people passing by shaking their heads and hurling insults also makes the reader think of Ps 22:7 (Mark 15:29). Likewise, the part where Jesus cried out, "My God, my God, why have you forsaken me?" especially recalls Ps 22:1 (Mark 15:34). Moreover, the description that some people gave wine vinegar to Jesus points the reader to Ps 69:21 (Mark 15:36). Finally, the report of the two thieves on each side of Jesus when he was crucified is connected with the prophecy written in Isa 53:9 (Mark 15:27). Through these references, Mark wrote that Jesus died on the cross while fulfilling the prophecies of the Bible. This shows that Mark inherited the view of Paul, who defined the gospel as the prophecies about Christ and applied it to the description of his crucifixion. Without doubt, this interpretation originated with the First Christians, who interpreted the death of Christ according to the Scriptures. Hereby, Mark made the crucifixion of Jesus happened according to the Scriptures a part of the gospel that is his life itself.

Mark described the death of Jesus as an incident that reflected the Pauline perspective on the sacrifice and redemption. As shown beforehand, according to Mark, Jesus' death on the cross is implicitly described as a guilt offering for many in the context of the prophecy of Isaiah about the Suffering Servant of YHWH. This is the redemptive death of Christ that Paul alleged for the first time in 1Cor(3), and then Galatians, Rom(1), and Rom(3). In addition, Mark mentioned that Jesus shed blood for many on the cross as he had prophesied at the Lord's Supper, which was described in the background of the Passover meal (Mark 14:24; Exod 12:1–14). This reflects the sacrificial death of Christ that Paul provided a theological basis for in 1Cor(2) and 1Thess(2). In addition, Mark made Paul's confession in 1Cor(3) that Christ died "for our sins according to the Scriptures" into the historical event that Jesus gave himself as a guilt offering for the people as the sacrificed Passover lamb. Thus connected with the prophecy of the Scripture, Jesus' death is described as an event of sacrifice and redemption. In this way, Mark reflects the influence of Paul regarding the redemptive and salvific death of Jesus Christ.

Mark saw the death of Jesus Christ on the cross as the climax of salvation history. This is shown through the actions of the people present when he was on the cross. The people passing by tempted Jesus to come down from the cross and save himself (Mark 15:30). The chief priests and the scribes mocked him by saying that he saved others but could not save himself, saying if he came down from the cross, they would believe in him as the savior (15:31–32). However, Jesus did not respond to this mockery, showing that he did not become a savior in that way. Though Jesus died on the cross, the Roman Centurion said that he surely was the Son of God (15:39). In this way, Mark conveyed the crucifixion as an event of God for the salvation of many people.

E. Other Documents

The other Gospels that inherited Mark's tradition also stay within this framework. In addition, the Deuteropauline epistles regard Jesus' death as the most important instruction for salvation. The General Epistles also understand the death of Jesus Christ to be a means of salvation. In this respect, his death took the central position in Christian doctrine.

Matthew basically followed Mark in describing the death of Jesus on the cross. However, Matthew added some texts in order to heighten the redemptive death of Jesus. First of all, by adding the phrase "for the forgiveness of sins" to the Markan text about the cup of wine at the Lord's Supper, Matthew provided a stepping-stone to understanding Jesus' death as the event of redemption (Matt 26:28; Mark 14:24). In addition, Matthew added some elements to the story of crucifixion in order to convey his intended lessons. For instance, Matthew mentioned the part where the people call Jesus the Son of God twice, and he quoted Ps 22:8 when the chief priests and the scribes reproach him (Matt 27:40, 43). Citing verses from Psalms, Matthew emphasized that all events occurred according to the Scriptures. Moreover, by drawing parallels between the event of the cross and the temptation in the wilderness, the author contrasted them with that of Adam. Matthew wrote that Jesus was tempted with something to eat (Matt 4:3; 27:34), something to see (4:6; 27:40), and desirable authority (4:9; 27:42–43), which runs parallel with Adam being tempted by the forbidden fruit that seemed delicious, looked good, and was desirable as a source of wisdom at the garden of Eden (Gen 3:6). Although Adam and Eve were expelled from the garden to face death because they gave in to temptation, Jesus overcame temptation and brought new life to the kingdom of God. In a contrast between the type, Adam, and the antitype, Jesus, Matthew added theological meaning to his death on the cross. It was not the end but the beginning of a new world God planned to give to the people. In this way, Matthew applied the typological approach to the crucifixion story in order to embrace the entire race with an allusion to Adam, the ancestor of all humankind. Matthew described Jesus as the new ancestor of all humanity and attributed a role of salvation to his crucifixion. In this sense, Matthew portrayed Jesus' death on the cross as a salvific event for the redemption for all humankind according to the Scriptures. In this respect, Matthew reached the culmination of the theological description of the death of Jesus based on the previous traditions passed down to him from Paul and Mark.

John described the crucifixion of Jesus Christ from a different perspective. First, although its descriptions are generally not much different from those of Mark and Matthew, John modified several texts by addition and omission. For example, John added stories about Pilate's attempt to make a deal with Jesus for his release (John 19:7–11), the Jews' appeal to the royalty of Caesar (19:12–16), their challenge against the notice fastened to the cross (19:20–22), a conversation between Jesus and his mother (19:25–27), and the event of the piercing of Jesus' side with a spear (19:31–37). On the other hand, John omitted the accounts of Simon of Cyrene carrying Jesus' cross, the Jews' attempts to tempt Jesus to come down from the cross, the confession of the Roman Centurion, and the tearing of the curtain of the temple. John delivered his own instructions by addition and omission of those found in Matthew and Mark.

Second, John also described the meaning of the death of Jesus from a redemptive perspective. Although Pilate announced Jesus' innocence three times, he could not help but hand him over to be crucified on account of the Jews' challenge (John 18:38; 19:4, 6). In this respect, John seems to emphasize the fact that Jesus was sentenced to death on the cross on account of political rather than ethical or religious reasons. It is, however, necessary to interpret his death in connection with John the Baptist's proclamation of Jesus as "the Lamb of God, who takes away the sin of the world" (John 1:29). In other words, John described Jesus as the guilt offering from a theological perspective, since Isaiah compared the guilt offering to a lamb from a metaphoric perspective (Isa 53:7). In this respect, unlike Mark and Matthew, John attributed a limited role to Jesus Christ as the guilt offering prophesied for the Suffering Servant of YHWH. As a result, John seemed to weaken the role of Jesus as the guilt offering compared to Mark and Matthew by omitting the indirect quotation from Isa 53:10 and by reducing the allusion to the Suffering Servant of YHWH.

Third, John also understood the crucifixion of Jesus in the background of the Bible. This is acknowledged by the phrase "that the Scriptures might be fulfilled" three times for the description of Roman soldiers' tearing of Jesus' clothes, his drinking of wine vinegar, and the piercing of his side with a spear without breaking his legs (John 19:24, 28, 36; Ps 22:18; 69:21; Exod 12:46; Num 9:12). The fact that these appear only in John implies that the author emphasized the fulfillment of the prophecies of the Bible in the crucifixion. This shows that John also adopted the hermeneutic principle of "according to the Scriptures" used by the First Christians, Paul, and Mark. John applied a quotation formula similar to Matthew's to the crucifixion of Jesus. In this respect, John combined the previous traditions and interpreted Jesus' crucifixion in the light of the prophecies of the Bible for his own theological purpose.

Finally, the crucifixion is described as the event that made Jesus say, "It is finished" (John 19:30). In this respect, John ascribed a meaning to the crucifixion that Jesus completed the will of God. John should be credited with a unique achievement in the fact that the death of Jesus on the cross was understood as the way of completing the will of God. Although John described the death of Jesus somewhat differently from Mark and Matthew, it was undeniably an event of redemption and salvation for all humankind.

The Deuteropauline epistles mentioned the death of Jesus Christ following the Pauline tradition. First of all, the cross of Christ was presented as a means of reconciliation with enemies in Ephesians (Eph 2:16). The cross was also described in Colossians as a way to reconcile all things, even the Gentiles, with God (Col 1:20–22). These two passages remind us of Paul's teaching on reconciliation through the cross of Jesus (2 Cor 5:17–19; Rom 5:9). Moreover, the cross was suggested as a way to cancel the legal indebtedness that condemned the people and to disarm the authorities from making a public spectacle of them (Col 2:14–15). In this, the cross is suggested as a way to avenge the persecution Christians suffered from the world. Finally, 2 Timothy simply mentioned the death of Jesus when it emphasized his resurrection from the dead (2 Tim 2:8). However, his death is less focused on than the resurrection. In this way, the Deuteropauline epistles paid attention to the cross of Jesus Christ, but interpreted it in a slightly different way from the Pauline theology of redemption.

Hebrews also described the death of Jesus Christ on the cross as the way of salvation. This is seen in the emphasis that those who have fallen away after believing in Jesus as the Christ cannot repent in order to become new again (Heb 6:6). This is because that person would be crucifying the Son of God all over again and subjecting him to public disgrace. It seems that the salvific effect of the death of Jesus only works once. Therefore, it is written that we should fix our eyes on Jesus, the pioneer and perfector of faith, who endured the cross for the joy set before him, scorning its shame (12:2). In this way, Hebrews presented the death of Jesus on the cross as an event of salvation; however, he did not use Bible prophecies for the death of Jesus on the cross.

First Peter is another document that described the death of Jesus Christ from a perspective of salvation. The author first acknowledged that God raised Jesus from the dead (1 Pet 1:3, 21). This is the historical description of his death, but the author notes that Jesus bore the sins of the people with his body on a tree (2:22–25). In this sense, 1 Peter followed the redemptive and salvific explanation of the death of Jesus on the cross begun by Paul. While doing so, the author taught that Jesus suffered once for our sins and became the righteousness for all of us who are unrighteous (3:18). It is written that the death of Jesus affected the whole world and all of mankind. Although 1 Peter firmly described redemption, it certainly expanded the previous tradition. In doing so, 1 Peter also referenced the Suffering Servant of YHWH found in Isaiah in connection with the death of Jesus. Even though his suffering was in spite of his innocence, he did not say a word in his own defense or complain

(1 Pet 2:23; Isa 53:7), and he bore the sins of many people with his body on the cross even if they were like sheep going astray (1 Pet 2:24–25; Isa 53:6, 10). Thus, Jesus' death on the cross became the path that led his disciples to God.

Luke also depicted the death of Jesus Christ as an event for salvation. According to Luke, Jesus understood his death as fulfilling the prophecies of the prophets through the predictions of his death (Luke 18:31–33). This reflects the gospel that was passed down from the First Christians to Paul and then to Mark. Furthermore, Luke added some elements to the redemptive nature of the death of Christ. This is shown when Jesus asked God to forgive the people at the cross, saying that they did not know what they were doing (23:34). However, Jesus was merely the mediator who worked for the redemption of other people. The salvific aspect is seen in the story about the two criminals who were crucified with him (23:39–43). Jesus promised the entrance of paradise to the criminal who admitted his wrongdoings and asked for salvation. Of course, questions arise concerning the nature of the paradise mentioned here, but this context established the death of Jesus on the cross as an event of salvation. In this way, Luke showed that the death of Jesus on the cross was the beginning of salvation; however, he weakened the aspect of "according to the Scriptures" by reducing the number of quotations and allusions to the prophecies of the Bible. Moreover, Luke changed the death of the Son of God in Mark and Matthew to that of the righteous one (23:47). It seems that Luke intentionally changed it. In this respect, the redemptive role of the death of Jesus was reduced in Luke compared with that in Mark and Matthew.

F. Conclusion

The death of Jesus Christ lies at the center of the gospel and is the climax of salvation history. Although Q and the first Christian gospel do not mention Jesus' cross, the First Christians merely left a theological statement about the death of Christ according to the Scriptures. However, Paul made it the core of Christian redemption and salvation. He described the cross as the means of redemption and salvation when his gospel and authority were challenged by the Gentiles, who had accepted the teachings of the apostles of Jerusalem over his. Paul was the first to explain the cross from a perspective of redemption and salvation. The Gospels especially changed the declaratory description of the death of Jesus on the cross into historical descriptions. They also taught their own lessons through these writings. Luke weakened the redemptive and salvific meaning of the death of Jesus compared with Mark and Matthew; however, most of the other writers followed the perspective of redemption and salvation. This was also the result of their theological interpretations. Through this process, the description of the death of Jesus on the cross, an element of the gospel, was formed and developed.

6

The Burial of Christ

THE ACCOUNT OF THE burial of Jesus Christ received relatively little attention. The burial of Jesus does not appear in Q. On the contrary, the First Christians only declared that Christ was buried without the hermeneutic principle of "according to the Scriptures." Paul inherited the tradition about the burial of Christ and simply interpreted it theologically in connection with baptism. Mark succeeded this and extensively described it as a historical event. In this, the description of the burial of Jesus reached its culmination. The other books of the Gospel, however, interpreted and described the burial of Jesus in different way. The descriptions about Jesus Christ's burial are relatively short compared to other events, especially his death. This was probably because there was not much to write about. Still, the element of the gospel relating to the burial of Jesus was formed from a short tradition and developed in its own way.

A. The First Christian Gospel

As Q does not write anything about the burial of Jesus, the First Christians also did not know much about the burial of Christ. Therefore, there was not much to interpret theologically. Nevertheless, the First Christians had to mention the burial of Christ for unknown reasons.

The First Christians simply proclaimed that Christ was buried (1 Cor 15:4). The burial could be included in the first Christian gospel "because it was the necessary stage between death and resurrection."[1] As the First

---

1. Barrett, *Commentary*, 339. Cf. Hooker, *Jesus and the Servant*, 120.

Christians did not attribuute a theological meaning to the burial of Christ, they did not describe anything about its process. The First Christians did not use the hermeneutic principle of "according to the Scriptures" in describing his burial—probably because they had already used it in relation to his death, they did not give it as much significance, or they were able to find no prophecy in the Bible about it. The reason for not using the expression "according to the Scriptures" could be that the First Christians considered the burial of Christ relatively less important than his death.

The First Christians' literary description of the burial of Christ is quite simple. They used a passive verb, ἐτάφη, to describe the burial as opposed to the active verb, ἀπέθανεν, used for his death. Obviously they could only use a passive verb in connection with his burial, since a person can only be buried by those who are still alive. It is noteworthy that there was no room for the divine intervention in the burial of Christ. Nevertheless, the burial of Christ seemed to be an important element of the gospel to the First Christians.

In conclusion, the burial of Christ did not receive much theological meaning. However, it was necessary for the First Christians to mention it. As shown above, the First Christians formed the first Christian gospel about the burial of Christ through these descriptions.

B. The Pauline Epistles

Paul inherited the tradition about the burial of Christ from the First Christians. He showed minimal interest in Christ's burial and did not write much about it. Rather, Paul connected it with Christian baptism from a theological perspective.

Paul would have known even less about the burial than the death of Christ. As a result, Paul simply mentioned the burial of Christ following the tradition of the First Christians in 1Cor(3). His burial would not have been different from others (1 Cor 15:4). Paul did not know much about the burial of Christ beyond what the First Christians had handed down to him. This is why Paul did not develop the description of the burial of Christ further.

Instead, Paul developed the burial of Christ theologically. For this, he connected Christ's burial to the rite of baptism in Rom(3). According to Paul, Christian baptism symbolizes being buried with Jesus Christ (Rom 6:3-4). It is noteworthy that Paul used the name Jesus in connection with the title Christ for the definition of baptism. This implies that Paul would have understood the burial of Christ to be a historical fact. At any rate, Christians baptized in the name of Jesus Christ spiritually die and are buried with him. This was an interpretation from Paul's theological perspective. In this sense, his burial received a new theological significance. Paul presented such assertions in Rom(3), which was written later than the other epistles. However, the historical circumstances that made Paul interpret the baptism under the light of the burial with Christ are unknown. The Roman Christians seemed to face a certain situation that ran the risk of death while believing and being baptized in Jesus Christ.

For a better understanding of the burial of Christ, it is necessary to take a look at Paul's theological expressions. Paul had already made a theological interpretation that those who were baptized into Christ had clothed themselves with Christ (Gal 3:27). The phrase "clothing with Christ" might be from the cloth for the baptismal ritual in the church. When the image of "clothing with Christ" refers to the unification with him, it means a new creation in Christ.[2] It can be related to being dead, buried, and reborn with Christ. Thus, later, "clothing with Christ" runs parallel with "being buried with Christ" concerning baptism in the Pauline epistles. Considering that Paul used "being buried with Christ" in Rom(3) later than "clothing with Christ" in Galatians, we can conclude that Paul's interpretation about baptism developed from clothing with Christ to being buried with him. In this way, Paul creatively interpreted the previous tradition from his own theological perspective and intention.

C. Mark

The First Christians simply related the burial of Christ, then Paul connected it to Christian baptism, but Mark was the first to describe it in detail and put it in its historical context. By doing so, the burial of Jesus Christ was interpreted as an event fulfilling the prophecy according to the Scriptures. In addition, Mark completed the explanation of the burial of Jesus with baptism. Hereby the description about the burial of Jesus developed most.

Mark presented many features in connection with the burial of Jesus Christ. First, the author introduced Joseph of Arimathea as a fulfillment of the prophecy of Isaiah (Mark 15:42–47). Joseph appeared to Governor Pilate, asked for the body of Jesus, wrapped it in linen, placed it in a tomb cut out of rock, and rolled a stone against the entrance of the tomb. Mark

---

2. Meeks insists that in the context of Gal 3:27–28, "The baptismal reunification formula thus belongs to the familiar *Urzeit–Endzeit* pattern, and it presupposes an interpretation of the creation story in which the divine image after which Adam was modeled was masculofeminine" (Meeks, "Image," 185). Paul seems to have the Adam typology in mind when interpreting the Christian baptism.

defined Joseph as a prominent member of the Council (with implied wealth) who was himself waiting for the kingdom of God. Therefore, Mark inferred that Jesus was the one who fulfilled the prophecy about the grave of the Suffering Servant of YHWH that he was assigned a grave with the rich in his death (Isa 53:9). Mark was able to write this way because the death of Jesus had already been interpreted in the context of the prophecy of Isaiah. Mark also applied Paul's perspective on the gospel to the description of Jesus' burial. Just as Paul defined the prophecies about Christ as the gospel, Mark wrote that the burial of Jesus had fulfilled the prophecies of the Scriptures. It is, therefore, highly probable that Mark framed the stories of Jesus' crucifixion between the two thieves and his burial in order to communicate that they fulfilled the prophecy about Jesus taking after the Suffering Servant of YHWH. Therefore, Mark, who saw the life of Jesus in its entirety as gospel, gave specific significance to his burial.

Second, Mark wrote that Jesus fulfilled his own prophecy about the burial. When Jesus was in the home of Simon the leper in Bethany, a woman came with expensive perfume and poured it on his head (Mark 14:3–9). At this, the disciples rebuked her, but Jesus proclaimed that she poured perfume on his body beforehand to prepare for the burial. Jesus also proclaimed, "Wherever the gospel is preached throughout the world, what she has done will also be told in memory of her." In fact, such behavior would have been rare in the customs of the time. Rather, those who passed away would be prepared for burial with spices and perfumes. But since Jesus was arrested suddenly and died right before the Sabbath, he was laid in his tomb in a hurry, so there was no time for the proper burial rites. So this woman, whether knowingly or unknowingly, prepared Jesus for burial. While Jesus prophesied about his suffering, death, and resurrection three times (8:31; 9:31; 10:33–34), he did not do so about his burial. This shows that Mark did not give great weight to the burial of Jesus, though he inherited the declaratory description about it from Paul and the First Christians. However, according to Mark, Jesus did predict his burial in the home of Simon the leper in Bethany. Thus, Jesus was described as a prophet, and his burial became an event that he himself fulfilled (15:42–16:4). Mark once more developed Paul's perspective on the gospel through such descriptions. The author wrote that Jesus Christ was a man who fulfilled the Bible's prophecies as well as his own.

Third, following Paul, Mark wrote that the burial of Jesus completed baptism. In the story of the sons of Zebedee, the cup is set in parallel with baptism (Mark 10:35–40). Without doubt, drinking the cup meant allowing oneself to die according to the will of God; in that context, then, being baptized also referred to dying and being buried with Jesus according to the will of God.³ In this way, Mark modified Paul's interpretation of the burial of Christ in connection with baptism into a historical event. Therefore, this story is also believed to have been created by Mark in order to deliver the hidden meaning of baptism passed on from Paul.

Fourth, Mark connected Jesus' burial with "being clothed," which was used by Paul for the description of baptism. For this, a story of a young man is introduced (Mark 14:51–52). Mark used linen (σινδών) as a linking word for the connection between baptism and burial. The young man who came to Jesus was wearing linen when he was arrested after his prayer at Gethsemane. The fact that the young man put on linen meant that he came to be baptized, considering the customs of the time (cf. Gal 3:27). However, when Jesus was seized and the young man felt threatened, he fled naked, leaving his linen garment behind. Later Mark stated that the body of Jesus was wrapped in linen. Therefore, linen became the link between Jesus and the young man. Hereby, Mark connected baptism with the burial of Jesus. Furthermore, the young man who put on a white robe also appeared at the empty tomb (Mark 16:5). This could mean that he came to Jesus' tomb determined to die and be buried with Jesus. However, he became the first witness to Jesus' resurrection. In addition, his white robe would have been made of linen as well. Mark introduced the notion that this young man fulfilled his baptism by the repetition of the descriptions about the linen and by connecting him with the theology of Paul, who saw baptism as dying, being buried, and being clothed with Christ. The young man was the person who fulfilled the words of Jesus: "For whoever wants to save his life will lose it, but whoever loses his life for me [Jesus] and for the gospel will save it" (Mark 8:35; Q⁴ 17:33). As a result, he is depicted as a true disciple. In this respect, Mark developed Paul's theology of baptism and burial. As a result, the story of this young man, probably created by Mark, became a part of gospel.

Fifth, Mark introduced the story of the women at the tomb from a negative perspective. They are depicted as those who did not understand the meaning of the burial of Jesus, although they bought spices for it (Mark 15:47—16:2). It is written that they watched helplessly while Jesus was laid in the tomb because there was nothing they could have done. Later, when the Sabbath was over, they went to the tomb with the spices they bought to anoint his body. At this point, they are revealed as those who had forgotten the words of Jesus, for he had already proclaimed that the perfume the woman poured on his body at Bethany was in preparation for his burial.

---

3. As for the eschatological death of Jesus through baptism in the Gospel of Mark, refer to Waetjen, *Reordering of Power*, 68.

In this respect, these women are contrasted with the woman at Bethany. They even forgot that Jesus prophesied they would meet at Galilee, and they were bewildered when the young man in the white robe told them about the prophecy (16:8). These women revealed unbelief in that they did not understand the death and burial of Jesus.

It is clear that Mark created several stories related to the burial of Jesus Christ. By doing so, Mark theologically developed Paul's statement about the burial in relation to being clothed and being baptized with Christ. Moreover, Mark biographically completed the last part of Jesus' life. In this way, Mark developed the concept of the burial of Jesus Christ as a part of the gospel.

D. Other Documents

Matthew and Luke also wrote about the burial of Jesus Christ. Although there are no major differences compared to Mark's description, the slight modifications show some varying interpretations. John, on the other hand, wrote an entirely different description of the burial. Once again the authors described the burial of Jesus according to their theological intention.

Matthew and Luke described the stories related to the burial of Jesus with different focuses. First, Matthew and Luke used the account of the woman pouring perfume differently. While she appeared in the same context in Matthew as she had in Mark (Matt 26:6–16), Luke described her in an entirely different context (Luke 7:36–50). Matthew used the event in connection with the burial of Jesus, but Luke used it as a story to convey gratitude for the woman's repentance and Jesus' forgiveness of sins. Therefore, the change in the image of the woman should be noticed. Matthew reflected the unusual customs of the Jews, as the book was written for the Jewish disciples, probably in Galilee, while Luke omitted those customs, suggesting the book was written for the Gentiles, probably in Ephesus of Asia Minor. This implies that Luke reduced the importance of the burial of Jesus. Second, the description about Joseph of Arimathea is also slightly different. Matthew deliberately added that Joseph of Arimathea was rich (Matt 27:57), which was not mentioned in Mark. This was done in order to concretely describe the fulfillment of the prophecy written in Isa 53:9, which mentioned the grave of the rich. In this way, Matthew could present that the burial of Jesus was done according to the Scriptures. Matthew reflected the perspective on the gospel he had received from Paul and Mark. Luke, on the other hand, wrote that Joseph was a member of the Council, a good and righteous man. It seems that he deliberately avoided the fact that Joseph was rich. Through this description, Luke weakened the image of Jesus as fulfilling the prophecy of Isaiah about the Suffering Servant of YHWH. As written above, each writer presented Joseph in his or her own ways.

John gave another meaning to the burial of Jesus Christ. First, he introduced the story of Mary, who poured perfume on him (John 12:1–8). In this part, Jesus explained that it was for the day of his burial in a compliment to Mary. In this way, John followed the description and interpretation of Mark and Matthew. Later, when Jesus died and was laid in the tomb, it is written that the body of Jesus was anointed with perfume again (19:36–41). This was done by Nicodemus, who brought a mixture of myrrh and aloe and applied it to Jesus' body. While doing so, it is written that his body was wrapped in strips of linen with the spices in accordance with Jewish burial customs. Therefore, John wrote that perfume was applied to the body of Jesus twice, adding his own tradition to that which had been adapted from Mark. Unlike Mark, who wrote about the actions of the women negatively in connection with the application of perfume to the body of Jesus, John wrote it positively through the actions of Nicodemus. This is the author's own theological interpretation. Second, John wrote that Jesus was laid in a new tomb in a garden. Emphasizing that the grave was new seems to be a way of showing respect and love for Jesus. Moreover, it reveals the beginning of a new era. However, there is no mention of who prepared the grave. This is made clear by the fact that Joseph of Arimathea is not mentioned at all. So it was that John interpreted that the death and burial of Jesus had little to do with the prophecy of Isaiah. Furthermore, John did not mention that the men who died with Jesus on the cross were criminals, which shows that his death and burial had nothing to do with the wicked. Overall, John weakened the intensity of the connection between fulfilling the prophecies of Isaiah and the burial of Jesus.

The Deuteropauline epistles inherited the Pauline concept of burial. Colossians described the circumcision done by Christ to be buried with him in baptism (Col 2:12). Colossians creatively interpreted the burial with baptism in different way from Paul. The author of Colossians adopted the theme of circumcision and applied it to the Pauline theology of baptism that had been interpreted under the light of the burial of Jesus. In this respect, the author of Colossians developed the Pauline theology of Jesus' burial. Nevertheless, the other authors of the Deuteropauline epistles did not develop the description of the burial of Jesus much.

E. Conclusion

In actuality, the tradition about the burial of Jesus Christ was not developed fully. While there is no mention of it in Q, the First Christians wrote simply that Christ was buried. Even Paul, who followed them, did not add anything since he did not know much about the historical facts related to the matter. He only revealed the interpretation that baptism meant dying and being buried with Christ. Later, Mark developed the gospel related to the burial of Jesus by creating the stories about the woman at Bethany and Joseph of Arimathea. While doing so, he wrote that the burial of Jesus fulfilled both the prophecies of Isaiah and his own. This reflected Paul's perspective on the gospel while conveying the burial of Christ as a part of the gospel. Also, Mark used the linen the young man wore as a linking word and connected baptism to the death and burial of Jesus; again, it is the result of developing Paul's theology. In this respect, Mark reached the culmination in the description of the burial of Jesus. The story about Joseph Arimathea was succeeded by Matthew, weakened by Luke, and practically abandoned by John. This was because each writer had his own image of Jesus he wanted to confess and convey. As discussed above, the tradition about the burial of Jesus started from a declaratory description and changed into a historical one. However, the amount of description given to the burial of Christ is less than that given to his death. The death and burial of Jesus is a historical fact because he was also a human. However, there is not much that is actually known about his burial. Nonetheless, more and more meaning was given to his burial. What is important here is the theological interpretations that were made based on this small historical fact. These examples show the process of how the gospel relating to the burial of Jesus Christ was formed and developed.

7

The Resurrection of Christ

THE GOSPEL RELATED TO the resurrection of Jesus Christ has gone through a process of development. The First Christians held that Christ was raised on the third day, according to the Scriptures. They were the first to confess it, considering the fact that Q does not mention the resurrection of Jesus. Inheriting the tradition, Paul stated the resurrection of Christ in theological terms, and Mark described it as the story of the empty tomb, though he could not have confirmed it as a historical event. Later, the other Gospels developed their accounts of the resurrection of Jesus as they added particular nuances according to their theological interpretations. The rest of the Christian Scripture also alleged the resurrection of Jesus declaratively. Although the resurrection is an event that cannot be proven beyond doubt, it is the center of the Christian faith. This chapter will show the process of how the elements of the gospel connected to the resurrection of Jesus were formed and developed.

A. Q

There is no mention of Jesus' resurrection in Q. However, Q mentioned the resurrection of the dead in the third redaction. In this respect, the third redactor revealed the Pharisaic characteristic. Nevertheless, it does not allude to the resurrection of Jesus at all.

Q mentioned the general resurrection two times in the third redaction. One is found in Jesus' response to the disciples of John with the present passive verb: "the dead are raised [ἐγείρονται]" (Q^3 7:22). The other is found in his teaching about the sign with the future verb: "The queen of the South will be raised [ἐγερθήσεται] at the judgment with this generation and condemn it," and "Ninevite men will arise [ἀναστήσονται] at the judgment with this generation and condemn it." (11:31–32).[1] It is noteworthy that a passive verb is used in 7:22 and 11:31, while the active meaning is adopted with the middle voice verb in 11:32. The third redactor seemed to convey that God is the agent for the general resurrection. It seems that Q mentions both the miracle of revitalization (7:22) and the general resurrection of the dead at the end of time (11:31–32). In this way, the third redactor revealed the interest in the resurrection.

The third redactor seems to be a Pharisee insofar as he or she mentioned the general resurrection of the dead. If the redactor had not been a Pharisee, he or she could not have attributed it to the teaching of Jesus. In addition, the third redactor cited the Bible verses that allude to Isa 29:18–19; 35:5–6 and 61:1 (Q 7:22). However, the redactor changed the citation according to his or her own theological purpose; in other words, he or she modified it to mention general resurrection. This implies that the redactor was a scribe well trained in biblical interpretation. If the redactor were not a Pharisaic scribe, it would have been difficult to mention the general resurrection and modify the biblical quotation for its description.

The general resurrection mentioned in Q does not imply anything about the resurrection of Jesus. If Jesus had actually risen from the dead, the third redactor wrote about it and gave it theological meaning. It seems that the resurrection of Jesus was not known to the redactor. From the fact that the general resurrection does not appear in the fourth redaction, it can be concluded that it did not draw consistent attention from the disciples of Jesus. Therefore, it can be said that the twelve apostles also did not know about the resurrection of Jesus at all. In this respect, Q says nothing about the resurrection of Jesus from a historical perspective.

B. The First Christian Gospel

The First Christians wrote about the resurrection of Christ. However, this does not mean that they witnessed the event firsthand. They simply made theological interpretations that he was raised on the third day according to the Scriptures.

The First Christians wrote about the resurrection of Christ for the first time (1 Cor 15:4). While the third redactor of Q dealt with the general resurrection, the First Christians confessed the resurrection of Christ based

---

1. Quotations are from Robinson et al., *Critical Edition*, 124, 252–53.

on the prophecies of the Bible. Although there are no prophecies found in the Bible that simultaneously deal with the death and resurrection of Christ, it seems that the First Christians had specific prophecies in mind. Hosea 6:1–2 is the only text in the Bible that has the words "third day" in connection with a man being raised from the dead.[2] However, we cannot say that this text was about the resurrection of Christ since this was clearly the word of God proclaimed to all people. Nevertheless, it is possible that the First Christians thought of this text as a prophecy about the resurrection of Christ. This interpretation could be achieved through their theological perspective because they are supposed to be from the Pharisees, who were trained to interpret the Bible and the Jewish tradition according to their theological purposes.

The First Christians used the passive verb for the resurrection of Christ. While the third redactor of Q used the present passive verb ἐγείρονται (Q^3 7:22), the future passive verb ἐγερθήσεται (11:31), and the future middle verb ἀναστήσονται (11:32), the First Christians adopted the perfect passive verb ἐγήγερται, referring to a previous event. When considering the phrase "on the third day," the First Christians would have had a certain event in their minds. In addition, they thought of God as the main agent responsible for raising Christ, as shown by the fact that the passive verb was used to say that Christ was raised back to life. Of course, the Jews preferred such descriptions, since they had a custom of not directly mentioning the name of God. Although a similar passive form was used in connection with Jesus' burial, people carried out the act.

It is not clear whether the resurrected Christ was the historical Jesus. The First Christians did not mention when and how the resurrection of Christ occurred. In addition, there is no point of contact between the historical Jesus and the resurrected Christ, because Q did not provide any hint about his resurrection. This implies that the First Christians would have sought to understand the resurrection of Christ by interpreting it theologically in the background of the Scriptures. However, there is no anointed servant of God who was raised from the dead in the Bible. There was no common ground between Q and the first Christian gospel regarding the resurrection of Jesus Christ.

The First Christians were able to accept the resurrection of Christ because of their religious and cultural background. They could make confessions about it based on the religious tradition of the Pharisees. The Pharisee

---

2. Crossan, *Cross That Spoke*, 93. Another verse that is suggested as a prophecy for the resurrection of Christ is Jonah 1:17. Referring to it, Matthew explains the resurrection of Jesus in Matt 12:39–40. It seems, however, that the First Christians did not have this in mind as a prophecy for the resurrection of Christ (Barrett, *Commentary*, 340).

group that formed after the Babylonian exile believed in the resurrection of the body, and they would have used verses like Hos 6:1–2 in order to convey such teachings publicly. If it were not the theological background for the resurrection of Christ, the First Christians could not use the phrase "according to the Scriptures." Therefore, the resurrection of Christ is closer to a theological event than a historical fact, based on their theological interpretations. In addition, as mentioned before, the First Christians are widely supposed to have been Jewish Christians who originally lived in the Diaspora, probably around Damascus in Syria. The Greek religion taught that when people died, their bodies and souls separated. Along with this, the majority of people in the Hellenized region learned that some of their heroes visited the world of the dead and that the dead also maintained relationships with the living. Although it is not certain, such cultural beliefs might have had an effect on the First Christians. In this way, the First Christians formed the gospel related to the resurrection of Christ.

C. The Pauline Epistles

Paul was familiar with the doctrine of resurrection since he was a Pharisee and Jew of the Diaspora. After achieving spiritual enlightenment about the Son of God at Damascus, Paul heard about the resurrection of Christ from the First Christians. It is, however, noteworthy that Paul did not extensively develop the instruction about the resurrection of Christ.

Paul inherited in complete form what the First Christians conveyed about the resurrection of Christ (1 Cor 15:4). However, Paul did not mention on which prophecy of the Bible the proclamation that "Christ was raised on the third day according to the Scriptures" was based. Had Paul completely communicated all that he had received, then it is most likely that he would have also believed Hos 6:1–2 to be the prophecy about the resurrection of Christ, probably following the First Christians. If so, that verse would have been part of the gospel for Paul.

Paul himself did not witness the resurrection of Jesus Christ firsthand either. He simply inherited the theological tradition that Christ was raised from the First Christians. It also seems that he never heard about the process of Christ's resurrection in detail. As a result, Paul never again talked about the tradition that Christ was raised on the third day according to the Scriptures in the rest of his epistles. Of course, Paul probably did not hear about the resurrection of Jesus from Cephas when he went up to Jerusalem around 38 CE; as a result, Paul did not mention the resurrection of Jesus from a historical perspective. He simply believed in and declared the resurrection to be fact.

Paul often mentioned the resurrection of Jesus Christ. His description of the resurrection appears in a similar manner throughout his epistles. At the beginning of his missionary work, Paul used the expression that God raised Jesus from the dead in 1Thess(1) (1 Thess 1:10). It is noteworthy that the name Jesus is used exclusively in connection with resurrection. This implies that Paul wished to acknowledge the historicity of Jesus' resurrection. Then Paul proclaimed that God raised the Lord in 1Cor(1). As a result, Paul focuses more on Jesus' resurrection than on his death (1 Cor 6:14). A little later, the resurrection of Christ was used as a basis for the general resurrection of the dead in 1Cor(2). Having been raised from the dead, Christ is defined as the first fruit among those who were raised from the dead (1 Cor 15:12–26). For this, the passive verb ἐγήγερται is used so as to reveal God's initiative in the resurrection of Christ. It is noteworthy that Paul adopted the passive verb, which had already been used by the third redactor of Q and the First Christians. Paul did not deal with the resurrection of Christ much at the beginning of his missionary journey.

After experiencing challenges and opposition from the Gentile Christians, Paul changed his thinking about the resurrection. First of all, Paul focused on the ability of Christ in 1Thess(2) when Paul said, "Jesus died and rose again" (1 Thess 4:14). This is the first case that the active verb ἀνέστη is used for the resurrection of Jesus in the Pauline epistles. This reminds the reader of the middle verb ἀναστήσονται, which carries the active meaning (Q^3 11:32). While the influence of Q on Paul is not certain in this case, it seems that he emphasized Jesus' ability to rise from the dead. And Paul once again emphasized Christ's ability in Phil(1) by mentioning the power of Christ's resurrection (Phil 3:10). In this case, the noun ἀνάστασις is used to allude to its verbal form used in Q^3 and 1Thess(2). When Paul heard that the Thessalonians and the Philippians had been in momentary turmoil but not shaken, he seemed to focus more on Jesus Christ's abilities regarding the resurrection.

A little later, in the middle of serious challenges and opposition by the Gentile Christians, Paul adopted the phrases used before. He proclaimed that Christ was risen after three days, according to the Scriptures in 1Cor(3). Reflecting the tradition of the First Christians, Paul used the divine passive form of verb ἐγήγερται once again (1 Cor 15:4). Moreover, Paul said that God raised Jesus Christ in Galatians (Gal 1:1), 2Cor(2) (2 Cor 4:14), and 2Cor(3) (13:4). It seems that Paul simply repeated what he had used to express God's initiative for the resurrection. Compared to his interpretation of the death of Christ, Paul did not develop his thinking about the resurrection much. This is supported by the fact that Paul did not frequently mention the resurrection of Jesus Christ.

Paul kept mentioning the resurrection even after the challenge had been diminished. In Romans, Paul delivered the theology of the resurrection of Jesus Christ in various ways. He used the noun form in the phrase of "resurrection from the dead" in Rom(1) (Rom 1:4). In addition, Paul once again used the expression that God raised Jesus Christ from the dead in Rom(1) (4:24), Rom(3) (6:4; 8:11), and Rom(4) (10:9). Moreover, it is noteworthy that Paul also describes Jesus Christ rising from death by himself in Rom(1) (8:34; 14:9) and Rom(3) (6:9; 7:4). As time passed, Jesus Christ's ability to rise from the dead was increasingly focused on. In the case of Phil(2), Paul did not mention Jesus' resurrection when he introduced the exaltation after Jesus' death on the cross (Phil 2:9). In this respect, as Paul got to the end of his missionary life, he came to use all kinds of expressions to describe the resurrection of Jesus.

It is necessary to explain why Paul did not develop the instruction about the resurrection of Jesus Christ much. One reason he might not have done so was because he was a Pharisee and accepted the doctrine that God will raise people from the dead at the end of the world as a common belief. Therefore, it seems Paul believed that God caused the event of the end when he heard about the resurrection of Christ from the First Christians. Particularly, Paul did not develop the theology of the resurrection as much as that of Christ's death when the Gentile Christians challenged him. This was probably because Paul did not know much about the resurrection of Christ and its theology was not developed much in the Bible, or his opponents did not raise questions about the resurrection of Jesus Christ. Probably, the latter was the case. Therefore, Paul did not need to answer them much. He simply kept the opinion that God raised Jesus from the dead. Thus, Paul did not mention the process of how Jesus was raised from the dead. In this respect, resurrection is more of an event of theological interpretation than a historical fact.

D. Mark

Mark did not directly verify the resurrection of Jesus Christ. It seems that he did not have sources that could accurately describe the resurrection. However, Mark did describe the resurrection of Jesus as a historical event, since he had inherited the theological interpretation about it from Paul.

Mark wrote that Jesus Christ fulfilled his own prophecy about resurrection. He prophesied three times that it would occur within three days after his death (Mark 8:31; 9:31; 10:33–34). Of course, these prophecies were created by Mark and delivered through the mouth of Jesus. In this context, the phrase "three days" proves that Mark inherited the tradition from the First Christians and Paul. Also, while Paul and the First Christians adopted the hermeneutic principle "according to the Scriptures," Mark developed this as Jesus fulfilling his own prophecy. This implies that Mark went beyond the First Christians and Paul, who interpreted the resurrection of Christ in the background of the Bible. Mark's description of Jesus fulfilling his own prophecy about the events following the resurrection also reflects the influence of the Pauline perspective on the gospel (14:28; 16:7). This too is the result of Mark developing Paul's perspective on the gospel and applying it to Jesus Christ.

Mark did not describe the resurrection of Jesus Christ with certainty. Therefore, the Gospel ends with the account of the empty tomb (Mark 16:1–8).[3] Mark indirectly described that Jesus was raised from the dead after three days, stating that Jesus rose on the day after the Sabbath. The first aorist passive verb ἠγέρθη is used instead of the perfect passive verb ἐγήγερται, which was used by the First Christians and Paul. With this verb, Mark emphasized the historicity of the resurrection of Jesus. The story ends with the women crying and afraid, which gives the impression that the account was not finished. In fact, no one actually witnessed the resurrection of Jesus. Mark introduced a young man as witness to Jesus' resurrection. This young man was the person who got rid of his linen and ran away when he saw the soldiers coming to arrest Jesus. However, there is no specific mention as to the young man's identity, the time he arrived at the tomb, how he rolled the stone away from the entrance, what he saw in connection with the resurrection, what occurred during the resurrection, etc. The resurrection was kept shrouded in mystery, for nothing was written in detail about those elements. The young man dressed in a white robe simply repeated to the women the prophecy that Jesus had told his disciples beforehand. He also told them to go to Galilee, where they would see Jesus Christ. However, it is not clear how the young man would have known the prophecy about the place where they should go after the resurrection. In this respect, Mark adopted an indirect means of describing Jesus' resurrection through a young man dressed in a white robe. This shows that Mark did not have an exact knowledge of the resurrection of Jesus. As a result, it seems that Mark could not describe the event vividly. He only created the story about the empty tomb, giving the impression that Jesus was raised from the dead.

---

3. As recognized by scholars, Mark originally ended at 16:8 (Cf. Brown, *Introduction*, 127).

However, Mark did seek to do his best when describing the resurrection of Jesus Christ. He was concerned that there was nothing written about the resurrection of Jesus in Q and that Paul actually preached about the resurrection. In other words, Mark was agonizing between the resurrection, which could not be proven historically, and the theological interpretation about this event. Ultimately, he wrote about this event by accepting the tradition of Paul, which sought to recognize the historicity of the resurrection of Jesus. Thus, Mark wrote about the women who visited the tomb and introduced the young man dressed in a white robe but did not make any further descriptions.

There was a reason, however, that Mark could not describe the resurrection clearly. This was because the description about the Suffering Servant of YHWH, which is regarded as the prophecy about his death and burial, did not mention resurrection. Nevertheless, based on the tradition of the First Christians and Paul, Mark made up his mind to describe the resurrection of Jesus as far as he could. In this respect, Mark completed the very last part of the life of Jesus Christ, namely the gospel, according to his theological purpose.

E. Matthew, John, and Luke

The resurrection of Jesus Christ was also mentioned by Matthew, John, and Luke. They wrote about the resurrection as a clear historical event compared to Paul's theological statements and Mark's indirect descriptions. The authors described Jesus' resurrection according to their own theological interpretations.

Matthew described the resurrection of Jesus Christ as a mysterious but historical event. This is shown where Matthew developed his resurrection into a transcendental event through the intervention of an angel, as he described it with more detail than Mark (Matt 28:1–10). Matthew wrote that an angel of the Lord came down from heaven, rolled back the stone, and sat on it. Therefore, the angel helped Jesus come out of the tomb after the resurrection. Matthew changed Mark's account of the young man dressed in a white robe into an angel. As a result, it seems that Matthew somewhat resolved many questions Mark had left surrounding the resurrection. Matthew also did not mention the process of resurrection. He simply wrote that Jesus had already risen from the dead when Mary Magdalene and the other women arrived at the tomb. It was written that the women were filled with joy instead of fear when they saw what had happened. However, they had not witnessed the resurrection either. It is noteworthy that the disciples did not take any role at the site of the resurrection. Still, it seems that Matthew wanted to verify the resurrection more concretely through such descriptions. As a result, it was written that an angel of the Lord proclaimed Jesus' resurrection and the guards at the tomb reported the event to the chief priests (28:11–15). Although Matthew inherited the mysterious aspect of the resurrection of Jesus from Mark, he attempted to show its historicity as best as he could. Matthew needed the historicity because of his belief in the presence of Jesus with his disciples until the end of the world, as it is written in 1:23; 18:20 and 28:20.

The Johannine documents also mention the resurrection of Jesus Christ. In John's description, further steps were taken (John 20:1–13). John also wrote that no one directly told Christ's followers that the stone at the tomb had been removed. When Peter and the other disciple went to the tomb, they saw that the body of Jesus was gone and that the strips of linen were lying there. However, none of them could have been a direct witnesses. In addition, John did not mention the phenomenon that occurred at the moment of resurrection. This shows that John did not have direct knowledge about the resurrection, just as Mark and Matthew did not. Moreover, the two angels that appeared at the tomb did nothing but sit where Jesus' body had been, one at the head and the other at the foot. By this, the angels give the impression that they were the guardians of Jesus. Through this description, John also demonstrated the resurrection of Jesus by the empty tomb. This was John's theological interpretation with the addition of Peter's visit to the tomb with the other disciples. Revelation deals with the expression "the firstborn from the dead," which also reminds readers of the Pauline expression that God raised him from the dead as "the firstfruits of those who have fallen asleep" (Rev 1:5; 1 Cor 15:20; cf. Col 1:18).[4] In this way, the Johannine documents developed the description of the resurrection of Jesus Christ at the end of the first century CE.

The Lucan documents also described the resurrection of Jesus Christ. In Luke, the appearance of the women is similar to that of the other Gospels (Luke 24:1–12). However, Luke described two men in clothes that gleamed like lightning being at the tomb. These two men rebuked the women for looking for the living among the dead. At the same time, they reminded the women of what Jesus had told them while he was alive. As John had, Luke also wrote that the women, remembering his words, told all this to the disciples. Peter then ran to the tomb, saw that it was empty, and left. In this respect, Luke reported their behavior more positively compared to Mark and Matthew, in which they did not appear at the tomb.

---

4. Shin, "Die paulinischen Auswirkungen," 823–24.

Luke did not overtly explain the status of the two men who appeared at the tomb. However, he had already mentioned that the two men Jesus met at the transfiguration were Moses and Elijah—those who had not experienced death (9:30). Elijah went up to heaven in a whirlwind, and Moses' body was never found (Deut 34:6; 2 Kgs 2:11). The Jews of the first century CE believed that Moses ascended to heaven and did not die (Ascension of Moses 10:11). Within this tradition is the description of Luke, who wrote that Moses and Elijah, who did not experience death, were present at the scene of resurrection. Through this description, Luke made Jesus' resurrection historically more distinct than it had happened according to the Scriptures.

In addition, Acts mentioned the resurrection of Jesus. Proclamation of his resurrection was the top priority to the apostles (Acts 1:22). This implies that Acts considered the resurrection of Jesus to be the most important issue. However, Acts preferred a declaratory statement to a descriptive narration, usually saying that God raised Jesus from the dead (2:24, 31; 3:15; 4:10; 5:30; 10:40; 13:37; 17:3, 31; 26:23, etc.). This expression reminds the reader of Paul's mention in his epistles. While Paul preferred the divine passive form of the verb to describe the resurrection of Jesus, Acts usually adopted the active form in order to emphasize God's power and authority to Gentile readers. In this respect, Acts showed its emphasis on the resurrection of Jesus. This is Luke's own theological interpretation of Jesus Christ's resurrection in the beginning of the second century CE. This kind of theological position made the author of the Lucan documents reduce the description of Christ's redemptive death in Luke.

F. Other Documents

The resurrection of Jesus Christ is also mentioned in other documents of the Christian Scriptures. They are also proclaimed according to the author's theological intention. Through such descriptions, Christianity maintained faith in the resurrection of Jesus Christ.

The Deuteropauline epistles mentioned the resurrection of Jesus Christ similarly to Paul. It is written in Ephesians that God exerted his power when he raised Christ from the dead (Eph 1:20; 2:5). It seems that Ephesians reflected Paul's perspective on the resurrection: God is its initiator with power as it is written in Phil(1). It is also written in Colossians that God raised Jesus Christ from the dead (Col 1:18; 2:12). The expression "the firstborn from among the dead" especially reminds readers of Paul's "the firstfruits of those who have fallen asleep" in 1Cor(2). Finally, in 2 Timothy it is described that Jesus Christ was raised from the dead (2 Tim 2:8). In this way, the disciples of Paul generally taught that God raised Christ from the dead. This shows that the authors of the Deuteropauline epistles reflected Pauline interpretations about the resurrection of Jesus Christ at the end of the first century CE.

Hebrews acknowledged the resurrection of Jesus Christ from a priestly perspective. This is revealed through the description of God, "who through the blood of the eternal covenant brought back from the dead our Lord Jesus, that great Shepherd of the sheep" (Heb 13:20). In this context, the expression "brought back from the dead" means the resurrection of Jesus. In addition, "the blood of the eternal covenant" reminds the reader of the blood sprinkled by the priest at the temple. In this way, Jesus' death led to his resurrection, and the two events' relationship to one another cannot be separated. However, the description of Jesus' resurrection significantly lost weight in Hebrews because he is believed to be in the heaven to which Jesus the high priest originally belongs.

First Peter wrote about the resurrection of Jesus Christ in connection with salvation. This is revealed when the author wrote that in his great mercy, God has given the people "new birth into a living hope through the resurrection of Jesus Christ from the dead" (1 Pet 1:3). This implies that Jesus' resurrection was the medium for giving Christians new birth into a living hope. In other words, Jesus' resurrection became the model for the general Christian resurrection. In addition, it is written that God raised Christ from the dead and glorified him (1:21). This means that the resurrection of Christ is the glory of God itself. Moreover, the resurrection of Jesus Christ gives a meaning of salvation to baptism (3:21). Of course, this refers to what the resurrection brings to the baptized. In this way, 1 Peter heightened the role of Christ's resurrection.

G. Conclusion

The resurrection of Jesus Christ is an event that resulted from the theological interpretation of the Christians of the early days. Q did not mention the resurrection of Jesus. If the disciples actually knew about his resurrection, they would have written about and given meaning to it. The First Christians began to preach the resurrection of Christ according to their theological interpretations. In this sense, they were the ones who established the tradition about Christ's resurrection according to the Scriptures. Paul inherited their tradition and proclaimed the resurrection of Jesus Christ; however, he proclaimed the event declaratively and did not describe it historically. Mark, on the other hand, developed this event into the story of the empty tomb.

Although there was no one who actually witnessed the resurrection of Jesus, Matthew, John, and Luke later mentioned people or angels who proved and expanded the event. In this way, they tried to describe the resurrection as a historical event. Acts especially ascribed top priority to the resurrection of Jesus. The remaining authors of the Christian Scripture also explain Jesus' resurrection according to their own theological intentions. In this way, the gospel related to the resurrection of Jesus was formed and developed. It was, however, not easy to describe Jesus' resurrection according to the Scriptures, since there were not many prophecies that fit that context. Nevertheless, Hos 6:1–2 is the best candidate for the resurrection of Jesus Christ.

8

The Epiphany of Christ

THE EPIPHANY OF JESUS Christ is the most difficult element of the first Christian gospel to cover, since it is difficult to corroborate. The twelve apostles could not have mentioned Jesus' epiphany in Q, since they did not mention his death and resurrection. On the contrary, the First Christians maintained that the resurrected Christ appeared; however, they did not explain how it happened. Nevertheless, it is included in the gospel. Paul inherited the tradition about the epiphany from the First Christians, then added the list of witnesses. He is then silent about it in the rest of his epistles. Later, the epiphany of Jesus Christ was written variously in each Gospel and given great significance in Acts. The epiphany is also the result of theological interpretations according to the various authors' perspectives.

A. The First Christian Gospel

The First Christians conveyed the epiphany of Christ. They simply wrote that he appeared. The phrase "according to the Scriptures" was not used in connection with the epiphany of Christ, which seems to suggest there were no prophecies that supported it. The First Christians also did not provide much detail about the epiphany of Christ, leaving out any information as to when, where, how, or to whom he appeared. They proclaimed the epiphany of Christ according to their own theological interpretation. Therefore, this event must be approached from a theological perspective rather than a historical one.

The First Christians taught that God directed the epiphany of Christ. This is shown in the first aorist passive form of the verb ὤφθη used for "appeared." The first aorist tense indicates that Christ appeared only once. It was not an event that happened continuously. The reason Christ appeared was because God made him do so. This is similar to the divine passive verb used for the description of the resurrection of Christ. They confessed the epiphany of Christ as an event caused by God.

The background from which the First Christians happened to confess the epiphany of Christ is unknown. They could have used the epiphany of God as a background (Isa 60:2), but that would not have been very persuasive. This is because the Jewish tradition had never identified the Christ with God. Otherwise, they might have been affected by the Greek myths learned in the Diaspora. The epiphany of Christ reminded readers of stories in which the heroes could appear in the human world as god-like figures after they died. It is, however, unlikely to describe the epiphany of Christ under the light of the Greek myths, especially when they confessed his death and resurrection based on the Bible. It seems that the First Christians created the statement about the epiphany of Christ.

In conclusion, without the background of the Bible, the epiphany of Christ seems to be the result of theological interpretation of the First Christians. It is also difficult to consider it a historical event. The First Christians' theological contemplation resulted in the theology about the epiphany of Christ.

B. The Pauline Epistles

Paul inherited the tradition about the epiphany of Christ from the First Christians and connected it to Jesus. It was a part of the gospel he proclaimed. Paul included himself in the list of witnesses to the epiphany. However, Paul did not mention much about the epiphany of Christ.

Paul inherited the epiphany of Christ as part of the gospel. He definitely introduced the tradition that was handed over from the First Christians as gospel in 1Cor(3) (1 Cor 15:1–2), and it includes the epiphany of Christ (15:5). This means that Paul understood the epiphany of Christ as an element of the gospel. However, Paul did not provide any scriptural reference to support the epiphany of Christ as part of gospel in his epistles at all. In this respect, Paul seems to have inherited the tradition from the First Christians, but he did not develop it further.

What Paul did provide was the list of witnesses to the epiphany of Christ. It is noteworthy that various groups of witnesses appear with the first aorist form of the verb here (1 Cor 15:5–8). Paul should have used the imperfect form of the verb so as to express the continual appearance of Christ to them in the past. However, Paul seemed to preserve the tradition inherited from the First Christians. The list includes various groups of people. Above all, Paul introduced Cephas and the Twelve.[1] Although the twelve apostles themselves did not mention the epiphany of Jesus in Q, Paul wrote that Christ appeared to the Twelve, which reminds readers of the twelve apostles introduced in the fourth redaction of Q. In this way, Paul tried to connect Christ to the historical Jesus by using the Twelve. It was, however, also Paul's theological attempt to connect them. In addition, Paul wrote that Christ appeared to more than five hundred of the brothers and sisters, and then to James. Moreover, he wrote that Christ appeared to all the apostles and to Paul himself, as to one abnormally born. Paul included as many witnesses as possible in order to show his intention to be acknowledged as one of them. By mentioning all the apostles in addition to the Twelve, Paul extended the boundary of apostles. This definitely reveals Paul's wish to be included in the group of apostles, which he expressed in 1Thess(1) (1Thess 2:7). In this way, Paul insisted that he also met Christ after he was raised from the dead. Nevertheless, it seems that he did not know much about the epiphany at all. This is the reason that Paul did not further develop the interpretation about the epiphany of Christ theologically.

Paul did not describe with confidence that Christ appeared to him. It would have been absurd for him to write that Christ has appeared to the Twelve when they, including Cephas Peter, did not even mention the death, resurrection, and epiphany of Jesus in Q. Nonetheless, Paul showed the urgency of presenting himself in the list of Christ's epiphany because this was the important link that connected him to Jesus. Paul had to assert that Christ, who was raised from the dead, appeared to him in order to emphasize his apostolic authority.

In fact, Paul did not meet with Jesus when he was on the earth. Since he was not one of Jesus' disciples, Paul's authority was often challenged. The most important thing in that situation was asserting that he had met Jesus.

---

1. Paul applied no title to "the Twelve ($\delta\omega\delta\varepsilon\kappa\alpha$)" in 1 Cor 15:5. This implies that Paul was not in good relationship with them when he wrote 1Cor(3). He knew that the Jerusalem Church sent some people to the Corinthian Church and made the Corinthians challenge him. In addition, "the Twelve" informs us of another historical fact. If Judas Iscariot had been one of the twelve apostles, it would have been impossible for Paul to mention "the Twelve" in 1Cor(3), which was written later than Q. At the same time, when we remember that 1 Corinthians was written earlier than Mark, it is then awkward to describe Judas Iscariot as one of the twelve disciples. It seems that Mark created the story about the betrayal of Judas Iscariot and did not deal with the story about the epiphany of Christ.

This is shown in the rhetorical question that Paul raised to the Corinthians in 1Cor(3), which reflects that the Corinthians asked Paul whether he had met the historical Jesus (1 Cor 9:1–2). Paul emphasized that he had met with Jesus who historically lived by using the title "Jesus our Lord." Nevertheless, Paul equivocated about his experience of meeting Jesus and did not describe the event clearly. Moreover, Paul said that the Corinthians acknowledged him as an apostle. In this sense, Paul could not have confidently asserted his meeting with the historical Jesus. Although Paul might have met the historical Jesus, he seemed to have no proof. This is why he had no recourse but to claim that the resurrected Christ appeared to him. Thus, the appearance of Christ is not mentioned in his other epistles.

In conclusion, Paul likely neither met the historical Jesus nor saw the resurrected Christ at all. However, having inherited the tradition from the First Christians, Paul used it to include himself among the witnesses in order to strengthen his apostolic authority to the Gentile Christians. Thus, Paul made no attempt at theological interpretation of the epiphany of Christ in the rest of his epistles.

C. Mark, Matthew, and John

Each Gospel presents the epiphany of Jesus Christ in different ways. The authors conveyed it according to their theological perspective while adding different stories to the tradition they followed. This resulted in different descriptions about the epiphany of Jesus Christ.

Mark did not describe the epiphany of Jesus Christ. This is in keeping with the fact that Jesus had predicted his suffering three times but did not say a single word about his epiphany. Mark only wrote that Jesus predicted that he would go ahead into Galilee after he had risen (Mark 14:28). Not having mentioned the epiphany in the three predictions, Mark could not describe it clearly after Jesus' resurrection at the end of the Gospel. Mark only indirectly conveyed Jesus' epiphany by describing the young man at the tomb saying they would see Jesus again in Galilee, while retelling the prophecy Jesus himself gave before his crucifixion (16:7). While Paul asserted that Christ appeared (ὤφθη) to the twelve apostles, Mark explained that the disciples had to see (ὄψεσθε) the resurrected Jesus in Galilee. Jesus became the object that the disciples had to seek out and meet. The implied epiphany of Jesus emphasizes the discipleship with which they had to follow Jesus after his resurrection even though he was not with the disciples in the world. Ultimately, Mark did not describe whether the disciples met him or not. He seems to simply presume Christ's appearance before them.

However, Mark did not mention any of the names on the list of witnesses to the epiphany given by Paul. In this sense, Mark had difficulty accepting the parts about Jesus' epiphany in the tradition Paul passed on to him. As a result, Mark did not develop the epiphany of Jesus asserted by the First Christians and Paul.

Matthew, unlike Mark, did describe the epiphany of Jesus Christ. The resurrected Jesus met the eleven disciples at a mountain in Galilee, was worshiped by them, and gave them the Great Commission (Matt 28:16–20). Some of the disciples doubted Jesus at that time, though they did confirm his resurrection and epiphany as they worshiped. This event was based on the account of Moses giving his last exhortation to the twelve tribes of Israel at Mount Nebo before he died (Deut 34:1–8). Matthew theologically interpreted the epiphany of Jesus through the Moses/Exodus typology. Matthew, to a certain degree, reflected the Pauline epistles; while Paul wrote that Christ appeared to the Twelve in 1Cor(3), Matthew wrote that Jesus had appeared to eleven of them. This was because he excluded Judas Iscariot. In this way, Matthew developed Paul's tradition as he described the resurrection and epiphany of Jesus as a historical event. This was the reinterpretation of the tradition surrounding the epiphany of Jesus that Matthew had inherited from Paul and Mark. Jesus' epiphany was important to Matthew because it strengthened the instruction that Jesus would be with his disciples until the end time.

John also described Jesus Christ's appearance after being raised from the dead. John described Jesus' resurrection and epiphany as a historical event, saying that many people touched his resurrected body (John 20:11–29). Mary stood outside the tomb crying after Peter and the other disciples confirmed the empty tomb and went back to the house. At that moment, the resurrected Jesus approached and called to her. Recognizing Jesus, Mary touched his resurrected body. This was the first case where someone touched the resurrected body of Jesus. It was written that he later appeared to his disciples, and at his second appearance, Thomas (who had doubted) confirmed the epiphany of Jesus by putting his finger in Jesus' hands and his hand into his side. In this, John communicated that not only Jesus' spirit, but also his flesh had been raised from the dead. It seems that John was refuting the Docetism that prevailed at that time. Probably John created the stories on the basis of the previous traditions that the resurrected Jesus appeared. This shows that John wrote the story about the epiphany of Jesus according to his theological need.

D. The Lucan Documents

The Lucan documents reported the epiphany of Jesus Christ after his resurrection. When they are read in sequence, his epiphany is revealed more clearly. In addition to the former tradition, the author listed more stories about Jesus in order to reveal his understanding of the epiphany.

Luke described the epiphany of Jesus Christ through several events. The most interesting is the story of Jesus meeting two of his disciples on the road to Emmaus (Luke 24:12–35). This account, told only in Luke, explains that these disciples returned at once to the disciples of Jerusalem after they met the incarnated Jesus. When they arrived, they heard the news from the other disciples that Jesus had already appeared to them as well. However, it seems that the two on the road to Emmaus were not included in the list of witnesses to the epiphany of Christ presented by Paul in 1Cor(3). Furthermore, the description of their return to Jerusalem was the main focus of Luke, showing the possibility that the author shaped the story of Emmaus according to his theological intentions. Interestingly, Luke omitted the prophecy of Jesus that he would meet the disciples in Galilee after his resurrection. Luke mentioned another event in which Jesus appeared to his disciples (Luke 24:36–49). Jesus let the disciples, who were frightened and distrustful, touch him (similar to the Johannine description that Thomas touched the resurrected Jesus) and even ate a piece of broiled fish. Here, Luke clearly described the epiphany of Jesus. This, as in the case of John, was written in order to defend against the Docetism prevalent around the end of the first century and the beginning of the second century CE.

Acts also mentions the epiphany of Jesus Christ in various places. He appeared often during the forty days after the resurrection and delivered instructions to the apostles (Acts 1:3–5). During that time, Jesus Christ "spoke about the kingdom of God." This implies that Jesus proclaimed the gospel even after the resurrection. His final appearance was at the ascension, which is only found in Acts (1:6–11). His disciples appeared as witnesses to it. Jesus' epiphany also became clear through the Great Commission. Probably, Luke also created this story on the basis of the Pauline tradition that the resurrected Jesus appeared to the Twelve in 1Cor(3). Nevertheless, it is clear that Acts seemed to describe Jesus' appearance as a historical event.

The epiphany of Jesus Christ is to be considered in light of Paul's spiritual enlightenment in Acts. As Paul neared Damascus, suddenly a light from heaven flashed around him, and he heard the voice of the resurrected Jesus of Nazareth (Acts 9:1–9). However, it is not clear whether such an event actually happened to him since Paul did not mention this event in his epistles. Acts was also influenced by Paul's theological interpretations in relating the epiphany of Jesus. Acts provided Paul with the condition for the apostleship when it described that Paul witnessed the resurrected Jesus on his way to Damascus. Actually, Paul was used to being challenged by the Corinthians with questions over whether he had met Jesus, as reflected in 1Cor(3). Thus, in Acts, the story about Jesus' epiphany to Paul was written as a theological compensation for the challenges Paul faced from the Gentiles in connection with his apostleship. As a result, it was written in Acts so that Paul would not need to defend his apostolic authority. According to the selection of the apostle to replace Judas Iscariot, an apostle had to be with Jesus the whole time, beginning from John's baptism to when he was taken up to heaven, and they had to witness his resurrection (Acts 1:21–22). Paul did not fulfill any of these conditions, so it was written in Acts that Paul was called as an apostle by Jesus himself, who appeared to him on his way to Damascus. Still, Paul did not witness the baptism of Jesus (although in fact, the other apostles did not witness the event either). Acts described Paul as an apostle according to his theological interpretation. The epiphany of Jesus Christ on the way to Damascus was mentioned again in Acts. Moreover, it was described as if Paul himself related it (Acts 22:5–16; 26:12–18). Of course, though there are some differences in the details, the fact that the epiphany of Jesus was written three times in Acts confirms that the event was given significant meaning. However, these events were also created by the author based on his theological interpretation of the previous tradition, probably handed over from Paul. In this sense, the gospel related to the epiphany of Jesus was given importance in Acts.

In conclusion, Luke should be credited with a significant achievement regarding the series of the epiphany of Jesus Christ. He created as many stories about it as possible, emphasizing its historicity. In addition, Luke provided the theoretic basis for Paul to be an apostle through Jesus' direct appearance before him. This shows that Luke also created the Lucan stories about the epiphany of Jesus for his own theological purpose.

E. Conclusion

The tradition about the epiphany of Jesus Christ was formed from theological perspectives. Even the twelve apostles did not know of this event, but it became known by the First Christians, who made theological interpretations from their point of view. Paul did not mention the event in detail but instead used the tradition about the epiphany of Christ to convey the content of the gospel and defend his apostolic authority. Even Mark only implied the event. Matthew and John, on the other hand, described Jesus' epiphany as a historical event through the description of Jesus' encounter with the disciples. The event was described in further detail in the Lucan documents, through which it seems the epiphany of Jesus became more of a historical fact. The other authors of the Christian Scriptures were strangely silent on the epiphany of Jesus Christ. Although the descriptions about his epiphany were different, each description was the result of the author's own theological interpretation. There was, however, no room to apply the hermeneutic principle "according to the Scriptures" to the epiphany of Jesus Christ because there is no prophecy about it in the Bible.

PART III

The Gospel of Q and Its Development

AFTER MEETING THE FIRST Christians, Paul went up to Jerusalem and met Cephas Peter and James, the Lord's brother. It is likely that this was the first time Paul learned how Jesus lived and taught. At that time, the third redaction of Q had probably been completed; therefore, Paul was aware that Jesus was identified theologically as the Son of God and the Son of Man. Paul could then identify Jesus as the Son of God about whom he had received the revelation at Damascus. In addition, he learned about the kingdom of God, which had been depicted in the first three redactions of Q. In this manner, Paul became familiar with various themes developed in Q and applied them to his interpretation of Jesus Christ and the kingdom of God. In particular, this allowed Paul to develop the concept of the ascension and the second advent of Jesus Christ on the basis of the role of the Son of Man. In this section, the kingdom of God, the ascension of Jesus Christ, and his second coming will be studied on the basis of the discussion in the prologue regarding the nature of faith, the chronological order of writings, and the concept of the gospel.

9

The Edenic Kingdom of God

SURPRISINGLY, THE MEANING OF the kingdom of God is not especially clear. The kingdom was first covered by Jesus in Q. However, it was not mentioned by the First Christians. Paul described the kingdom of God, but he did not provide many details. Nonetheless, he sought to convey the character of the kingdom of God. Later, the Gospels connected the kingdom of God specifically with the gospel. What is important here is the kingdom of God as an idea, but in fact, there are no verses that explain it clearly. However, toward the end of the first century CE, the kingdom of God was graphically compared with the garden of Eden. This reflects increasing interest in the form of the kingdom of God. In this way, the gospel about the kingdom of God was interpreted from a theological perspective.

A. Q

The kingdom of God was first mentioned in Q. The term "kingdom of God" does not appear in the Bible or in the intertestamental writings penned prior to the first century CE.[1] Although the concept of the kingdom existed since ages past, its explanation was not clear.[2] Q is the first document that mentioned the kingdom of God in various ways.

---

1. Collins, "Kingdom of God," 81.
2. The thought of being ruled over God is revealed in Judg 8:23, which was a perspective passed on to the Jews from very long ago. On the other hand, though the word "your kingdom" was used in Ps 145:13, the word "kingdom of God" was not used yet.

Various tenses are used to describe the kingdom of God in Q. In fact, it seems the notion about the kingdom of God was not established at that time. To begin, the first redactor used the present tense verb ἐστίν to describe the kingdom of God (Q¹ 6:20b). This implies the present aspect of the kingdom of God; then, the poor belong to the kingdom of God. From that perspective, the kingdom of God relates to the economic affluence that gives contentment to the poor. Generally then, according to the first redactor, the kingdom of God stands for the situation or circumstance that gives contentment to those who look for a better life. In this respect, the historical Jesus was supposed to proclaim the kingdom to the marginal people from a socio-religious perspective.

The second redactor also mentioned a kingdom that was not yet fully established. This was described with a perfect tense verb ἤγγικεν, relating that the kingdom had come near (Q² 10:9). It was also explained that people should pray for the kingdom to come to the world using the first aorist active imperative verb ἐλθέτω (11:2). This also reflected the wish for the kingdom to come in the near future. Furthermore, the kingdom could be confirmed by the miracles of demons being exiled with the finger or Spirit of God using the first aorist active indicative verb ἔφθασεν (11:20). In this, the kingdom is a place that can only be experienced when certain preconditions are met. Thus, the disciples of Jesus must live by pursuing that kingdom (12:31). All these statements describe a kingdom of God that has not yet fully arrived but soon will. In this respect, the time of the kingdom's coming was postponed to the near future in the second redaction.[3] According to the second redactor, Jesus was merely an announcer for the kingdom of God.

Third, the kingdom of God reveals a mysterious characteristic in the third redaction. The third redactor described the kingdom of God through parables (Q³ 13:18–21). The kingdom is a mysterious place that cannot entirely be explained by humans. How to enter the kingdom is not depicted; however, it can be surmised that those who wait for the Son of Man will enter it because the kingdom is inevitably related to his coming. This is shown by the fact that the texts about his coming (12:39–40, 42–46; 17:23–24, 26–27, 30, 34–35) surround the texts about the kingdom (13:18–21, 24–27).

Also, the expression that God reigns was used in Ps 146:10. However, it seems that these psalms were also added in the first century BCE or the first century CE to the book of Psalms.

3. This is why the second redactor used the future tense for the second and third Beatitudes (Q² 6:21), which were added to the first one belonging to the first redaction (Q¹ 6:20b). To my view, the fourth beatitude belongs to the third redaction, which focuses on one's attitude toward Jesus, the Son of Man (Q³ 6:22–23b), and rest of it belongs to the fourth redaction (Q⁴ 6:23c). In this way, the Beatitudes reveal their redactional stages.

In other words, they constitute an *inclusio*; from literary perspective, this strengthens the relationship between the kingdom of God and the coming of the Son of Man. In this way, Christians' attitude toward the Son of Man, probably Jesus, stood for the condition for entering the kingdom. In this respect, Jesus, the Son of Man, was focused on in association with entering the kingdom of God. In addition, according to the third redactor, the kingdom of God is a place where a person can enter through something that is compared to gate or door (13:24–27).

Finally, the fourth redactor described the transcendental aspect of the kingdom of God. It is a place in which a hierarchical system exists among the residents (Q^4 7:28), and people are eager to enter (16:16). The kingdom of God is likely a realm of residence. In addition, it is a place where Abraham, Isaac, Jacob, and others went, but also a transcendental world where many people would join them (Q^4 13:28–30). It seems that the persecuted and martyred prophets, namely the disciples of Jesus, would enter into it (6:23c; 11:47–51; 13:34–35). It was described as a realm that had existed somewhere else and would be completed in the indefinite future. The kingdom could be contrasted with the prison in the depths of the earth where the corrupted angels are in custody until the end of the world, as it was written in the second century BCE (1 En 18:14).[4] At any rate, the kingdom of God conveyed the eschatological and transcendental characteristics in the fourth redaction.

The four characteristics of the kingdom of God are the result of redaction. Jesus, as reflected in the first redaction, proclaimed that the kingdom of God had already arrived, but later redactors edited Q by describing that the kingdom would come in the future, since it did not arrive as quickly as they expected. This shows that understanding about the kingdom of God changed, and the reality of the kingdom of God was not completely known in Q. The people of that time had a general notion about the kingdom of God, but the image of the kingdom traditionally shared by the Jews was tacitly proclaimed by Q in the first stage of the formation of the gospel related to the kingdom of God. The kingdom of God went through a process of redaction over a short period from the late twenties to the early forties CE.

The role of Jesus was not clearly depicted in connection with the kingdom of God in Q. He proclaimed the kingdom, but the specific role he played was not described any further. In this, Jesus was presented more as a messenger than a savior. He was probably not different from other

---

4. The Book of Watcher, the first book of 1 Enoch, is composed of chapters 1–36. It is supposed to have been written between 170–150 BCE (Isaac, "1 Enoch," 1:7; Barker, *Lost Paradise*, 14; Knibb, "1 Enoch," 174; and Collins, *Apocalyptic Imagination*, 36).

Jewish wisdom teachers and prophets who proclaimed religious and spiritual teachings to the people.

B. The Pauline Epistles

Paul mentioned the kingdom of God, but he covered a smaller amount of detail than might be expected. Like Q, Paul did not describe the reality of the kingdom. Taking this into consideration, it seems that the notion of the kingdom of God was not complete at that time. However, Paul understood it in connection with the Spirit after he had faced the challenge from the Gentile Christians.

At the beginning of his missionary journey, Paul did not teach the Gentile Christians much about the kingdom of God. For example, it was mentioned only once in 1Thess(1). Paul simply said that God called the Thessalonians into the kingdom of God and glory (1 Thess 2:12). Placed in parallel with glory, the kingdom of God shows the reader its glorious aspect. Paul then declared that those who were called by God would live a holy life (4:7), focusing on the authority of God to call his people and make them holy. In considering both texts in combination, it can be concluded that those who were promised to enter the kingdom lived a holy life. In this respect, holiness is indirectly related with the kingdom of God. From the facts of God's authority to call his people and that holiness is the top priority for them in the Bible, we can conclude that Paul applied the Jewish concept of the conditions for entering the kingdom of God to the Thessalonians.

Paul mentioned ethical behavior in connection with the inheritance of the kingdom of God in 1Cor(2).[5] He taught that the unrighteous would not inherit it (1 Cor 6:9–10). The list of the unrighteous shows the ethical aspect of behaviors from a religious point of view: sexual criminals, idolaters, thieves, the greedy, drunkards, etc. People can avoid these behaviors by observing the Law, or at least following common sense. It is noteworthy that Paul introduced a list of wrongdoing instead of belief in Jesus Christ for the condition to inherit the kingdom. It is, however, to be remembered that the list above includes more extended elements than that in 1Thess(1) (1 Thess 4:3–6) and 1Cor(1) (1 Cor 6:15, 18). This demonstrates that Paul was definitely within the Jewish tradition when he taught the Gentiles about

---

5. It is necessary to look at 1 Cor 15:24–25, which is supposed to belong to 1Cor(2), because it could be suggested as the verse in which Jesus Christ and the kingdom are related. However, it seems that the kingdom is an intermediate place that will be fulfilled when it is entirely handed over to God after the end has come. It is similar to the millennium presented in Revelation (Rev 20:1–15). As for the influence of Paul to Revelation, refer to Shin, "Die paulinischen Auswirkungen," 834–47.

the kingdom of God at the time of writing 1Cor(2). In addition, Paul articulated his notion that a person could make him or herself cleansed, holy, and righteous by the name of the Lord Jesus Christ and in the Spirit of God (6:11). The phrases "by the name of the Lord Jesus Christ" and "in the Spirit of God" appear for the first time in connection with the religious status of people in terms of salvation. At any rate, this shows that Paul started becoming interested in the Spirit regarding the inheritance of the kingdom of God in 1Cor(2).

After Paul heard the news that the Gentile Christians faced turmoil caused by outsiders, he paid more attention to the kingdom of God. Paul revealed some characteristics related to this matter in 1Cor(3). The kingdom is not a matter of talk, but of power (1 Cor 4:20). Here, power refers to miraculous phenomena through the Spirit of God, since Paul already used the word "power" for that meaning by putting it in parallel with the Spirit (2:4).[6] Insofar as the kingdom is verified by the spiritual power, it can be related with the kingdom described in Q^2 11:20, where the finger or Spirit of God resulted in the exorcism of demons. It is, however, noteworthy that the characteristics of the kingdom began to be defined in connection with the Spirit during the period of conflict between Paul and the Gentile Christians sponsored by the Jerusalem apostles. Paul seemed to remind the Corinthians of their experience in receiving the Spirit of God and confirming the kingdom of God among them so that they might remain in the gospel he proclaimed. Regarding the condition for its inheritance, Paul said that the kingdom could not be inherited by flesh and blood (1 Cor 15:50). The flesh and blood used here ultimately stands for the essence of unrighteousness—the nature that resists God. Paul seemed to turn his eyes from the unrighteous behaviors in 1Cor(2) to the nature that causes unrighteous behavior in 1Cor(3) as the condition for not inheriting the kingdom of God. This kind of description was made because Paul had experienced serious challenge from the Corinthians, which was also a challenge against God.

Paul also dealt with the kingdom of God in Galatians in connection with the Spirit. He insisted that those who do the works of the flesh could not inherit the kingdom of God (Gal 5:19–21). For this, Paul listed unrighteous works in much more detail than in 1Cor(2). In Galatians, flesh is for the first time contrasted with the Spirit (Gal 3:3; 4:29; 5:16–17; 6:8) since the flesh was introduced as the nature that resists God in 1Cor(3). In this way, Paul developed his understanding of the flesh and the Spirit in connection with the kingdom of God. Ultimately, righteous people living by the Spirit

6. Paul mentioned the spirit and miracles together in Gal 3:5. In addition, it is described in Rom 1:4 that this spirit cannot be separated from the resurrection of Jesus Christ.

of God, will inherit the kingdom. In this respect, Paul emphasized people's spiritual condition in Galatians more than the righteous and ethical behaviors in 1Cor(2) as the conditions for inheriting the kingdom. The kingdom of God is a place people can inherit according to their spiritual condition (Gal 5:21–22). However, Paul did not reveal its characteristics in Galatians at all.

Paul introduced the characteristics of the kingdom of God in Rom(1). He wrote that it is not a matter of eating and drinking, but of righteousness, peace, and joy in the Holy Spirit (Rom 14:17). In this sense, the kingdom of God is the complete spiritual condition that is possible to enjoy in this world. In other words, the kingdom of God stands for a peaceful and stable fulfillment of one's spiritual capacity. This description could be the result of the influence of Q, since the lesson that the kingdom could be confirmed when demons are exiled by the finger or Spirit of God displays spiritual power (Q^2 11:20). This is, however, somewhat different from the transcendental and eschatological aspect of the kingdom of God in the fourth redaction (Q^4 13:28). It is noteworthy, however, that as time passed, the kingdom of God was increasingly characterized in connection with the Spirit of God.

Paul did not explain in detail the reality of the kingdom of God. The kingdom was only described as the capacity for peace enjoyed in the power of the Spirit. This is a different place from the paradise—namely, the garden of Eden—in the third heaven mentioned in 2Cor(3) (2 Cor 12:1–4). Paul was supposed to enter the paradise only once through a mysterious phenomenon. Paradise, unlike the kingdom of God, was a transcendental world believed in by the Jews, as written in the book of Parables, one of the five books in 1 Enoch written in the middle of the first century CE (1 En 37:5; 39:3–4, 8; 60:23; 61:8).[7] In this respect, the kingdom of God can be enjoyed during life in this world. The reason for this interpretation is that Paul probably shared the notion of the contemporaneous Jews reflected in the second redaction of Q. Paul rarely reflected the instruction in the fourth redaction of Q regarding the kingdom of God, since he did not accept its transcendental aspect.

Paul mentioned the role of Christ in connection with the kingdom of God. He taught that the righteous would inherit the kingdom of God (1 Cor 6:11), then wrote that a Christian is justified before God by faith in Jesus Christ (Gal 2:16; Rom 3:22). In other words, faith in Jesus Christ makes a person righteous so that he or she can inherit the kingdom of God. In this respect, the role of Jesus Christ in inheriting the kingdom of God was getting stronger as time passed. However, his role is indirectly connected;

---

7. As for the composition date of the book of Parables, see Collins, *Apocalyptic Imagination*, 143; and Mearns, "Dating," 368–69.

in other words, such descriptions are the result of Paul taking further steps than Q, which described Jesus as the messenger of the kingdom. Paul indirectly suggested the Christian attitude toward Jesus Christ as a means of inheriting the kingdom of God during the last part of his missionary journey. In conclusion, the Gentile Christians' challenge made Paul regard a personal relationship with Jesus Christ more as the condition for inheriting the kingdom of God.

C. Mark

Mark related the kingdom of God in close connection with the gospel. He inherited the idea of the kingdom from Q and described it while applying Paul's perspective on the gospel. It also seems that he referred to the garden of Eden, and in so doing, tried to define the reality of the kingdom of God.[8]

Mark described the condition for entering the kingdom of God in connection with the gospel. For this, Mark asked for repentance and faith in the gospel (Mark 1:15). While Paul thought of the gospel as the prophecies about Jesus Christ and taught that those who believed in the gospel would be saved in Rom(1), Mark taught that people who believed in the gospel would enter the kingdom of God. Jesus Christ was more directly connected to entering the kingdom of God, since Mark thought of Jesus Christ's life itself as the gospel. While Paul preached that those who believed in Christ become righteous and that the righteous would inherit the kingdom of God, Mark taught that believing in Jesus—that is, living by the ways he taught and demonstrated—was the way to enter the kingdom of God. Mark took further steps than Paul did in regard to the kingdom of God's connection with Jesus and the gospel. The belief in Jesus—that is, the gospel itself—is the condition for entering the kingdom of God.

Mark planted the clue that connects the kingdom of God to the garden of Eden from the beginning. For this, Mark quite possibly inherited the idea from Paul that Jesus proclaimed repentance and belief in the gospel since the kingdom of God had come near and the time had come (Mark 1:15). While Paul wrote that God sent his Son through a woman "when the time had fully come [ὅτε δὲ ἦλθεν τὸ πλήρωμα τοῦ χρόνου]" (Gal 4:4), Mark conveyed that the coming of the kingdom of God was the moment when "the time has come [πεπλήρωται ὁ καιρός]." Paul emphasized the duration from prophecy to fulfillment by using χρόνος, but Mark focused on the moment

---

8. Fawcett suggests the opinion that the kingdom of God described in the Synoptic Gospels refers to the garden of Eden. However, he does not describe this matter in detail (Fawcett. *Hebrew Myth*, 261–62).

of fulfillment by using καιρός. In addition, Mark changed the noun form to the verb form regarding πληρόω. While Paul understood the Son of God as the descendent of a woman in the context of the garden of Eden by the phrase "when the time had fully come" (Gen 3:15), Mark understood the kingdom of God in connection with the garden of Eden by using the phrase "the time has come." These instances make the connection between Paul and Mark even stronger. This interpretation is strengthened by the fact that the proclamation of the kingdom follows the temptation of Jesus in the wilderness, which alludes to that of Adam and Eve in the garden of Eden (Mark 1:12–13; Gen 2:18—3:24).[9] While Paul thought of the kingdom of God and paradise (the garden of Eden) as different places in 2Cor(3), Mark tried to connect these two. The garden of Eden became the model for the kingdom of God in Mark. In this respect, Mark seemed to apply Paul's perspective on the gospel to the description of the kingdom of God.

Mark continued to reference the garden of Eden when connecting the kingdom of God with repentance. People must first repent in order to enter the kingdom of God (Mark 1:15). This was a theme that Paul also thought important, although it was not closely related with the kingdom in his epistles.[10] However, according to Mark, repentance is an element that connects the kingdom of God to the garden of Eden from which Adam and Eve were exiled because they did not repent from their sin of eating the forbidden fruit. As a result, Mark presented repentance as the precondition for entering the kingdom of God and provided a clue to connect the kingdom to the garden of Eden. For this purpose, Mark attempted a typological approach. Therefore, Mark should be credited with a significant achievement regarding the typological understanding of the kingdom of God in connection with the garden of Eden.

Mark also added agricultural elements in order to connect the kingdom of God to the garden of Eden. First of all, Mark intentionally reveals the relationship of the kingdom of God through this agricultural aspect by inserting the phrase "secrets of the kingdom of God" between the parable of the Sower and its interpretation (Mark 4:3–9, 11, 14–20). Then, Mark added the parable of the Seed Growing Secretly (4:26–29). In addition, the parable

---

9. Jeremias, *New Testament*, 1:61. This will be dealt with more in detail in chapter 12.

10. Paul proclaimed that the unrighteous would not inherit the kingdom of God (1 Cor 6:9–10), which means that only the righteous would inherit the kingdom of God. Also, Paul said that those who have sinned earlier—that is, via impurity, sexual sin, and debauchery—had to repent (2 Cor 12:21). This is the lesson that people can only inherit the kingdom of God by becoming righteous through the repentance of their wrongdoings.

of the Mustard Seed came from Q (Mark 4:30–32; Q³ 13:18–19). Adding such horticultural elements implies an attempt to connect the kingdom of God with the garden of Eden. Mark's intention is strengthened by the fact that the parable of the Leaven originated from Q (Q³ 13:20–21) but was not accepted into the description of the kingdom because the leaven does not have anything to do with the garden of Eden.[11]

Mark continued to refer to the garden of Eden by writing about high mountains. This was revealed in the description that the kingdom of God has come with power at the high mountain (Mark 9:1–8). As Jesus promised to show the kingdom, Peter, James, and John experienced it on that mountain for a moment. In the Jewish tradition, a high mountain is connected to the garden of Eden, which led to the tradition that a temple is on the high mountain and that temple functions as the garden of Eden (Ezek chapters 40–47; especially 40:2; 47:6–12).[12] Later, the garden of Eden was described as relating to the high mountain in the intertestamental writings as well (1 En 18:6–8; 24:4–6; 25:5–6; 32:1–3; Jub 4:26, etc.). Based on the Jewish tradition, Mark probably connected the kingdom of God and the garden of Eden when he described its experience on the high mountain.

Mark included another allusion to the garden of Eden in the words of Jesus at the Lord's Supper. Jesus said that he would not drink again of the fruit of the vine until the day when he would drink it anew in the kingdom of God (Mark 14:25). Thus, Mark described that Jesus refused to drink the wine mixed with myrrh offered at his crucifixion (15:23). He refused once again on the cross when a man tried to offer a sponge with wine vinegar and another person said to just leave him alone (15:36). These examples are included to fulfill Mark's intention that Jesus would keep his promise not to drink wine until the day when he would drink it anew in the kingdom of God. It should also be noted that the kingdom of God is related to the wine that is made of the fruit of the vine because it reminds readers of the plants in the garden of Eden. According to Jewish tradition, the vine was one of the typical plants found in the garden (1 En 32:4; 2 En 8:6, etc.). Following that tradition, vines were engraved on the front doors of the temple in Jerusalem (*Jewish Antiquities*, 15:395; *Jewish War*, 5:210–211). This implies that the Jews at that time identified the Jerusalem temple with the garden of Eden. Mark also connected the vine with the kingdom of God, and so alluded to

---

11. Although Mark put the Parable of the Lamp on the stand in the middle of texts that refer to the kingdom of God, it is not directly connected with the kingdom (Mark 4:21–22). This parable was adopted from Q (Q³ 11:33), but it was not related to the kingdom of God there either. It seems that the element of the lamp is unrelated to the garden of Eden.

12. Himmelfarb, *Ascent to Heaven*, 73; and Fawcett, *Hebrew Myth*, 256.

the garden of Eden by mentioning the vine and kingdom at the Lord's Supper. In this respect, Mark figuratively delivered the Edenic kingdom of God.

Mark also tried to define the kingdom on the basis of previous traditions. Although Jewish tradition never used the kingdom of God in connection with the garden of Eden, the Hymn of Thanksgiving identified the Qumran community with a garden (1QH 8:4, 6, 16, 21–23).[13] This shows their hope that the garden of Eden be realized in their community.[14] While Paul did not understand the kingdom of God in the context of the garden of Eden, Mark knew about the Qumran tradition and attempted to apply it to the kingdom of God. This is why Mark planted the horticultural elements into the description of the kingdom. Therefore, it seems that Mark adopted the term "kingdom of God" from Q and tried to connect it for the first time with the garden of Eden according to the Jewish tradition.

In conclusion, Mark should be credited with a significant achievement in connecting the kingdom of God to the garden of Eden through agricultural allusions, the theme of repentance, the motive of high mountains, and the images of the vine and the temple. Although the attempt was not sufficiently clear, Mark was the first author who imposed the Edenic aspect to the kingdom of God from a typological perspective.

D. Matthew

Matthew used the term "kingdom of heaven" more than "kingdom of God."[15] This implies that the kingdom of God was connected with something that belonged to heaven. Most likely this meant the garden of Eden, which was kept in heaven until the end of the world.[16] In this respect, Matthew advanced one step further than Mark in describing the kingdom of God.

Matthew assigned the proclamation of the kingdom to various groups of people. John the Baptist was the first to proclaim the coming of the kingdom in Matthew (Matt 3:2), while the disciples of Jesus were committed to announce it in Q (Q^2 10:9), and Jesus was the only herald in Mark (Mark 1:14). In Matthew, not only Jesus Christ but also the disciples proclaimed the approaching of the kingdom (Matt 4:17; 10:7). Thus, Matthew was able

---

13. It seems that the Hymn of Thanksgiving (1QH) was written around 100 BCE (Rowley, *Jewish Apocalyptic*, 8; and Collins, *Apocalyptic Imagination*, 119).

14. Charlesworth, *Jesus*, 149. He argues for the possibility that the Hymn of Thanksgiving affected the formation of the Markan Parable of the Wicked Tenants regarding the self-understanding of Jesus as the Son of God (Mark 12:1–12).

15. While the kingdom of God appears four times, the kingdom of heaven was used thirty-two times in Matthew.

16. Cf. Ra, "Return," 253–311.

to describe that the kingdom has been forcefully advancing toward the world from the days of John the Baptist (11:12).[17] It seems that Matthew combined all the traditions from Q and Mark and used them creatively according to his theological need.

Matthew introduced righteousness as the condition for entering the kingdom of God or heaven. According to Matthew, a Christian must earn righteousness by keeping the teachings of Jesus in order to enter the kingdom of heaven (Matt 5:20; 7:21–23). This reminds readers of Paul's emphasis on "being righteous" by faith in Jesus (Gal 2:16; Rom 3:22) and the righteous entrants into the kingdom (1 Cor 6:9–11; Gal 5:19–21). In addition, Matthew taught that the tax collectors and the prostitutes who accepted the path of righteousness asserted by John the Baptist are entering the kingdom of God (Matt 21:31). In this sense, Matthew demonstrated a unique theology that not only Jesus Christ, but also John the Baptist could lead people to the kingdom of God. Matthew's emphasis on righteousness in connection with Jesus seems to reflect the influence of Pauline theology on the condition for entering the kingdom, although Jewish tradition generally emphasized righteousness before God.

Matthew dealt with the coming of the kingdom of God to the world. He inherited this tradition from Q, and it was also shown in the example of prayer (Matt 6:10; Q^2 11:2). In addition, experiencing the kingdom of God at the high mountain also explains that the kingdom will come to this world (Matt 16:27—17:8; Mark 9:1–8). Moreover, at the renewal of all things when Jesus Christ, the Son of Man, sits on his glorious throne, the kingdom is the place into which this world will change (Matt 19:28; Q^4 22:30). In this sense, the kingdom of God is to be completed in a newly changed world. Using the traditions from Q and Mark, Matthew developed his thinking on the coming of the kingdom of God to the world.

Matthew also connected the kingdom of heaven to the garden of Eden. Using the Jewish tradition and Mark, Matthew taught that the garden of Eden, which has been preserved in heaven, will come to this world. The Jews of that time thought the garden of Eden was kept in heaven. For example, in the forties CE, the book of Parables explained that the paradise had been kept in heaven (1 En 39:3–4; 60:23). In addition, in the fifties, Paul thought paradise—that is, the garden of Eden—was in the third heaven (2 Cor 12:1–4). Moreover, in the seventies, it was written that the paradise had been preserved in the third heaven (*Apocalypse of Moses* 37:5–6; 40:1). Finally, in the nineties, it was written in Revelation that the garden of Eden was kept in the

---

17. Many versions translate the Greek verb βιάζεται in a passive voice; however, it is argued that it must be translated in a middle voice (Verseput, *Rejection*, 94–96).

midst of the Holy City, the New Jerusalem in heaven (Rev 21:1—22:5; cf. 2 En 8:1; 42:3). It seems that Matthew also believed the garden of Eden was kept in heaven on the basis of such traditions, and Matthew more frequently described it as the kingdom of heaven rather than the kingdom of God. While Paul did not identify the paradise, the garden of Eden, in the third heaven with the kingdom of God, Mark tried to connect it with the kingdom of God. Matthew then took the next step by implying that the kingdom of God was kept in heaven on the basis of the contemporary Jewish tradition.

Matthew left many clues in order to connect the kingdom of heaven to the garden of Eden. First, he strengthened the agricultural or horticultural aspects. Such aspects are revealed through parables. For this purpose, as Mark had done, Matthew located the phrase "the secret of the kingdom of heaven" in between the parable of the Sower and its interpretation (Matt 13:11). Then Matthew not only used the parable of the Mustard Seed used by Q and Mark (Matt 13:31–32) but also included more agricultural parables. For instance, he omitted the parable of the Seed Growing Secretly, but added the parable of the Wheat and Weeds (Matt 13:24–30). While doing so, he clearly distinguished the good and evil that reminds readers of the tree of the knowledge of good and evil in the garden of Eden. Moreover, Matthew added the parables of the Hidden Treasure and the Workers in the Vineyard, which also show agricultural aspects (Matt 13:44; 20:1–16). Matthew took the Markan parable of the Evil Tenants, which was not related to the kingdom of God, and connected it to the kingdom (Matt 21:33–41; Mark 12:1–12). Matthew connected horticultural parables to the kingdom of heaven as much as possible in order to assosciate the kingdom of God with the garden of Eden.

Another way Matthew connected the kingdom of heaven and the garden of Eden was through the themes of forgiveness and judgment. The parable of the Unmerciful Servant can be an example of forgiveness, and the parables of the Net and of the Sheep and the Goats can be examples of judgment (Matt 13:47–50; 18:21–35; 25:31–46). The fact that these parables only appear in Matthew strengthens the connection between the kingdom of heaven and the garden of Eden. The parable of the Talents can also be included here because it carries the theme of judgment (25:14–30). These parables distinguish good and evil by contrasting the different fates each one faces in the end. Such themes reflect the case of Adam and Eve, who did not forgive one another after eating the forbidden fruit and were judged by God. In other words, the kingdom of heaven is a place that can be entered by the judgment of God when people forgive one another. In this sense, entering the kingdom of heaven is a process of returning to the garden of Eden by retracing the steps of exile.

Matthew referred to the garden of Eden while applying clues to the kingdom of heaven unused in the other Gospels. First, he emphasized that the kingdom existed since the creation of the world (Matt 25:34). The kingdom prepared since the creation of the world was an expression only used in Matthew, which implies that the kingdom is the garden of Eden.[18] This interpretation could be supported by the Jewish tradition. It was stated around one hundred BCE that the garden of Eden was created on the third day of God's creation of the world (Jub 2:5–7), and this belief was preserved in the first century CE (2 En 31:1–2). On the other hand, as time passed, in the nineties, the Jews began to believe that the garden was created before the creation of the world (4 Ezra 3:6). At the end of this trend, Matthew probably believed that the kingdom of heaven existed since the creation of the world, alluding to the garden of Eden. Second, Matthew newly described that the kingdom of heaven was related to weddings, doors, and treasures (Matt 13:44–46; 22:1–10; 23:13; 25:1–13). Except the theme of the wedding, which originated in Q (Q^4 14:16–24), most of these only appear in Matthew.[19] These elements are connected to the wedding of Adam and Eve, the fence of the garden, and all kinds of treasure in it. In this sense, Matthew implied the kingdom of God was the garden of Eden, believed to be kept in heaven. Here, he shows the typological theology that the events of the beginning will come again at the end. Therefore, Matthew, following Mark, further developed the gospel that understood the kingdom of God to be the garden of Eden in heaven.

In conclusion, Matthew is the first person who attributed the heavenly aspect to the kingdom of God. Following the Jewish tradition, Matthew planted many allusions to the kingdom of God in order to connect it to the garden of Eden: the horticultural aspect, the images of mountain and door, the motives of forgiveness, judgment, and wedding, and the theme of good and evil. In this way, Matthew described the transcendental and eschatological aspect of the kingdom of God in the context of the garden of Eden.

E. The Johannine Documents

The Johannine documents list various descriptions of the kingdom of God. While John defined the lordship of the kingdom of God as Jesus Christ, Revelation dealt with the eschatological New Jerusalem in relationship

---

18. Cf. Gnilka, *Matthäusevangelium*, 2:372–373; and Luz, *Das Evangelium*, 2:337.

19. Luke did not use Q 14:16–24 in connection with the kingdom of God (Luke 14:16–24). This strengthens the intention of Matthew, who used it for the description of the kingdom of heaven in order to allude to the garden of Eden.

with the garden of Eden. This shows a radical change in the description of the heavenly kingdom.

First of all, John intermittently mentioned the kingdom of God. It is a place that no one can enter unless he or she is born again of water and the Spirit (John 3:3, 5). In this way, John wrote that the kingdom of God is a reality that is totally different from the world we live in now. Then, John conclusively stated that Jesus claimed a kingdom that is not of this world (18:36). It seems that the kingdom of God is a transcendental place. Referring the lordship of the kingdom to Jesus, the author of the prologue to John later identified him with God (1:3). However, John did not clarify the reality of the kingdom of God. As time passed, there was a tendency to attribute this transcendental aspect to the kingdom of God at the end of the first century CE.

Revelation does not often mention the kingdom of God, which is directly addressed in only two instances. The kingdom of God is contrasted with the secular world but identified with the kingdom of Christ (Rev 11:15). In this, Revelation is in line with John in its description of the lordship of the kingdom. In addition, the kingdom of God is placed in parallel with the salvation and power of God (12:10). This also shows that the kingdom as a transcendental place. It appears that Revelation followed John in its description of the characteristics of the kingdom while stopping short of clarifying its reality.

Later, in order to clarify its reality, Revelation mentioned a transcendental space that would come from heaven. This is the Holy City, the New Jerusalem, which could be the kingdom of God and may include the garden of Eden in its midst (Rev 21:1—22:5). Clues that refer to the garden of Eden are found in the image of the Holy City. First, the wall that surrounds it could be compared to the fence around the garden of Eden (Rev 21:12-21). Also, the precious stones used to build the wall could refer to the jewels and gold produced in the garden of Eden. Moreover, in the New Jerusalem, a river of the water of life flows down out of heaven, and on each side of the river stands the tree of life, which bears twelve types of fruit. This stands for the tree of life at the center of the garden of Eden (22:1-2). In addition, the Holy City descending from heaven is compared to the garden of Eden in that there were no more curses; the garden of Eden was the place where the first curse was given (22:3). The Holy City is a place brighter than the sun, where only the glory of God is revealed (22:5). The Jewish tradition taught that such themes were also the reflection of the garden of Eden before the fall of Adam and Eve (1 En 58:3; 2 En 42:3-4). The description that the throne of God and the Lamb will be in the center of the city means that they are the lords of the garden of Eden. Therefore, Revelation wrote that Jesus, the Lamb of God, was contrasted with Adam; and that the Holy City, the New Jerusalem that would come in the end, was connected to the once-lost garden of Eden. In this sense, Adam and the garden of Eden were used as the background to describe Jesus and the Holy City, the New Jerusalem, probably as the kingdom of God. The descent of the New Jerusalem from heaven is unique in Revelation. When the Holy City, the New Jerusalem, comes down from heaven at the end of time, the garden of Eden will accompany it in its midst (21:1–2; 22:1–5). As shown in the description of the kingdom of heaven in Matthew, the heavenly aspect of the garden of Eden was dominant in the Jewish tradition of the first century CE. While Matthew mentioned the ultimate coming of the kingdom to the world, Revelation dealt with the descent of the New Jerusalem, which is to be accompanied by the garden of Eden. Therefore, the gospel about the Edenic kingdom of God from heaven was developed in Revelation as well.

F. Other Documents

Other documents also deal with the kingdom of God in various ways. However, they do not suggest new aspects of the kingdom or provide many details. This implies that it was difficult to define the characteristic and form of the kingdom of God at the time of writing.

The Deutropauline epistles also dealt with the kingdom of God. By defining idolaters as those who could not inherit the kingdom of Christ and God, Ephesians put Christ in parallel with God (Eph 5:5). Similar to John and Revelation's description of the kingdom of Jesus Christ, Ephesians exalted Christ to the height of God. Colossians announced that God rescued people from the dark influence of evil and brought them into the kingdom of the Son he loved (Col 1:13). The author gradually emphasized the lordship of the Son in connection with the kingdom, even though the kingdom of God was still mentioned (4:11). Next, 2 Thessalonians mentioned the kingdom of God while defining those who would be worthy to enter it (2 Thess 1:5). Thus, the kingdom is connected with the righteousness of God. On the contrary, having placed God in parallel with Jesus Christ, 2 Timothy mentioned the kingdom of Christ Jesus (2 Tim 4:1). This again emphasizes the lordship of Jesus Christ over the kingdom. The author focused more on the lordship of Jesus Christ than the kingdom at the end of the first and the beginning of the second century CE but did not concretely define the reality of the kingdom.

The General Epistles also dealt with the kingdom of God. For instance, in Hebrews, righteousness represents the characteristics of the kingdom of God (Heb 1:8) and that kingdom will not be shaken (12:28). This was written for the purpose of strengthening the Christians' faith when faced with suffering under persecution by the Roman Empire. In addition, James introduced the idea that those who love God will inherit the kingdom of God (Jas 2:5); however, its characteristics are not defined because no more information is provided. On the contrary, 2 Peter mentioned the eternal kingdom of our Lord and Savior, Jesus Christ (2 Pet 1:11). While describing its eternal quality, 2 Peter emphasized Jesus Christ as the Lord of the kingdom. As time passed, there was a tendency to focus more on Jesus with regard to the lordship of the kingdom. Nevertheless, writers hesitated to define the characteristics and reality of the kingdom.

Luke mentioned the kingdom of God more than any other Gospel, adapting all the content of the traditions he inherited at the beginning of the second century CE. First, Luke presented the kingdom of God as a present as well as futuristic form. He used the present possessive form to say that the kingdom of God belongs to the poor (Luke 6:20). As it was shown through the event on the Mount of Transfiguration, the kingdom of God is a place that can be experienced briefly on earth (9:27–36). In addition, the kingdom can be found when God drives out demons by his finger (11:20; cf. 9:2; 10:9). Moreover, Luke taught that the kingdom of God is present even in the midst of the Pharisees, who are hostile to Jesus and his disciples (17:21). Luke emphasized that the kingdom of God could be enjoyed in this world in the present. However, Luke explained that the kingdom of God was still something to be realized in the future. The kingdom of God was a place that should be proclaimed to be near (Luke 10:9; 21:31), a place that should be explained through parables (13:18–21), a place where feasts would be held (13:29–30), a place that would not appear at once as expected (19:11), and a place that should be waited upon (23:51). In this sense, the kingdom of God is a place of the future that has yet to arrive. In order to describe the kingdom of God, Luke used all of the sources he inherited regarding its tense.

Second, Luke described the kingdom of God as an intact place. In the kingdom, demons were driven out by the finger of God (Luke 11:20), and the sick were healed (9:2; 10:9). The kingdom belonged to children (18:16–17), and many people from all directions could enter it (13:28–30). It was also a place to feast (13:29–30; 14:15; 22:16–18, 20). Luke described the kingdom of God as the most intact place, collecting sources from Q, Paul, and Mark.

Third, Luke defined the kingdom of God with a vague allusion to the garden of Eden. Like Mark and Matthew, Luke also adopted the horticultural parables, the images of wedding and gate, and theme of eschatological judgment to connect them. In addition, if possible, the dialogue between Jesus and the thief on the cross could be suggested as an example of characterization of the kingdom because Jesus referred to paradise in response to the thief's asking for "your kingdom" (Luke 23:42–43). In this text, "your kingdom" is related to paradise; however, it is not clear whether "your kingdom"—that is, the kingdom of Jesus—is indeed the kingdom of God, since Luke never identified Jesus with God. It is noteworthy that as the end of the first century CE approached, the lordship of the kingdom changed from God to Jesus Christ in John, Revelation, Ephesians, Colossians, 2 Timothy, and 2 Peter. There is a possibility that in Luke, "your kingdom" could refer to the kingdom of God, that is, paradise. However, there is no definite evidence in Luke itself to connect "your kingdom" to paradise. According to Luke, paradise—that is, the garden of Eden—is a place a righteous person's spirit can enter after they die. Although the genealogy of Jesus Christ goes back to Adam (3:23–38), Luke did not clearly reveal the Edenic kingdom of God.

G. Conclusion

The descriptions about the kingdom of God differed according to the era. They were the same in that the kingdom of God was described as ultimately reigned by God, but the details of these explanations were slightly different. Each author made his or her own theological interpretation for this purpose. Jesus was the first to use the term "kingdom of God," although he did not accurately define it. As a result, his disciples and other Christians made a variety of interpretations. In Q, the kingdom of God is introduced for the first time and defined at last as an eschatological and transcendental place. Paul meant the kingdom of God to be the enjoyment of the condition of spiritual completion, since he thought of the kingdom of God and the garden of Eden as separate places. Mark, on the other hand, was the first to attempt to connect the kingdom of God to the garden of Eden, and Matthew connected the two more clearly by emphasizing its heavenly aspect. Finally, Revelation states that the heavenly kingdom includes the garden of Eden in its midst. By contrast, Luke would accept a vague relationship between the two. Clearly, interpretations about the kingdom of God varied greatly. Each author of the Christian Scripture surely made his or her own theological interpretation about the kingdom of God according to need, and we can conclude that understandings of the kingdom of God developed in light of such transitions.

10

The Ascension of Jesus

THE ASCENSION OF JESUS, the Son of Man, developed without leaving behind many traditions. While the First Christians did not mention Jesus' ascension, Q dealt with the transcendental role of the Son of Man, who was understood to be Jesus. Paul himself did not know much about the event. However, judging from Paul's description of Jesus' exaltation at the right hand of God in heaven, it seems that Paul presumed his ascension. Mark and Matthew did not mention the ascension of Jesus, but they presumed it in their description of coming of the Son of Man. In fact, the only details about the event come from the Lucan documents that describe the image of the resurrected Jesus ascending to heaven after staying in the world for forty days. The ascension of Jesus was theologically interpreted more from the perspective of faith than that of history.

A. Q

The ascension of Jesus is not clearly described in Q. It is only presumed through the coming of the Son of Man as an eschatological agent at the end of the world. The description of the ascension of Jesus is depicted in the background of the book of Daniel.

Q seems to presume the ascension of Jesus, hinting that if a person acknowledged or disowned the Son of Man, then he would likewise acknowledge or disown that person at the time of judgment (Q^3 12:8–9). In the context of the third redaction, the Son of Man refers to Jesus, while the choice between acknowledging or disowning means the judgment at the end of time. In this respect, the Son of Man is not merely a human being; rather, the eschatological role features the Son of Man as a transcendental being. Considering Q's claim that the Son of Man will come to this world in order to judge people (12:39–40; 17:23–24, 26–27, 30), it seems that he will stay somewhere until that time comes. Although the third redactor presumed the Son of Man would go to a transcendental place first, details of his trip were not provided. In this way, Q imposed a theological meaning to Jesus, the Son of Man, casting him as a transcendental figure.

For the presumption of the ascension of the Son of Man, it is necessary to see how the third redactor was able to describe it, considering the use of the title. The title "Son of Man" does not appear in the first redaction. On the other hand, the second redactor used it in substitution for the first person (Q^2 9:58; 11:30).[1] In this case, Jesus, the Son of Man, refers to an earthly figure. The third redactor used the title in three different ways. First, when the title "Son of Man" was interpolated into the main texts of the first redaction, it referred to the earthly figure (Q^3 6:22; 7:34). Second, when the title was added into the main texts of the second redaction, his features were ambivalent (12:8–9); in other words, his role is interpreted differently depending upon the identity of ἄγγελοι of God. If the term ἄγγελοι refers to "the angels," the Son of Man would also be a transcendental figure. On the other hand, if it refers to "the messengers," he would be an earthly figure. To my judgment, the third redactor used it for a transitory role in this context for the next step. Third, in the main texts of the third redaction, the Son of Man appears as a transcendental and eschatological figure in the apocalyptic context (12:39–40; 17:24, 26, 30).[2] Finally, in the fourth redaction, the Son of Man is defined as the one subordinate to the Spirit (Q^4 12:10).[3] This implies that the Son of Man was not yet a divine being in Q. The above observation informs us that the Son of Man was imbued with a transcendental quality at the stage of the third redaction, so that his ascension might be presumed and possible.

---

1. Vermes, *Dead Sea Scrolls*, 162–68. There is also an opinion that the title "Son of Man" did not refer to a person in general sense at the time of Jesus (Owen and Shepherd, "Speaking Up," 81–122).

2. "Building on Philipp Vielhauer's view that the apocalyptic Son of man sayings do not go back to Jesus himself," Helmut Koester argues for their late appearance in Q (Robinson et al., *Critical Edition*, lx). Cf. Koester and Robinson, *Entwicklungslinien*, 129, n. 66.

3. The relationship between the Spirit and the Son of Man is accordant with that between the Spirit and Jesus in the temptation story written ahead of this text in the fourth redaction of Q (Q^4 4:1–13; 12:10). In other words, Jesus, the Son of Man, is described as the one subordinate to the Spirit at the final stage of Q redaction.

The theological background for the transcendental features of the Son of Man comes from the Bible. Above all, the title "Son of Man" reminds readers of "one like a Son of Man" in Daniel. The "one like a Son of Man" came with the clouds of heaven, approached the Ancient of Days, and was given all authority (Dan 7:13–14). All these things happened to him in heaven. A similar text is found in the book of Parables, presumably written in the forties CE, a little later than Q. The Son of Man is depicted as a righteous agent who was chosen by the Spirit, reveals all the secrets, and will pass judgment on kings and earthly rulers (1 En 46:2–6). The Son of Man is a transcendental and preexistent figure who has existed before the creation of the world (48:3, 6; 62:7). In this case, however, his ascension is not necessary, because he stayed in heaven where he belonged.

In conclusion, it seems that the book of Parables ascribed more developed features to the Son of Man than Daniel did to the "one like a Son of Man." On the other hand, the third redactor of Q revealed less developed features of the Son of Man than the book of Parables. However, Q was unique in mentioning the coming of the Son of Man to the world in detail. In this respect, the Son of Man in Q is different from the "one like a Son of Man" in Daniel and the Son of Man in the book of Parables. Although the third redactor described the Son of Man in the context of the "one like a Son of Man" in Daniel, the redactor added his or her own theological interpretation about the Son of Man's coming to the world. In this respect, the redactor believed that Jesus, the Son of Man, had returned to the heavenly place before he would come again at the end. The third redactor thought of heaven as the place to which the Son of Man went and from which he would return at the end. Therefore, it can be concluded that the ascension of the Son of Man to heaven is presumed in the third redaction from a theological perspective, not a historical one.

B. The Pauline Epistles

Like Q, Paul did not mention the ascension of Jesus Christ. He only presumed it by mentioning that Jesus is at the right hand of God and will eventually come again. In this sense, Paul only references the exaltation of Christ, not the ascension of Jesus.

Paul did not mention the ascension of Jesus Christ. Rather, he only presumed it through the second coming. As described in 1Thess(2), when Christ comes from heaven, the dead in him will rise first, while those who are still alive will be caught up together with the resurrected people in the clouds to meet the Lord in the air, and they will be with the Lord forever (1 Thess

4:13–17). The promise that Christ will return from heaven suggests that Christ ascended to heaven after his first coming. Such a description reflects that Q influenced Paul. While the third redactor of Q presupposed the ascension of the Son of Man from the belief that he will come to the world, Paul also presupposed the ascension of Jesus by writing that the Lord will come down from heaven. It is, however, noteworthy that Paul never applied the title "Son of Man" to Jesus because the Gentile Christians could not understand the Jewish title. Paul could apply the tradition to Jesus because the Son of Man was described as the transcendental and eschatological figure in Q.

Paul wrote more about the exaltation of Jesus Christ than his ascension in the last part of his missionary journey. In Rom(1), Paul described Jesus Christ at the right hand of God, where he intercedes on behalf of his people (Rom 8:34). The Jews traditionally thought of the right hand of God as the position of power (Ps 110:1), and Paul proclaimed the authority of Christ based on this tradition. The words written in Psalms became part of the gospel for Paul in the sense that he thought of them as the prophecy and connected them to the exaltation of Christ. In this respect, the gospel related to the ascension of Jesus was replaced by his exaltation. Therefore, Paul should be credited with a significant achievement regarding the exaltation of Christ.

In conclusion, Paul seemed to share the concern about the ascension of Jesus Christ he inherited with the tradition from Q. However, as time passed, Paul preferred Jesus' exaltation to the ascension. This indicates that he did not know much historically about the ascension of Jesus Christ.

C. Mark and Matthew

Mark and Matthew did not mention the ascension of Jesus Christ. Mark especially could not have done so, since he did not clearly describe Jesus' resurrection and epiphany. However, like the others, Mark and Matthew presumed the ascension of Jesus by describing his exaltation. In this sense, while Mark applied the theology of Q and Paul, Matthew also used all the previous traditions.

Mark mentioned only the exaltation of Jesus Christ, describing it in the process of the interrogation by the chief priests in the yard of Caiaphas (Mark 14:60–65). When the high priest Caiaphas asked whether Jesus was the Christ, the Son of the Blessed One, he affirmed it by saying he would be sitting at the right hand of the Mighty One and would come on the clouds of heaven. This means that Jesus was higher than the high priest and that he himself would pass judgment upon the chief priests, who were sitting in the throne over him. Understandably then, the high priest Caiaphas became angry, tore his clothes, and condemned Jesus for blasphemy. The exaltation of Jesus is revealed in this dialogue.

However, Mark did not explain how Jesus would go up to the right hand of God, which is supposed to be in heaven, or the process of his ascension. In this way, Mark minimized the theme of ascension and succeeded Paul regarding the exaltation of Jesus. Mark was influenced by Q and applied the title "Son of Man" to Jesus, mentioning the judgment. However, he followed Paul in defining Jesus as Christ and describing Jesus' coming in connection with the clouds after staying at the right hand of God. Mark inherited the sources and theology of Q and Paul, then reinterpreted them in his own way. In this way, Mark considered the exaltation of Jesus as a theological event, presupposing his ascension, though he did not describe it clearly.

There was a reason Mark emphasized the exaltation of Jesus Christ instead of his ascension. Written around seventy CE, Mark reflected the destruction of the Jerusalem temple by the Roman troops. In this circumstance, Mark introduced Jesus as the new authority who would substitute for the high priest of the temple and the Jewish society. For this, using the tradition of Q and Paul, Mark described that Jesus had been at the right hand of God and would come as the Son of Man. In other words, Mark seems to have created the story of interrogation before the high priest Caiaphas. This then story became part of life of Jesus. In this way, the story about Jesus' exaltation became part of the gospel in Mark.

Matthew combined all the traditions he inherited relating to Jesus' exaltation. Like Mark, Matthew did not describe the ascension. First, he mentioned what Jesus would do in front of God in heaven (Matt 10:32–33). This was passed on to him from Q, which wrote that whoever acknowledged or disowned the Son of Man in front of people would be acknowledged or disowned before the messengers of God. However, Matthew referred to the heavenly role of Jesus, the Son of Man, after his departure from the world by adding the term "heaven." In this way, Matthew made the ascension of Jesus more possible than Mark had. Second, Matthew mentioned that the followers of Jesus would be taken as well (24:40–41). This was also taken from Q, which promised that the people of God would be taken in the end. Matthew does not talk about the place where Jesus will take the disciples at the end, but the contextual understanding that the Son of Man will come from heaven indicates that heaven is the destination (24:29–31). In this way, Matthew once again presumed the ascension ahead of the second coming of Jesus. Third, according to Matthew, Jesus proclaimed in front of many, including the high priest Caiaphas, that they would see the Son of Man sitting at the right hand of the Mighty One and coming on the clouds of heaven (26:64). This followed Mark and came indirectly from Paul (Mark 14:62; Rom 8:34; 1 Thess 4:16–17). In this, Matthew reflected the exaltation of Jesus in a way that implies the ascension ahead of his sitting at the right hand of God.

There was a reason that Matthew did not mention the ascension of Jesus at all. It was because of the theology of presence that the resurrected Jesus would be with his disciples to the very end of the age. In fact, Matthew emphasized immanence more than ascension, especially by using the word "Immanuel" to give meaning to his conception through the Holy Spirit (Matt 1:23). Matthew also emphasized immanence through the promise that wherever two or three believers gather in Jesus' name, he would be there with them (18:20). Finally, Jesus Christ promised to be with them until they finally fulfilled the commission to spread his teachings to all the nations of the world (28:20). Jesus' presence beside the disciples is a very important theme in Matthew. In this sense, Matthew did not describe the ascension of Jesus, which would mean his absence in the world. Thus, Matthew cannot but indirectly refer to the ascension of Jesus according to his theological purpose.

D. Other Documents

The ascension of Jesus Christ was mentioned in other documents as well and interpreted according to the author's theological intention. They passed on the tradition about Jesus' ascension and thus affirmed its place in the gospel. However, the theme of ascension culminated in the Lucan documents based on the prophetic tradition.

John presumed the ascension of Jesus Christ in different way from the Synoptic Gospels. The Gospel starts with the description that no one has ascended to heaven except the one who descended from heaven—that is, the Son of Man (John 3:13). This means that Jesus Christ will return to the place he originally belonged. John, for the first time, clarified the place from which Jesus, the Son of Man, came and to which he will go. In other places, John also wrote Jesus' question about the place where the Son of Man will ascend in connection with the place from which he came in the subjunctive form (6:62). Once again, this emphasizes the original place to which Jesus belonged. The fact that John used the title "Son of Man" for the ascension of Jesus makes it possible to conclude that the tradition begun in Daniel and used by Mark is reflected here. Then, according to John, Jesus definitely informed his followers that he would go to God the Father (16:7,

17, 28; 17:11). In this way, John presumed the ascension of Jesus rather than describing it concretely. Nevertheless, John developed the description of the ascension more clearly than Mark and Matthew had.

The Deuteropauline epistles also implied the ascension of Jesus Christ. Ephesians also states that God seated Christ at his right hand in heaven and gave him every kind of authority (Eph 1:20–21). This reminds readers of both traditions of Dan 7:13–14 and Ps 110:1. Above all, Ephesians reflects the Pauline theology of exaltation in Rom(1). In addition, Jesus Christ was proclaimed as the one who ascended to heaven (Eph 4:9–10). Ephesians emphasizes the term "heaven" for the description of the ascension of Christ. Thus, Ephesians seems to combine both themes of ascension and exaltation. In Colossians, it is written that Jesus Christ was seated at the right hand of God (Col 3:1). Colossians followed Paul's belief that Christ was exalted to be seated at the right hand of God. The tradition about the ascension and exaltation of Jesus was passed on until the very end of the first century CE. However, the Deuteropauline epistles did not contribute much to the description of the ascension of Jesus.

The ascension of Jesus Christ was mentioned in Hebrews. This is revealed in the proclamation that he is a great high priest, the Son of God, who ascended to heaven (Heb 4:14). Moreover, Jesus was the one who sat down at the right hand of the Majesty in heaven (1:3; 8:1; 10:12; 12:2). His sitting at the right hand of God was discussed in Hebrews more times than in any other document. In this way, the exaltation of Jesus was emphasized in Hebrews, as in Paul and Mark. The ascension of Jesus was described in Hebrews according to the principle that what is from heaven is the original form, and what is of this world is a mere shadow. The lesson here is that Christ's ascension to be a high priest in heaven is a return to the original, perfect form. Jesus is keeping his place as an eternal high priest, where he should be. This theology is unique to Hebrews, which is the result of influence by neoplatonism.[4] Unfortunately, the process of Christ's ascension is not mentioned at all in Hebrews, illustrating the view that the things of heaven are ideal and those of the world are negative. The ascension of Jesus was described in Hebrews, emphasizing his exaltation. This also causes the view of Christ's ascension to be taken from a theological perspective rather than a historical one, showing the further development of the gospel about the ascension of Jesus. Hebrews shows that the faith in the ascension of Jesus had spread throughout Christianity around the end of the first century CE.

---

4. Brown, *Introduction*, 691–92. Brown believes that Hebrews was not directly influenced from Philo, but was rather influenced by the contemporary tendency of the New Platonism.

The Lucan documents also dealt with the exaltation and ascension of Jesus Christ. They are the only documents in which Christ's ascension is described historically. Luke briefly described the ascension in saying that Jesus had blessed his disciples before leaving for heaven (Luke 24:50-51). Then Acts described the ascension of Jesus in exceptional detail. He gave the Great Commission and was taken up to heaven after promising his disciples the presence and power of the Holy Spirit (Acts 1:6-11). It seems that Luke took the same perspective as John, Hebrews, and Ephesians, which all favored heaven as the place of ascension. In addition, the absence of Jesus would be replaced by the presence of the Holy Spirit. When the ascension happened in Acts, two men dressed in white stood beside the disciples and prophesied that Jesus would come back from heaven in the same way he had left the earth.

Jesus' ascension was described as a historical event in Acts. The Bible's account of Elijah's ascension provided the theological background for the ascension of Jesus in Acts. First, the two men dressed in white who stood beside Jesus' disciples when he ascended are Moses and Elijah. They appeared at the Mount of Transfiguration and at the tomb of the resurrected Jesus (Luke 9:29-30; 24:4). The reason they were able to appear when Jesus Christ ascended to heaven was because they also had not experienced death. Moreover, the promise concerning the Spirit was based on what happened when Elijah ascended: Elisha asked for a double portion of Elijah's spirit. In this sense, the ascension of Elijah was used as a theological background for the description of Jesus' ascension in the Lucan documents. Luke should be credited with a unique achievement in his description of the ascension of Jesus Christ in the background of Elijah and Elisha.

E. Conclusion

The account of Jesus Christ's ascension is closely related to his exaltation, although the ascension for his exaltation was not mentioned from the beginning. Daniel 7:13-14 became a theological background, especially insofar as the description of the "one like a Son of Man" was changed into "the Son of Man" in Q, while Paul applied its concept to Jesus. Mark and Matthew inherited the theological interpretations of Q and Paul and applied them to Jesus. As the Jewish notion of the right hand of God as the position of dignity and exaltation was increasingly applied to Jesus, interest in his exaltation began to grow toward the end of Paul's missionary journey. However, heaven attracted more interest from a theological point of view as the place of Jesus' returning in John, Ephesians, and Hebrews at the end of the first century CE. On the other hand, Jesus' ascension to heaven was described historically for the first time in the Lucan documents, using the ascension of Elijah as a theological background. The Lucan tradition about the ascension of Jesus was formed at a very late time and was influenced by his exaltation. In this sense, it shows radical change. This is not a matter that can be proven or disproven historically. It is a theological event to which the ascension of Elijah and the vision of Daniel were applied. Therefore, Christians must accept the ascension of Jesus as a matter of faith. In conclusion, the ascension of Jesus Christ should be interpreted more from a theological perspective than from a historical one.

11

The Second Advent of Jesus

THE SECOND ADVENT OF Jesus Christ is an eschatological event that has yet to occur, and as such, it is the theological interpretation of a future occurrence. Q mentions that the Son of Man will come in the future, but the First Christians said nothing about the second coming of Christ. In spite of this, Paul inherited the tradition of Q and mentioned the return of the Lord Jesus many times. For this purpose, Paul incorporated the second advent of Jesus Christ into the gospel while utilizing the Bible as a background. Also, Mark adopted Paul's theology and added that Jesus had prophesied about his coming, though not clearly. Later, Matthew adopted this interpretation, but Luke weakened it considerably. Through this process, the gospel about the second coming of Jesus was formed and developed from a theological perspective, not a historical one.

A. Q

The second advent of Jesus is not directly mentioned in Q. Rather, it only wrote that the Son of Man would come in the future. Considering the context, the Son of Man stands for Jesus. It can be confirmed by looking at the Bible.

The phenomena that will occur in the future were described in the third redaction of Q. First, the third redactor taught that believers must be alert, since the time of the Son of Man's coming is unknown (Q^3 12:39–40). Traditionally, the coming of the Son of Man referred to the end of the world. The eschatological events that will happen at his coming were described as well (17:23–24). It is written that the Son of Man will come as if lightning struck in a split second from one side of the sky to the other. Judging from the Jewish tradition, this is what will happen when the divine being comes to the world. However, the people will not be prepared when the Son of Man comes and will enjoy pleasure like the time before the flood (17:26–27, 30). Ultimately, many people will be destroyed on that day—that is, the end of the world. In this way, the third redactor implicitly identified the Son of Man with Jesus and applied transcendental qualities to him from an apocalyptic perspective. The third redactor introduced another event that will happen at the time of the Son of Man's coming. For instance, there will be a distinction between the people being taken and those being abandoned (Q^3 17:34–35). It is noteworthy that the third redactor used a man and a woman for the description of rapture, as it was already used for the description of the kingdom of God through parables (Q^3 13:18–20). The Son of Man will take the chosen people to the place he comes from—probably a heavenly place. The division of people is an aspect of the eschatological judgment. In this respect, the coming of the Son of Man is described from the eschatological perspective in the third redaction of Q. This was possible because the third redactor imposed a transcendental quality to the Son of Man from a theological perspective, not from a historical one.

The third redactor took the Bible as the background for the description of the Son of Man. As discussed above, the title "Son of Man" reminds readers of the "one like a Son of Man" in Dan 7:13–14. Daniel saw in a vision this "one like a Son of Man" led into the presence of God on clouds. God gave authority, glory, and sovereign power to him and made every person worship him. This was to demonstrate that he would be given authority in heaven and would enjoy it in this world. In Q, however, the title "one like a Son of Man" was modified to "the Son of Man," and the events that would come to pass when he comes were described in different ways. His coming was described in the apocalyptic perspective, and he was given authority to take the chosen people and to abandon the rest. The third redactor seemed to think back to the account of Enoch when describing the people chosen by the Son of Man (Gen 5:24). Enoch walked faithfully with God and was taken by him, though how and where God took him was not mentioned. If this event was used as a theological background, the people who will be chosen by Son of Man are in parallel with Enoch, who was taken by God. In this respect, combining the traditions from Genesis and Daniel, the third redactor thought of heaven as the transcendental place from which the Son of Man would come and to which he would take the chosen people. Through the implication that the Son of Man alludes to Jesus, the coming of the Son of Man was developed into the lesson that Jesus will return in the future. However, this was not described directly but rather through the theological interpretation of the second advent of Jesus as the Son of Man. This shows how the third redactor in Q formed the gospel about the second advent of Jesus.

B. The Pauline Epistles

Paul was the first to proclaim the second advent of Jesus Christ. He followed the tradition about the coming of the Son of Man from Q and developed it into the second coming of Jesus. However, Paul did not develop it much after the Gentile Christians challenged his authority and his gospel.

Paul described the second advent of Jesus Christ at the beginning of his missionary life in 1Thess(1). It is said that Paul was waiting for the Son of God from the heaven (ἀναμένειν τὸν υἱὸν αὐτοῦ ἐκ τῶν οὐρανῶν) (1Thess 1:10). His coming can be identified as the second one because the Son of God was Jesus Christ, who lived and died on earth but was resurrected and was believed to have ascended to heaven. The coming of the Son of God is related to rescue from the coming wrath. What is important is the fact that his coming is accompanied by the eschatological judgment. It seems that Paul received the tradition about the second advent of Jesus from Q based on the fact that the coming of the Son of Man seemed to be applied to the second coming of Jesus. However, Paul did not use the title "Son of Man" because the Gentile Christians were unable to understand the Jewish title. It was replaced by the Son of God, which was also known to the Gentiles. Of course, Paul thought of the Son of God as the one he received revelation about from God on his way to Damascus.

Paul expressed his strong hope for blamelessness at the coming of the Lord Jesus Christ in 1Cor(1). For this, Paul uses the term "appearance [ἀποκάλυψις]" (1 Cor 1:7). The Corinthians should be blameless in the eschatological judgment that will take place on the day of his coming (1:8). Paul taught the Corinthians to live blamelessly in order to prepare for the eschatological judgment that will be held at the coming of the Lord Jesus Christ. Such blamelessness is in accord with the instruction that the Corinthians must keep their bodies holy because they are the temple of the Spirit (3:16). Paul did not specify how to be blameless; however, he seems to assert that the Corinthians could be blameless by observing the Law (11:2; 14:21, 34). Of course, this blamelessness is contrasted with the pleasure of the world enjoyed at the time of coming of the Son of Man as described in the third redaction of Q. Yet it is noteworthy that Paul did not describe the phenomena that will occur at the time of the second coming at all in 1Cor(1).

Later, Paul mentioned the second advent of the Lord theologically in 1Cor(2). Paul taught that those who eat the bread and drink the cup at the Lord's Supper should proclaim the Lord's death until he comes (ἄχρι οὗ ἔλθῃ) (1 Cor 11:26). The coming of the Lord was connected with the proclamation of the death of Christ, and Paul described the eschatological phenomena that will mark the time of coming of Christ (15:23–24). At that time, he will deliver his kingdom to God the Father. However, Paul did not mention when, where, or what would happen during the coming of Jesus except a short assertion that Christ and his followers would be raised. It could be said that Paul was able to deal with the general resurrection using influence from Q (Q^3 11:31–32). At any rate, this is Paul's first description of eschatological phenomena. In this respect, Paul consistently believed in the second advent of Jesus and waited for the end of the world in 1Cor(2).

Paul extensively developed this view on the second advent of Jesus Christ in 1Thess(2). He asked the Gentile Christians to prepare for the second advent in terms of their ethical and religious status. According to Paul, they must be holy and blameless before God at the coming of the Lord Jesus (τῃ παρουσίᾳ τοῦ κυρίου ἡμῶν Ἰησοῦ) (1Thess 3:13; 5:23). The word παρουσία appears as a technical term for the first time in the Pauline epistles. Paul strengthened their prescribed status further by adding "being holy" to "being blameless" mentioned in 1Cor(1). Moreover, Paul described the phenomena that will accompany the second coming of the Lord (1 Thess 4:13–17). At his coming, a loud command will be accompanied by the voice of the archangel and the trumpet call of God. According to tradition, his coming is depicted as that of a divine being (Exod 20:18; Ezek 1:24, etc.). At any rate, in this part, the coming Lord stood for Jesus, and then Paul equated Jesus with Christ by using parallelism in the phrases "those who have fallen asleep in Jesus" and "the dead in Christ." Of course, Paul understood the return of Jesus to be an event caused by God. He revealed this through the teaching that God will bring with Jesus those who have fallen asleep in him. In other words, God will bring Jesus and those who are resurrected together. This means that Jesus' second coming will happen in the air. The eschatological phenomena described here show a more advanced understanding than that in 1Cor(2).

Paul's description of eschatological phenomena reveals Q's influence. This is somewhat different from the description found in Q that the Son of Man will come to the world. While Q taught that the people of God will be taken from the earth by the Son of Man (Q 17:34–35), Paul taught that the followers of Jesus will go up to heaven and meet him there at the end (1 Thess 4:17). Paul seemed to apply the sources and theology of Q surrounding the

Son of Man to Jesus and his followers from an apocalyptic perspective. In particular, the description that "the Lord will come like a thief in the night" reminds readers of that found in Q (1 Thess 5:4; Q³ 12:39). Another element to be examined is the phrase "word from the Lord." Paul proclaimed that he spoke according to the word of the Lord while teaching about the Lord's second coming (1 Thess 4:15). This seems to refer to the teachings of the Lord Jesus, which Paul had learned from Q through Cephas when he visited Jerusalem around 38 CE. As demonstrated, the third redactor of Q implicitly identified Jesus with the Lord (Q³ 6:46; 7:6–7; 10:2; 12:42–46; 13:25) and taught about the future coming of the Son of Man (12:39–40, 42–46; 17:23–24, 26–27, 30, 34–35). Paul saw such teaching as the word of the Lord, and based on this view, he taught about the second coming of the Lord Jesus. The above discussion verifies Q's influence on Paul regarding the second advent of Jesus Christ.

Paul briefly implied the second advent of Jesus Christ in Phil(1), where it is said that the Philippians should wait for (ἀπεκδεχόμεθα) the Savior from heaven (Phil 3:20). The Savior from heaven refers to the Lord Jesus Christ coming from heaven described in 1Thess(2). It is noteworthy that his coming is related to salvation in that the Lord Jesus Christ is identified as the Savior from heaven. Although Paul did not describe Christ's second coming in detail, he definitely had his belief in it in his mind. However, it is noteworthy that Paul's description of the second coming of the Lord Jesus Christ was critically diminished in Phil(1).

At last, Paul maintained the instruction about the coming of the Lord through 1Cor(3). He believed that the Lord would eventually come again (ἕως ἂν ἔλθῃ) to this world (1 Cor 4:5). According to Paul, Jesus Christ will come and "bring to light what is hidden in darkness and will expose the motives of men's hearts." This reveals a crucial aspect of the eschatological judgment. Interestingly, this saying is reminiscent of Q³ 12:2–3 regarding the disclosure of hidden things. Moreover, it is noteworthy that this saying is followed by the instruction about the juridical and eschatological role of the Son of Man before the messengers of God in the third redaction (Q³ 12:8–9). Once again, this strengthens the possibility that Paul learned about the coming of the Son of Man and his juridical role from Q and that he applied them to Jesus and his eschatological judgment. Paul once again mentioned the coming of the Lord in the form of prayer when he said, "Come, Lord! [μαράνα θά]" with an emphatic tone (1 Cor 16:22). Paul seemed to wait desperately for the coming of the Lord so that he could pass the judgment upon the Corinthians who had challenged him and ultimately God. The fact that Paul waited for the coming of the Lord is strengthened by the fact that this prayer appears at the end of the letter. In this way, Paul developed the instruction about Jesus' second advent, reflecting the influence from Q in 1Cor(3).

Paul refrained from mentioning the second advent further in the rest of his epistles. After he faced serious challenges from the Corinthians, he began to avoid mentioning the second advent of Jesus. No text about it has been found in the letters written later than 1Cor(3). It was probably because Paul would not have liked to use the instruction of Q as much as possible and wanted to be independent from the instruction of the Jerusalem apostles. This shows how the instruction about the second coming of Jesus disappeared in the latter part of his missionary journey.

The description of the second advent of Jesus Christ was based on the biblical event. Paul received the tradition about the coming of the Son of Man from Q and ultimately Dan 7:13-14. The coming of the "one like a Son of Man" was applied to the Son of Man in Q, and Paul applied the Son of Man to Jesus Christ. Paul changed the apocalyptic coming of the Son of Man as if lightning struck in a split second from one side of sky to the other in Q into the coming of the Lord Jesus Christ from heaven with a loud command, the voice of the archangel, and the trumpet call of God. In addition, the promise in Q that the Son of Man will take the chosen people was replaced by predictions of the rapture of people in the clouds to meet the Lord in the air in the Pauline epistle. This shows Paul interpreting the second coming of Jesus as the fulfillment of Dan 7:13-14, in which Jesus played the role of the "one like a Son of Man." Paul took a further step than Q by implying that Jesus is the Son of Man based on these verses. In this respect, Dan 7:13-14 became part of the gospel to Paul.

C. Mark and Matthew

Mark and Matthew taught that Jesus Christ himself proclaimed his second advent. This is revealed during his interrogation by the high priest Caiaphas. However, the theme of the second coming lost its influence in Mark and Matthew's description of the life of Jesus. At any rate, both were dependent upon the traditions from Q and Paul.

Mark taught that Jesus Christ would come back to this world as the Son of Man. First, while he was preaching about the end of the world, Jesus declared that the Son of Man will come in clouds with great power and glory (Mark 13:26). This seems to be the modified form of Paul's description that Jesus will come from heaven in 1Thess(2). It is noteworthy, however, that the theme of Jesus' coming ultimately originated in Q and was then used by Paul, even though Mark avoided Q's apocalyptic description that the Son of

Man would come as if lightning struck in a split second from one side of sky to the other. Second, Mark mentioned the coming of the Son of Man in the midst of the interrogation by the high priest Caiaphas (14:62). Mark taught that people will see the Son of Man sitting at the right hand of the Mighty One and coming on the clouds of heaven. In this context, the Mighty One refers to God, the "Ancient of Days" written about in Dan 7:13–14. Their connection is strengthened by the mention of clouds and the title "Son of Man." As a result, Mark proclaimed that Jesus himself is the one who will come and judge the chief priests and the high priest Caiaphas. Mark added this to all that Paul wrote about what would happen when the Lord Jesus comes again in 1Thess(2). They both wrote that these events would take place at the end of time; however, while Paul wrote that the Lord Jesus would come in the air, Mark followed Q by teaching that the Son of Man would come to the world. In this sense, Mark strengthened the connection with Dan 7:13–14 more than Q did. This is how Mark developed the gospel in connection with the second advent of Jesus as part of Jesus' future life.

Matthew also mentioned the second advent of Jesus Christ on the basis of Q, Paul, and Mark. First, it began with the description about the coming of the Son of Man. In general, Matthew followed Mark's description of the coming of Jesus. However, there are also differences between them because Matthew used more sources from Q and Paul than Mark. Jesus will come such that, as with a flash of lightning, all the people in this world will be able to see him (Matt 24:27; Q^3 17:24). Moreover, a sign will appear at his coming on the clouds accompanied by a loud trumpet call (Matt 24:31; 1 Thess 4:16). However, people will ignore this sign and seek pleasure (Matt 24:37–39; Q^3 17:26–27, 30). Nevertheless, people must be ready for his coming like a thief in the night (Matt 24:44; Q^3 12:40; 1Thess 5:4). Matthew used sources from Q, Paul, and Mark. Second, Matthew described the coming of the Son of Man in the middle of the eschatological parables (Matt 25:31), saying the Son of Man would come with all the angels and sit on his glorious throne. Matthew inherited such sources from Q and Paul (Q^4 22:30; 1 Thess 4:16). Third, Matthew also mentioned that the Son of Man would be seated at the right hand of the Mighty One and come on the clouds of heaven in the end, as Mark did (Matt 26:64; Mark 14:62). Matthew reinforced the description about the second coming of Jesus, inheriting the theology of Q, Paul, and Mark.

In conclusion, Mark and Matthew explain that Jesus Christ, coming as the Son of Man, will be an arbitrator. However, they show differences in the intensity of their descriptions because of their own theological interpretations. In this way, the teachings about the second coming went through many changes and developments, though the second advent of Jesus will only be completely understood when he actually comes. In this respect, the second advent of Jesus should be understood from a theological perspective, not from a historical one.

D. The Johannine Documents

The second advent of Jesus Christ was described from a different perspective in the Johannine documents than the Synoptic Gospels. This is revealed through the teaching that Christ will prepare a place, then come back to take his disciples. The Johannine documents show various perspectives about the second coming.

John clearly stated that Jesus would come again, explaining that Jesus went to his Father's house to prepare a place for his disciples so as to come back and take them with him (John 14:2-3, 28). In this context, the place stands for somewhere in heaven (3:13; 6:62). Going to that place is relevant to his ascension, but coming back to take his disciples is relevant to his second coming. How and when he will go and come, however, is not mentioned. Moreover, John did not connect his coming with the title "Son of Man," which was used for the ascension of Jesus. In this sense, John shows a different tradition from the Synoptic Gospels.

The second advent of Jesus Christ is prominently mentioned in Revelation, which proclaimed that the second coming will happen in the end and that Jesus will come back to this world as an arbitrator. He will come with the clouds, and every eye will see his coming, even those who pierced him (Rev 1:7; John 19:34). Thus, Jesus' second coming includes judgment for those who harmed him. However, he was not yet described as the Son of Man, though the understanding that he will come back to this world for judgment at the end was inherited from Q and passed on through Mark. Mark's proclamation that Jesus will come on the clouds of heaven was accepted by Matthew, rejected by John, but recorded in Revelation. This reference also used Dan 7:13-14 as a theological background. In addition, Revelation deals with the coming of the Lord in the future. This is shown in the context that Jesus promised his coming, and the disciples responded by confessing their willingness to wait (Rev 22:20). This reminds readers of Paul's declaration that the Lord will come soon in 1Cor(3). In this respect, the tradition about the coming of the Lord in the future was strengthened in early Christianity, while his second coming was expanded as a worldwide event. Revelation made its own theological interpretation as well.

The second advent was described in 1 John, which was written in the beginning of the second century CE. It is revealed that when the Lord appears, members of the Johannine community will be confident and unashamed before him at his coming (1 John 2:28). This is similar to Paul's description, which states his wish that the Christians would be blameless and holy in the presence of God when the Lord Jesus comes in 1Cor(1) and 1Thess(2). Of course, 1 John did not mention its relationship to Paul in detail, but it was clearly revealed that John succeeded Paul's theological interpretation about the second coming of Jesus. In this way, the gospel about the second advent of Jesus developed gradually.

In conclusion, the Johannine documents succeeded previous instruction about the second advent of Jesus. Paul had abandoned it after being challenged by the Corinthians, but the authors of the Johannine documents picked it up and used it. The reason that the authors of the Johannine documents described it was probably due to persecution under the Roman Empire.

E. Other Documents

The second advent of Jesus Christ was not mentioned much in other documents. Although it was described in Hebrews and 1 Peter, the accounts are relatively weak. The Lucan documents in particular reduced the number of descriptions regarding the second coming. It is another theological topic that has been interpreted according to the author's intention.

The Deuteropauline epistles mentioned the second advent of Jesus Christ in the form of fragmentary descriptions. In Colossians it is written that Christ, who is life, will appear (Col 3:4). This refers to Christ's second coming in that this mention comes after his death, resurrection, and exaltation. In addition, it was described in 2 Thessalonians that the Lord Jesus would be revealed from heaven in blazing fire with his powerful angels (2 Thess 1:7; cf. 1:10; 2:1, 8). The blazing fire seems to describe the divine aspect of the Lord Jesus. Moreover, it was also written in 1 Timothy as well that the Lord Jesus Christ would appear again (1 Tim 6:14). However, no description has been found regarding his role at the time of his coming. Finally, the expectation of his appearance is affirmed in 2 Timothy (2 Tim 4:1, 8). The author was certain of the eschatological judgment at the time of the second coming of Christ Jesus. The Deuteropauline epistles often dealt with the second advent of Jesus, but did not show well-organized instruction about it.

Hebrews is also interested in the second advent of Jesus Christ. First, it explained that God would bring his firstborn into the world again (Heb 1:6). It was written that Christ would appear a second time, not to bear sin, but to bring salvation to those who are waiting for him (9:28). How he will appear is not explained. However, the description surrounding his second coming had to be weakened in Hebrews, since he ascended to heaven where he belonged as the perfect high priest. In this respect, Hebrews minimized the instruction about the second coming of Jesus Christ according to the writer's theological interpretation.

The second advent of Jesus Christ was also treated with great interest in 1 Peter. This is revealed in the encouragement given to Christians to maintain their faith (1 Pet 1:7, 13). The second coming was mentioned along with the teaching that the proven sincerity of their faith, which is said to be of greater worth than gold and endures even though refined by fire, may result in praise, glory, and honor. It was taught that judgment and reward would be given when he comes again. Christians were encouraged to maintain their faith until the end with the teaching that the grace of God is like a precious jewel and that God's grace would be given in reward to the recipients of 1 Peter, who were supposed to be under the persecution by the Roman Empire. This shows that the gospel about the second advent of Jesus Christ was maintained continuously, but not uniformly.

Luke described the second advent of Jesus Christ based on the tradition of Q and Mark. First of all, the author inherited the sources from Q teaching that the Son of Man will come like a thief at an unexpected time (Luke 12:39–40; Q^3 12:39–40), and second, that he will come like a flash of lightning so that all the people in this world will be able to see him (Luke 17:24; Q^3 17:24). Luke preserved the apocalyptic description about the coming of the Son of Man. Third, Luke taught that the Son of Man would come in a cloud with power and great glory (Luke 21:27; Mark 13:26-27). However, Luke only vaguely described where the Son of Man would come from and omitted the apocalyptic description that angels would accompany him. Fourth, Luke omitted any reference to the coming of the Son of Man during Jesus' interrogation by the chief priests (Luke 22:69; Mark 14:62). Compared with Mark and Matthew, Luke considerably weakened the apocalyptic descriptions of the end.

The second coming of Jesus also appears in Acts. The second coming is revealed in that the two men who were with the disciples when Jesus ascended to heaven said he would come back in the same way they saw him go into heaven (Acts 1:11). This implies that Jesus will come down on clouds, making up for the omission of this account in Luke. In addition, it was written that God will send the predestined Jesus from heaven when he restores everything (3:20–21). These few references show that the least interest was paid to the second coming in the Lucan documents. In this way, faith in the second coming of Jesus endured through the end of the first century and the beginning of the second CE.

F. Conclusion

The understanding of the second advent of Jesus Christ began to blossom through the story of the fulfillment of Dan 7:13–14. The tradition about the "one like a Son of Man" was changed into the "Son of Man" in Q, which implied he was Jesus. Then, Paul substituted the Son of Man with the Son of God, the Lord, or Jesus Christ, and explained this identification in detail. His coming is described in detail, along with various phenomena that will occur at that time. However, Paul's concern about the second advent of Jesus rapidly diminished and disappeared after the Gentile Christians challenged his authority and gospel. Moreover, Mark noted that Jesus Christ called himself the Son of Man and wrote that he was the godlike figure prophesied about in Daniel who will descend on clouds. The second advent of Jesus was proclaimed as a worldwide phenomenon that would be seen by everyone, as the confession about his coming was accepted in Matthew and the Johannine documents as well as in the Lucan documents. The writers of Hebrews, 1 Peter, and some of the Deuteropauline epistles also accepted the advent of Jesus Christ. In this sense, the gospel about the second coming of Jesus gradually developed as a theological event, but not so strongly as other elements of the gospel.

PART IV

The Pauline Gospel and Its Development

PAUL DEVELOPED OTHER THEMES based on traditions beyond what he had inherited from Q and the First Christians. This was made possible through the principles of biblical interpretation he had learned as a Pharisee from the Jewish tradition. Paul created and developed themes in the gospel such as the Adam Christology, the birth of Jesus Christ, the theology of redemption, and the Lord's Supper. The authors of the Gospels followed Paul and developed the accounts in their own style. The content of the gospel expanded further based on this creative application. In this part, the themes created by Paul will be studied on the basis of the discussion in the prologue regarding the nature of faith, the chronological order of writings, and the concept of the gospel.

12

The Adam Christology

LIKE OTHER PARTS OF the gospel, the comparison of Jesus Christ with Adam has gone through a process of formation and development in Christian tradition. For the first time, Paul used the Adam typology to explain the status and role of Christ. In this he was the first to use the hermeneutic principle of "according to the Scriptures" for the Adam Christology. In this way, Paul introduced Christ as the savior of humanity. Later, the theological work connecting Jesus to Adam was developed more substantially in the Gospels. Mark used the Adam Christology inherited from Paul minimally, while Matthew made further developments and, in this way, communicated that Jesus is the savior for all people. While John applied the Adam typology to the resurrected Jesus, Luke weakened it. So it was that the portion of the gospel that interprets Jesus Christ in the light of Adam was formed and developed.

A. The Pauline Epistles

Paul used the Adam typology in order to explain the status and role of Jesus Christ. He introduced Christ in contrast with Adam, who is able to save people. Paul was the first to develop the Adam Christology based on the Jewish tradition.

Paul compared Jesus Christ to Adam in order to describe his life-giving role for the first time in 1Cor(2). The life is inevitably related to the resurrection of Christ (1 Cor 15:12–28, 35–49). First of all, Paul was able to use the Adam typology because Adam and Christ were "human being [ἄνθρωπος]," literally "*adam* [אדם]" (15:21). Adam and Christ appear to contrast death and life, for they were the sources of both in their own way (15:22).¹ In this context, the title Christ is used instead of Jesus, showing that Christ acted out the theological role of giving life to people rather than that Jesus did the same work historically. The comparison between the death of Adam and the life of Christ seems to be based on Gen 3:19, since God had proclaimed death to Adam and Eve in the garden of Eden, and as such, this verse became for Paul the gospel related to the Adam Christology. Later, Adam and Christ are once again compared in the role of giving life and death. For this, Paul distinguished the spiritual body (σῶμα πνευματικόν) from the natural body (σῶμα ψυχικόν) (15:44); then, he wrote that Christ, the last Adam, became a life-giving spirit (πνεῦμα ζωοποιοῦν) while the first Adam became a living being (ψυχὴ ζῶσα) (15:45). Finally, Paul stated that the natural body (τὸ ψυχικόν) had come first, then the spiritual body (τὸ πνευματικόν) came (15:46). With this contrast, Paul showed that Adam was a man of the natural from whom death stemmed and that Christ was a man of the spiritual from whom life stemmed. In this way, Adam and Christ are contrasted in the role of giving life or death. This description was based on the event by which God formed a man from the dust of the ground, breathed into his nostrils the breath of life, and made him a living being (Gen 2:7). Then Gen 2:7 became part of the gospel for Paul, as it was a prophecy about Christ's role in becoming the life-giving spirit. The reason that Paul adopted the Adam typology for the description of the general resurrection was probably that the Corinthian Church was generally composed of Gentiles. He taught that just as Adam was the ancestor of all humankind, so Christ is the new ancestor of all the people of the world from a spiritual perspective. In this way, Paul wanted the Corinthian Christians to continue in faith in Christ so they could receive life. The resurrection signifies the eternal life given by Christ in contrast with the death given by Adam. Paul should be credited with a significant achievement in applying the Adam typology to Christ.

Second, Paul drew another contrast between the sin of Adam and the grace of Christ in Rom(3). Though the sin of Adam brought death, the gift of grace given by Jesus Christ flows abundantly (Rom 5:14–15). In this, the sin of Adam is starkly contrasted with the grace of Christ. In this context, Paul used the name and title "Jesus Christ," comparing him to Adam while defining him as a man—that is, Adam.² While being compared to Adam, Jesus Christ was introduced as the man who gives life to death (5:17–18). The gift of grace is identified with life. As a result, Paul made Adam the type

---

1. Cf. Beker, *Paul*, 100.
2. Scroggs, *Last Adam*, 92; and Wright, "Adam in Pauline Christology," 371.

and Jesus Christ the antitype. Compared to the Adam-typological explanation in 1Cor(2), Paul extended its scope from the matter of the natural and spiritual bodies to that of sin and grace in Rom(3). As the Roman Christians got to know the essence of faith through their dialogue with Paul, they came to consider sin and death in comparison with life as the gift of Christ. Written in the late days of Paul's missionary life, Rom(3) is the epistle in which the Adam Christology was more developed.

Third, Paul made an allusion to Adam in Phil(2). It is found in the christological hymn (Phil 2:5–11).[3] Paul said that Christ Jesus "made himself nothing" by humbling himself. Thus, God exalted Jesus Christ by giving him the name above every name. No one is exempt from comparison with Jesus. This indicates that Jesus Christ received the authority to reign through the humility and service that Adam should have shown before God but failed to in the garden of Eden. Even if this christological hymn carries allusions to the various objects in the Bible,[4] it cannot be denied that Adam is one of them, considering the theme of making oneself nothing and the radical contrast between humbleness and exaltation.[5] Jesus Christ, who was humble but exalted, is radically contrasted with Adam, who attempted to become like God by taking the forbidden fruit in the garden of Eden. Paul implicitly adopted the typological approach to depict Jesus Christ in contrast with Adam. Because the christological hymn was adopted at the very end of Paul's life, it can be understood as his conclusion regarding the Adam Christology.

Paul applied the typological interpretation of the Jews to Jesus Christ. The Jews often described their leaders using the Adam typology. For instance, this is reflected in the *Hymns of Thanksgiving* left by the Qumran community (1QH 8:4, 6, 16, 21–23). The community is compared to a garden, which alludes to the garden of Eden, while their leader, the Righteous Teacher, is likened to the gardener who waters the garden.[6] In addition, the members of Qumran community were compared to the trees in the garden.

3. Cf. Martin, *Carmen Christ*, xx–xxi, 116–19, 128–33, 142–43, 152–53, 161–64.

4. Some scholars criticize the Adam typology in this case. Cf. Hurst, "Re-enter," 449–57. Seeley argues that the hymn is composed of various allusions to Isa 45, the stories of the Suffering Righteousness, and Greco-Roman ruler worship (Seeley, "Background," 49–72). Critical scholars, of course, raise the possibility that Phil 2:5–11 was added at the beginning of the second century CE. Even if such points are correct, this demonstrates that Christ was continuously confessed in connection with Adam in the Christianity of Paul.

5. Seo, "Der historische Jesus," 479–84. Cf. Brown, *Introduction*, 492. Although Brown does not support the Adam typological interpretation of Phil 2:5–11, he lists it among the various interpretations available.

6. Charlesworth, *Jesus*, 148.

In this respect, the author of the hymn, the Righteous Teacher, used the Adam typology in order to deliver the instruction about the ideal feature of community. On the basis of Jewish tradition he probably learned as a Pharisee, Paul was able to apply the Adam typology to Jesus Christ, the leader of Christianity, for the first time.

In conclusion, Paul was the first to apply the Adam typology to Jesus Christ on the basis of the Jewish tradition he likely learned as a Pharisee. The more time passed, the more advanced Adam Christology Paul suggested. The contrast between life and death was enhanced to be equal to that between Adam's sin and Christ's grace, then that between the very nature of God and the appearance of the servant. The Adam Christology was adopted to show that Jesus Christ is the Savior for all humanity. This is how the gospel regarding the Adam-like Jesus Christ was formed.

B. Mark

Mark neither mentioned Adam nor directly compared him to Jesus Christ. Mark does, however, remind readers of Adam in describing several events. Mark received the Adam Christology from Paul and applied it figuratively while describing the life of Jesus. Mark seemed to create certain stories to describe Jesus Christ from a typological perspective.

The story about the baptism of Jesus is the first text to which the Adam Christology was applied in Mark (Mark 1:9–11). It derived from Q (Q^3 3:21–22) and was based on the Israelites crossing the Red Sea. Yet Mark slightly edited this story to compare Jesus to Adam. For this, Mark changed the opening (ἀνοίγω) of heaven (Q 3:22) into its tearing (σχίζω) in order to make a connection with the curtain of the temple, which had been torn during Jesus' death on the cross (Mark 1:10; 15:38). As shown in the description of the kingdom of God (see chapter 9 [x-ref]), the intertestamental writings often described the temple in connection with the garden of Eden. This indicates that the tearing of heaven at the time of baptism and the rending of the curtain of the temple is to be understood in the context of the garden of Eden, where Adam and Eve had lived but from which they were finally expelled. In this way, Mark provided a stepping-stone for the connection between Jesus and Adam.

In addition, the Spirit of God can be understood as a basis for their connection. The description that the Spirit descended on Jesus at his baptism is contrasted with the breath of life given to Adam by God (Mark 1:11; Gen 2:7). Mark used it to remind believers of Paul's description that the last Adam became a life-giving spirit, while the first Adam became a living being in 1Cor(2). As a result, having taken the story about the baptism of Jesus from Q, Mark changed it into a theological basis to draw the contrast with Adam. Moreover, Jesus Christ heard a voice from heaven saying that he was the Son who was loved, as Adam often heard the voice of God in the garden of Eden and was also considered to be the son of God as the first created man. Just as Paul reminded readers of Adam when he introduced Jesus Christ as the Son of God in light of Gen 3:15 (Gal 4:4–6), Mark also alludes to Adam by introducing Jesus as the Son of God. These two texts of Paul and Mark share the term "spirit" in common. Under the influence of Paul, Mark left references to Adam in the story about the baptism of Jesus.

Second, Mark compared Jesus and Adam using the story about temptation (Mark 1:12–13). The temptation story derived from Q (Q^4 4:1–13) and was based on the Israelites testing God as they roamed the wilderness for forty years. Mark, however, extensively edited these verses and adapted them so as to compare Jesus with Adam. The wilderness where the temptation occurred was undoubtedly contrasted with the garden of Eden.[7] Adam had to work hard in a land covered with thorns and thistles after he was driven from the garden of Eden (Gen 3:17–18). Furthermore, the forty days of the temptation also suggest a comparison between the two. For this purpose, although the tradition about forty days originated in Q, readers would be familiar with Jubilees' account that Adam was led into the garden of Eden forty days after he was created (Jub 3:9, 15). Mark probably inherited this Jewish tradition and applied it to the description that Jesus had spent forty days in the wilderness before he proclaimed the coming of the kingdom of God (Mark 1:12–15). As discussed, Mark placed Jesus' proclamation of the kingdom just after the temptation so the kingdom of God might be interpreted as the garden of Eden. Moreover, the danger of his temptation in the midst of wild animals contrasts with Adam's experience of peacefully naming the animals (Gen 2:19). The appearance of the angel is another element that invites comparison between Jesus and Adam. When Adam sinned after being tempted, Cherubim drove Adam and Eve out of the garden to the place of death (3:24). In the case of Jesus, an angel helped him to overcome temptation and to sustain his life. Finally, the word ἐκβάλλω was commonly used in order to explain that Adam was expelled from the garden in Genesis (*LXX*) and Jesus was driven to the wilderness in Mark. This made the comparison between Jesus and Adam even more possible. Ultimately, Adam was tempted, sinned, and was exiled from the garden of Eden, a peaceful and blessed place, and so brought death to the people. In contrast, Jesus Christ

---

7. Jeremias, *New Testament*, 1:61. There are some scholars who criticize the Adam typology in this case. Cf. Best, *Temptation and the Passion*, 8.

overcame temptation in a dangerous wilderness, leading the people back to life. In this respect, Mark seems to have inherited the Adam Christology from Paul and applied it to the story of the temptation of Jesus. Just as Paul used the Adam typology based on the comparison between death and life in 1Cor(2), so too did Mark in drawing the comparison between Jesus and Adam through temptation.

Third, Mark compared Jesus and Adam in terms of obedience during temptation. This is revealed in the account of Jesus praying at Gethsemane (Mark 14:32–42). Above all, the location on the Mount of Olives invites comparisons with the garden of Eden, which is believed to have been located on a mountain according to Jewish tradition (Ezek 40:2; 47:6–12; 1 En 24:4—25:6; Jub 4:25–26; 8:19). Particularly, the Mount of Olives is believed to be located opposite Mount Zion, on which the Jerusalem temple stood. In Mark, the Mount of Olives was introduced as the place that replaces the temple on Mount Zion. Thus, the Mount of Olives provides a stepping-stone for a comparison between Jesus and Adam in that the mountains were related to the garden of Eden. In addition, it is noteworthy that Jesus called God "*abba*, Father [αββα ὁ πατήρ]" while praying at Gethsemane. Ahead of Mark, Paul had already applied this vocative form to the Galatians, emphasizing their filial relationship with God in that the Son of God is indirectly related to Adam as a descendent of a woman (Gal 4:4–6; Gen 3:15). Paul once again applied the vocative form "*abba*, Father" to the Roman Christians in Rom(3) (Rom 8:15). Having inherited the Pauline tradition, Mark put this vocative form into the mouth of Jesus when he prayed at Gethsemane. In this respect, Mark described Jesus in a filial relationship with God that is to be understood in light of Adam in the garden of Eden. Moreover, Jesus prayed that the cup of death might pass from him and then continued praying that it be done by God's will. This prayer could be contrasted with Adam's attitude as he earned death by eating the forbidden fruit according to his own will and desire (Gen 2:17; 3:1–6). Death came from his disobedience to God's will in the garden of Eden (3:19). Although Adam and Eve faced death since they were forbidden access to the tree of life (3:22–24), Jesus was given a chance to reach life through his crucifixion and resurrection by obeying God's will at Gethsemane. Mark compared Jesus and Adam while introducing life and death as the result, based on the theme of obedience and disobedience. The theme of obedience was once used in connection with the Adam Christology in Phil(2). It seems Mark probably took it from Paul and applied this theme to Jesus praying at Gethsemane. Finally, temptation is an important element in Jesus' prayer at Gethsemane because it makes possible the connection between Jesus and Adam. Jesus' prayer at Gethsemane is similar to Jesus' temptation in the wilderness.[8] The description of Jesus telling his disciples "not to fall into temptation [ἵνα μὴ ἔλθητε εἰς πειρασμόν]" implies Jesus' own effort to avoid the temptation. This saying seems to have been created on the basis of the fifth petition of the Lord's Prayer in Q, "Lead us not into temptation [μὴ εἰσενέγκῃς εἰς πειρασμόν]," which follows the second petition about the kingdom of God (Q^2 11:2, 4). Thus, it seems that the prayer at Gethsemane in Mark replaced the Lord's Prayer. Using the sources of Q and Paul, Mark created the account of Jesus' prayer at Gethsemane and applied the Adam typology to him.

Fourth, Mark implicitly applied the Adam typology to the crucifixion of Jesus (Mark 15:21–41). For this, Mark created the story of crucifixion at Golgotha as salvific event that opened the way from death to eternal life. For the typological interpretation, Mark depended on Paul, who taught that the cross of Christ worked both as a curse and as the means of redemption (Gal 3:1, 13). In other words, Mark compared the cross to both the tree of the knowledge of good and evil and the tree of life in the garden of Eden; while the former brought death, the latter would give eternal life. In this sense, Mark contrasted Jesus with Adam in the area of life and death, which was originally developed by Paul in 1Cor(2). This is how Mark developed the Adam typology in connection with the crucifixion of Jesus at the climax of his life. Through such descriptions, Mark developed the gospel comparing Jesus to Adam.

In conclusion, Mark planted many clues that hint at the Adam Christology. The events of Jesus' life are listed according to the biographical order of Adam in the garden of Eden. The Spirit's descent upon Jesus at the baptism is in contrast with the breath of God given to Adam at the time of his creation. Then, Jesus' temptation in the wilderness runs parallel with that of Adam in the garden of Eden. In addition, Jesus' prayer to obey the will of God at Gethsemane is contrasted with Adam's disobedience to God while being seduced by the serpent. Finally, Jesus' crucifixion is contrasted with the fate of Adam and Eve. In this respect, Mark deliberately used the traditions of Q and Paul and created some accounts of Jesus so they could remind readers of the events surrounding Adam in the garden of Eden in terms of life and death. Mark should be credited with a significant achievement in applying the Adam-typological perspective to the life of Jesus Christ.

---

8. Senior, *Passion of Jesus*, 77–79.

C. Matthew

Matthew also used the Adam Christology on the basis of the previous traditions. The author did not speak of Adam; however, he did explain Jesus' status and role compared with Adam. Matthew brought together the Adam Christology of Paul and the references to Adam used by Mark. The Adam Christology reaches its culmination in Matthew.

Matthew used the Adam typology in order to describe the status and role of Jesus Christ. First, the author compared Jesus and Adam by describing the baptism in parallel with death and the temptation in parallel with the crucifixion.[9] While the events of baptism and temptation originated in Q, those of crucifixion and death came from Mark. Mark had already edited the stories of baptism and temptation and added to those of crucifixion and death to recall Adam in the tradition about Jesus. Matthew followed such theological interpretations and applied them to the four events of Jesus in more detail. In addition, the six antitheses teach how to walk backward through the steps of Adam's corruption. Moreover, Matthew applied the Adam typology to the disciples—that is, becoming eunuchs for the sake of the kingdom of heaven. Matthew offers the reinterpretation that both Jesus and his disciples were those who recovered the nature of Adam before the fall in the garden of Eden. When looking at the sources used by Matthew, we find traces of reinterpretation for the Adam Christology. In this way, Matthew described Jesus Christ as the Savior who leads all humankind from death to life from a typological perspective.

1. Baptism and Death

In many regards, Matthew described the events of baptism and death in parallel with each other (Matt 3:13–17; 27:45–57). These two events may appear different on the surface, yet they contain both similar and contrasting elements. In this way, the comparison between Jesus and Adam is made possible. Having inherited them from Mark, Matthew strengthened their relationship by alluding to the events of Adam in the garden of Eden.

First, descriptions about the Spirit commonly appear. According to Matthew, Jesus was baptized with the Spirit of God descending like a dove from heaven (Matt 3:16), and he gave up the Spirit when dying on the cross (27:50). It is important to notice that the same word, πνεῦμα, is used for the Spirit in both texts. The Spirit descended on Jesus from heaven like a dove,

---

9. Ra, "Return," 178–252. As for the chiastic structure of Matthew, see Lohr, "Oral Techniques," 403–35.

which was used in contrast with the breath of life breathed into the nostrils of Adam in Mark, following the Pauline tradition. On the other hand, in Matthew, the Spirit descended on Jesus like a dove out of the water, which reminds readers of the chaotic circumstances before the creation (Gen 1:2). This can be explained when we consider how Matthew used the previous traditions. When he adopted the story about the baptism of Jesus from Q^3 3:21–22, Matthew planted many allusions to the creation. In particular, Q originally used the Hebrew term יונה (Jonah), which means "dove." According to the second redactor of Q, Jonah the prophet was a sign against the Ninevite men (Q^2 11:30). In this respect, Jonah was an icon for the divine judgment upon the Gentiles. In this vein, the third redactor used the Spirit like Jonah (dove) and added the heavenly voice with allusions to Ps 2:7 and Isa 42:1, which delivers the meaning of judgment upon the Gentiles. Finally, the third redactor depicted Jonah as the prophet of eschatological judgment (Q^3 11:32). It seems there was some wordplay between the Hebrew word "Jonah" (יונה) and the Greek word "dove" (περιστερὰ) when Q was translated from Hebrew into Greek before its use by Mark. However, Matthew took the Spirit descended upon Jesus like a dove from Q because Matthew was written in Greek. In addition, Matthew understood the dove to be a symbol of innocence (ἀκέραιος) (10:16). In other words, the Spirit like a dove refers to the divine agent who gave an innocent nature to Jesus at the baptism. This could mean the innocent nature before the fall of humanity in the garden of Eden. In addition, the description of the baptism graced by the Spirit like a dove could be connected with the description of before the creation, when the Spirit of God appeared on the water in the form of a bird, as the word "hovering over [מרחפת]" implies. If this connection is possible, Matthew saw what happened in the beginning as the old creation and the baptism of Jesus as the new. Matthew inherited the tradition of Mark, who drew a contrast between the breath of life breathed into the nostrils of Adam and the Spirit that descended upon Jesus in the form of a dove; however, Matthew changed the Markan contrast into that between the old and new creations. In this sense, it can be said that Matthew provided a stepping-stone for the comparison between Jesus and Adam according to his theological purpose.

Second, Matthew conveyed the communion between heaven and earth. The opening of heaven at the baptism means that God made a path of communion with the world (Matt 3:16). The opening of tombs at the death of Jesus also implies that God made a path of communion between heaven and earth (27:52). This is strengthened by the description that the rocks split, the bodies of many holy dead people were raised to life, and they went into the Holy City; in other words, they were given new life, and again, the path leading to heaven (27:52–53). These two descriptions share the common theme of removing the obstacle and starting communion with God, who leads people to eternal life. In this respect, these two descriptions can be contrasted with the account that God built a fence around the garden of Eden in order to prevent Adam from eating the fruits of the tree of life (Gen 3:22–24).

The theme about the opening of the garden and communion with God is frequently found in the Jewish tradition. The Jewish documents show this desire for life, and interpretations especially connect it with the tree of life in the garden of Eden (Ezek 47:12; 1 En 24:3–25:5; 4 Ezra 8:11, etc.). It is also written that the "new chief priest" who was the apocalyptic missionary, in contrast with Adam, would give fruit from the tree of life to the righteous (TLevi 18:11). Revelation explained that Jesus would give the fruit from the tree of life to the Christians of Ephesus who restore their first love (Rev 2:7). Based on the trend of this tradition (though he did not concretely speak of the fruit of the tree of life), Matthew compared the opening of the road leading to eternal life with the opening of heaven, the opening of graves, and so on. While Adam was exiled from the garden and faced death because of his disobedience, Jesus opened the path from earth to eternal life in heaven through obedience. In this respect, it can be said that the death and resurrection of Jesus played the role of providing fruit from the tree of life in Matthew.

Third, similarities and differences between the events of baptism and death appear, since Jesus was proclaimed as the Son of God in both events. A voice from heaven said, "This is my [God's] Son, whom I love; with him I am well pleased," when he arose from the water after being baptized (Matt 3:17). By contrast, the Roman centurion and those guarding Jesus confessed that he was the Son of God when they saw him die on the cross (27:54). While the former was a proclamation made from above, the latter was a confession from below. The Gentile centurion relayed the proclamation from heaven to the whole world. Thus, this became a proclamation to all humankind. Although they are in contrast with each other, they both share the common element of referencing the Son of God. It is, then, possible to compare Jesus Christ with Adam, who is considered to be the first created man, the son of God. Adam heard the sound of the Lord God calling to him "Where are you?" and he said to the Lord God, "I heard you in the garden" (Gen 3:8–10). The dialogue indicates the communication between Adam and God. Therefore, Jesus and Adam have a few primary things in common. In this respect, Matthew compared Jesus Christ with Adam from a typological perspective.

2. Temptation and Crucifixion

Matthew compared Jesus Christ to Adam in another way by describing the events of the temptation and the crucifixion in parallel (Matt 4:1–11; 27:32–44). Although they are different accounts, a dozen common elements can be found between them. These elements cause readers to see the author's intended allusion to Adam and his temptation in the garden of Eden. In this way, Matthew effectively presented typological interpretations.

To begin, Jesus was called the Son of God in both events. The tempter recognized him as the Son of God and addressed him accordingly (Matt 4:3, 6). The devil probably heard the heavenly voice at the baptism of Jesus and used the title here. In the same manner, many people, including the chief priests, called Jesus Christ the Son of God when he was on the cross (27:40, 43). This title appeared while they were mocking Jesus and trying to trap God into saving him. Since Adam was the first to be created by God, Matthew also saw him as the son of God. In this sense, the filial relationship with God is found primarily between Jesus and Adam for their comparison.

Second, Adam and Jesus run parallel in the fact that they were both tested. Jesus Christ was led by the Holy Spirit into the wilderness to be tempted by the devil (Matt 4:1). In the same manner, Jesus was tempted to come down from the cross during his crucifixion (27:40–42). This recalls Adam, who was led into the garden of Eden and consequently fell into temptation (Gen 3:1–6). Matthew formed a typological relationship between Adam and Jesus using the theme of temptation. This kind of typological work, having already been attempted in Mark's description of the temptation event, was followed by Matthew.

Third, the comparison between the temptation of Jesus and Adam becomes even clearer with the tempter. Matthew specifically used the word "tempter" (Matt 4:3). Ultimately, the devil, identified as Satan at last, is the one who appeared here as the tempter (4:1, 3, 5, 8, 10). Along with this, Matthew introduced those who were passing by during the crucifixion as tempters (27:40). The chief priests, the scribes, and the elders joined in this group (27:41). Matthew also made the criminals who were crucified with Jesus join in as well (27:44). These people were tempters used by the devil. Matthew wrote this with the serpent that tempted Adam and Eve in the garden of Eden in mind (Gen 3:1–6). Later, around 160 BCE, Jubilees depicted the serpent as the tempter (Jub 3:17); in addition, around 70 CE, the serpent was defined as the devil (*Apoc. Mos.* 16:1; 17:1; cf. 7:2–3). Moreover, at the end of the first century CE, it was described that the same devil tempted Eve (2 En 31:3–6). On the basis of Jewish tradition, in Matthew the devil alludes to the serpent in the garden of Eden. In this respect, Matthew attempted a typological interpretation in order to place Jesus in parallel with Adam and identify him as the new ancestor of humankind.

Fourth, the tempter used the words of God while tempting his victims. The devil quoted Ps 91:11–12 (Matt 4:3), and the Jewish leaders cited Ps 22:8 or Wis 2:16–18 (Matt 27:43). The latter was used only in Matthew, which reinforced the parallelism. This could also be understood in connection with the temptation of Adam, because the serpent used the words of God, though he distorted them (Gen 3:4). Such a description is also succeeded in Jub 3:18 and *Apoc. Mos.* 17:5. According to my judgment, such traditions were known by Matthew and were used to describe that Jesus was tempted with the words of God. In this sense, there is a parallel between those who tempted Jesus and the serpent in the garden of Eden.

Fifth, the events of the temptation in the wilderness and the crucifixion are similar. Jesus was extremely hungry, and the bread he was offered was what he desperately needed (Matt 4:3–4). This temptation reappeared when he refused to drink the wine mixed with gall at the cross, to his extreme suffering (27:33–34). The verb for "to drink" was used twice along with the verb "taste," which emphasizes that this temptation was related to his mouth. This temptation also runs parallel with the first reaction of Eve, who represented Adam. When she saw the forbidden fruit in the garden of Eden, the food looked tempting (Gen 3:6). In this sense, the parallelism between Jesus and Adam is possible from a typological perspective.

The second temptation can also be interpreted in the same context. The devil took Jesus to the pinnacle of the temple in Jerusalem (Matt 4:5–7). He commanded Jesus to throw himself down with the assurance that God would command the angels to come and save him. This was an opportunity for Jesus to test God and see the results with his own eyes. This kind of temptation also appeared during the crucifixion (27:40–42).[10] The crowds passing by and the Jewish leaders enticed Jesus to come down from cross, saying that if they saw God save him, they would believe that he was the Son of God. The tempters wanted to see this feat with their own eyes. Such parallelism is connected with Adam, whose wife, Eve, noticed the fruit was pleasing to the eye when she observed it after the serpent's temptation (Gen 3:6). The temptations Jesus faced in the Jerusalem temple and on the cross are essentially identical with the temptation of Adam and Eve in the garden of Eden.

The third temptation also connects Jesus with Adam. The devil took Jesus to a high mountain, showed him the kingdoms of the world and their splendor, and told him to bow down and worship him (Matt 4:8–10). The

---

10. Weber, *Kreuz*, 180–81.

devil was offering the authority to rule the world in this temptation, and this is essentially what appears in the event of the cross. Many people said that they would accept Jesus as the king of Israel if he came down from the cross and saved himself (27:42). The title "king of Israel" does appear significantly in this context, which is also related to authority. Matthew described the temptation on the high mountain and that on the cross in parallel. This kind of parallelism is again connected to the temptation Adam faced in the garden of Eden. When Eve saw the forbidden fruit, she desired its wisdom in order to have something more than the authority God had given to her (Gen 3:6).[11] This was also about having the authority to rule. Ultimately, Matthew showed that the temptation to receive undue authority that Adam and Eve faced was repeated by Jesus. In conclusion, the descriptions above show that the three temptations Jesus faced run parallel with those Adam and Eve faced from the serpent and the forbidden fruit. Although Adam fell into temptation and committed sin, bringing death to people, Jesus overcame temptation and gave life to people, as represented by the resurrection.

Sixth, Jesus' response to the three temptations also shows a typological relationship with Adam. In every case of temptation, he defeated the devil with the words of God (Matt 4:4, 7, 10), especially those found in Deuteronomy (Deut 6:13, 16; 8:3). In line with Jesus' first answer, he fulfilled his own words by living by the word of God. Contrary to this, during Jesus' temptation on the cross, he said nothing. In this way, Jesus coped with those who tested him using the words of God. Ultimately, this image was contrasted to that of Eve in the garden of Eden: she did not live according the words of God, and even sought to modify them. Adam, represented by Eve, is contrasted with Jesus regarding their attitude toward the words of God. This also reveals Matthew's intention in comparing Jesus to Adam.

Seventh, the places where the temptations took place are contrasted. The wilderness where Jesus was tempted was desolate, similar to Golgotha, where he was dragged to be executed on the cross. These places are contrasted with the garden of Eden, the rich and beautiful land where Adam was tempted. While Adam failed in the midst of perfect surroundings, Jesus overcame temptation even in a desolate place. Through this description, Matthew portrayed Jesus as the one contrasting with Adam.

Eighth, the description about forty days is also important in connection with these places. This is because the Jews of the intertestamental period left the record that Adam lived for forty days outside the garden of Eden before he entered. It is written in Jubilees around 160 BCE that Adam stayed for forty days in the place he was created, then was led into the garden of Eden

---

11. Fawcett, *Hebrew Myth*, 106. Cf. Aalders, *Genesis*, 1:102.

(Jub 3:9). Such tradition was developed around the sixties CE through the description that Adam and Eve repented for forty days outside the garden of Eden after their exile (*Apoc. Mos.* 29:10–11).[12] Moreover, it was written in 2 Enoch (a bit later than Matthew's Gospel around 90–95 CE) that Melchizedek was led into the garden of Eden forty days after his birth, demonstrating the influence of Jubilees (2 En 72:1). Matthew, who probably knew about this tradition, connected the garden of Eden with the tradition surrounding the forty days and the wilderness. When this story was taken from Q (Q⁴ 4:1–13), the term "forty days" alluded to the forty years that the Israelites spent in the wilderness after the Exodus. However, following Mark (Mark 1:12–13), Matthew also applied this to the forty-day period Adam and Eve spent before entering the garden. As a result, the place where Jesus Christ was tempted is closely related to the garden of Eden.

Ninth, Jesus was connected to the temple in the events of temptation and crucifixion. Although the Greek words ναός and ἱερός are different, they refer to the same temple (Matt 4:5; 27:40). Thus, the two events were connected through the mention of the temple. The emphasis on the temple is also connected to the garden of Eden, since the garden from which Adam was exiled was described in relation to the temple beginning with Ezekiel and throughout the documents of the intertestamental period. For example, Ezekiel depicted the temple in relation to the garden full of trees and fruit (Ezek 40:2; 47:12). According to 1 Enoch, "seven mountains" was a place that resembled the garden of Eden, and people would enter the temple of YHWH after the judgment there (1 En 18:8; 24:4–6; 25:5–6). According to Jubilees, the description that Adam was led into the garden of Eden after forty days following his creation was an attempt to connect the garden with the holy temple (Jub 3:9, 19; 4Q426). Moreover, grapes and Cherubim, which symbolized the garden of Eden, were drawn on the doors of the holy temple built by King Herod in the first century CE, showing that the holy temple symbolized the garden of Eden and offered protection for those who entered (*Ant.*, 15:395; *J.W.*, 5:210–11). Matthew thought of the temple of Jerusalem as the place of temptation, based on the traditions of the time, and connected it with the garden of Eden.

Tenth, the image of mountains is also indispensable for the garden of Eden. The high mountain is also connected with Golgotha, presumed to be located at a high place near Jerusalem. This element can also be connected to the garden of Eden. Although Genesis does not say that the garden was on a high mountain, later tradition located it there. For example, Ezekiel

---

12. As for its composition date, see Pokony, "Temptation Stories," 121; and Charlesworth, *Messiah*, 31.

described a garden in a vision, reminding readers of the garden of Eden (Ezek 47:12). It is important, however, to keep in mind that the vision was one of those seen on the high mountain (40:1–2). Later, in the intertestamental documents, the high mountain had been connected with the garden of Eden since the second century BCE. The "seven mountains," which were considered to be an apocalyptic place, were introduced as the high mountain, and that place took the form of the garden of Eden (1 En 24:4–25:6). The garden of Eden had already developed into a tradition in the form of a high mountain from early Jewish tradition. In addition, the garden of Eden ran parallel with Mount Zion and Mount Sinai and was added in the form of a mountain in Jubilees (Jub 4:25–26; 8:19). Moreover, it was described in the Christian tradition of Revelation that the New Jerusalem, which came down out of heaven, was put on a mountain great and high, and the garden of Eden was included in that city (Rev 21:10; 22:2–4). Judging from such tradition, it seems that Matthew was aware that the garden of Eden was connected to a high mountain, and he had no difficulties referring to the garden of Eden, since this was selected to be the place of temptation for Jesus. In this sense, Matthew referred to the garden of Eden through the descriptions about the high mountain.

Eleventh, the conclusion of the temptation events can also be connected to the garden of Eden, as demonstrated through the different types of angels. Adam and Eve, who fell into temptation, were exiled from the garden of Eden by Cherubim (Gen 3:24), but Jesus was attended to by the angels when his temptation was over (Matt 4:11). This comparison is further supported by the fact that while Mark described the angels' support during the forty days of Jesus' temptation (Mark 1:14), Matthew redacted the Markan description into the angels' support after the temptation was over. Although the attendance of angels is not directly mentioned in the event of the crucifixion, they did come to the tomb and attend him after his resurrection (Matt 28:2). Therefore, the angels showed contrasting manners toward Adam and Jesus at least.

Twelfth, Matthew presented Jesus as the one obeying God. He overcame the temptation of bread even though he was in hunger, and proclaimed instead that man shall live on every word that comes from the mouth of God (Matt 4:4). He also responded that God should not be put to the test and should only be worshiped and served, showing a God-centered mind (4:7, 10). Jesus followed the will of God even to his death as he prayed at Gethsemane (26:36–46; 27:50). This is complete obedience to the will of God, which is contrasted with Adam and Eve's disobedience to God in eating the forbidden fruit in the garden of Eden and not taking responsibility when confronted by God (Gen 3:6-7; 3:11-21). In this exact sense, Matthew contrasted Jesus with Adam.

In conclusion, Matthew presented the parallelism and contrast between Jesus and Adam. This is the result of following and developing the declaratory descriptions of Paul and the indirect descriptions of Mark. Matthew described the events of baptism, temptation, crucifixion, and death in parallel, making the contrast even more apparent. In this respect, Matthew described Jesus as the one who, unlike Adam, obeyed God, restored the garden of Eden, and will ultimately lead others to life.[13] Matthew presented Jesus as the Savior—that is, the new ancestor of all humankind—while comparing him to Adam, the old ancestor. Matthew's description runs according to his typological interpretation, and he developed the Adam Christology in order to explain the status and role of Jesus Christ. In this sense, Matthew applied to Jesus Christ the Adam Christology that had been transmitted to him from Paul through Mark.

3. Six Antitheses

Matthew left the reference to Adam in the six antitheses (Matt 5:21-48). The six antitheses recorded in the Sermon on the Mount are written in the following order: murder, adultery, divorce, oaths, sacrifice, and love for humanity. They present the means of retracing the steps of Adam's corruption and restoring the original nature in the garden of Eden God created at the beginning of the world. In this sense, Matthew applied the Adam typology to the disciples.

The six antitheses were written in connection with the description in Genesis. The first antithesis is about murder—that is, taking a life by physical force (Matt 5:21-22). However, in equating murder with annoying one's brother, Matthew made an allusion to the murder that occurred between the first brothers, Cain and Abel (Gen 4:1-7). The reconciliation of the brothers taught by Jesus alludes to the restoration of the relationship between the first brothers. The reconciliation among them, namely the disciples of Jesus, is an essential precondition for entering the Edenic kingdom of God.

---

13. M. Eliade introduces the symbolism of the World Tree, saying, "The Cross made from the wood of the Tree of Good and Evil, is identified with, or replaces, the Cosmic Tree." In the early Patristic period, the fathers believed that Adam's tomb was on the Mount of Golgotha, where Jesus Christ was crucified. Thus, it has been believed that the blood of Jesus went down from the cross to the skull of Adam and cleansed his sin. In this respect, the cross was considered the tree of life (Eliade, *History of Religious Ideas*, 2:402). This kind of early Christian tradition is based on the interpretation of the crucifixion in the Synoptic Gospels.

The second antithesis is about adultery, relating to sexual relationships (Matt 5:27). This could refer not only to the pure condition of Adam and Eve, who did not feel embarrassed even though they were naked, but also to sexual intercourse that leads to conception (Gen 2:24–25; 3:6–10; 4:1). According to Matthew, not looking at a woman lustfully is a way of avoiding adultery. In this way, the disciples can recover the nature of Adam and Eve before the fall in the garden of Eden regarding sexuality.

The third antithesis is about divorce (Matt 5:31). In principle, divorce is prohibited, except in cases of marital unfaithfulness. The marriage of man and woman reminds readers that Adam and Eve were the first couple (Gen 2:18, 21–23). Divorce breaks the marital relationship that God established in the garden of Eden. Thus, keeping faithfully to one's marriage is a way that disciples can observe the commandment of God issued in the garden of Eden.

The fourth antithesis is about oaths (Matt 5:33). According to Matthew, Jesus taught his disciples to let their "yes" be "yes" and "no" be "no," for "anything beyond this comes from the evil one" (5:37). This reminds readers of the occurrence between the serpent and Eve in the garden of Eden. God made an oath to Adam and Eve that they would certainly die if they ate the fruit from the tree of the knowledge of good and evil (Gen 2:16–17). However, the serpent lied to Eve and led her to ignore the divine oath, saying that even though she ate from the tree, she would not die (3:4). She only had to say "no" to the serpent; however, she said more than what she was supposed to say. As a result, Adam and Eve were exiled from the garden and ultimately faced with the fate of physical death. Thus, according to Matthew, Jesus' instruction about oaths leads Christians to the way of recovering the nature of Adam and Eve before their fall.

The fifth antithesis teaches the disciples not to resist an evil one (Matt 5:38–39a). Rather, they have to voluntarily help the evil one by doing something more than what they are asked for (5:39b–42). This is how to overcome the evil one. This reminds the reader of the tree of knowledge of good and evil (Gen 2:9). After taking its fruit, Adam and Eve were overcome by the evil one, the serpent, and then rebuked one another (3:11–14). When the disciples of Jesus overcome the evil one, they observe the commandment of God and recover the nature of Adam before the fall in the garden of Eden.

The sixth antithesis refers to love for humanity, demonstrating that God, the Father of heaven, bestows grace upon everyone (Matt 5:43, 45). This reminds readers that all humans share Adam and Eve as their ancestors and should therefore love one another as family (Gen 2:8). Matthew taught that all humans should restore the nature of Adam given by God at the beginning of creation. Although the previous interpretations are not thorough enough, they can reasonably be accepted from a typological perspective.

Matthew deliberately enumerated the six antitheses in the present order. This seems to be a comparison to the articles of the Law of Moses, but actually, there is a much more significant meaning.[14] They teach us how to retrace the steps of Adam's fall. The disciples of Jesus are those who restore the nature of Adam and Eve before their fall, and this is the way to enter the kingdom of heaven, which is identified with the garden of Eden. In this way, Matthew applied the Adam typology to the disciples, since he described Jesus from an Adam christological perspective. Matthew should be credited with a unique achievement in creatively applying the Adam typology inherited from Paul through Mark to the disciples.

4. The Eunuchs for the Kingdom

Matthew left another allusion to Adam with the phrase "eunuchs for the kingdom of heaven" (Matt 19:12). This is a *hapax legomenon* in Matthew, which means that this appears only once in the Bible.[15] This has long vexed interpreters; however, I would argue that Matthew taught the disciples to regain the nature of Adam and Eve before their fall in the garden of Eden.

There have been several attempts in order to define the meaning of eunuchs for the kingdom of heaven.[16] However, they did not avoid certain

---

14. The six antitheses have been understood to have a deep connection with the Ten Commandments. The first antithesis refers to the sixth commandment, the second to the seventh commandments, and the fourth to the ninth commandments. Thus, they were written according to the order of the Ten Commandments. However, the rest of them do not correspond to the order insofar as the eighth commandment, which should have been next, was omitted; and the third antithesis about divorce suddenly appears between the second and fourth. Strictly speaking, the order of the six antitheses is not directly connected to that of the Ten Commandments. Also, the fifth and sixth antitheses were not related to the Ten Commandments. Moreover, the commandment about false oaths in the fourth antithesis is only slightly similar to the description about false witnesses in the ninth commandment. The order of the six antitheses should be explained from a different perspective, while being skeptical as to whether or not they were composed with the Ten Commandments in mind.

15. Sand, *Reich Gottes*, 55. The phrase "eunuchs for the kingdom" has no parallel in other Jewish literature (Allison, "Eunuchs," 3).

16. Their arguments can be summarized as follows: the renunciation-of-marriage view, the celibacy-of-the-divorced view, and the rules-of-using-the-plumbing view. He summarizes as follows. The first view argues that Matt 19:10–12 advocates "the renunciation of marriage" and promotes "celibacy for the sake of the kingdom"; the second view indicates that the eunuchs for the kingdom refers to "the husband whose wife has been put away, requiring him to consecrate himself to a celibate life (at least until his

critiques.¹⁷ Thus, William F. Luck suggests that becoming eunuchs for the kingdom of God centers on a person's ability to control his or her sexual life.¹⁸ In other words, the eunuchs for the kingdom are those who got married but engaged in limited sexual intercourse with only their spouse and without ever committing adultery. It is, however, important to remember that the term "eunuchs" refers to those who are unable to, cannot, or do not have sexual intercourse. Using Mark 10:2-12, Matthew admitted the necessity of marriage on the basis of Gen 2:24, but he added this phrase for a special purpose. In this respect, a well-controlled sex life is not an adequate interpretation for the enigmatic eunuch saying either. Thus, it is necessary to focus on the particular purpose of the word "eunuch."

I would argue for an alternative interpretation in the background of Adam in the garden of Eden.¹⁹ First of all, as shown earlier, it is noteworthy that the kingdom of God or heaven refers to the garden of Eden in Matthew. Then, the eunuchs for the kingdom of heaven seem to be related to the person in the garden of Eden. Moreover, the eunuchs refer to those of much stricter ascetic lifestyle—that is, an asexual life. At this moment, it is necessary to take a look at Paul's interpretation regarding asexuality because it provides a theological background for the meaning of the eunuch saying. For example, based on the analysis of the term παρθένος in 1Cor(2), John C. Hurd argues that there were female spouses who married but refused to engage in sexual intercourse with their husbands in order to keep themselves pure and holy before God (1 Cor 7:25-40).²⁰ According to Hurd, this interpretation explains all the difficult problems regarding the identity of παρθένος. Thus, Hurd calls it "spiritual marriage" and defines these women as "holy virgins." However, Hurd does not explain why the holy virgins would not engage in sexual intercourse with their husbands.

In regard to this, I would argue that Paul thought of the holy virgins under the light of the marital relationship between Adam and Eve before their fall. Adam and Eve were not believed to have had sexual intercourse there (Gen 2:24).²¹ This could be supported by the early Jewish tradition

---

former wife dies)"; and the third view suggest that Jesus teaching on marriage "is only intended for those who get married" (Luck, *Divorce*, 150-53). For a brief history of interpretation of Matt 19:12, see also Sand, *Reich Gottes*, 23-24.

17. In order to see my critiques of the three interpretations listed in the main text, see Ra, "Return," 338-42.

18. Luck, *Divorce*, 153.

19. In order to see my argument, see Ra, "Return," 343-48.

20. Hurd, *Origin*, 169-78.

21. Westermann, *Genesis 1-11*, 233. On the contrary, there are some scholars that argue that Adam and Eve in the garden of Eden provide the etiological basis for the

that Adam and Eve's first sexual encounter occurred after the first jubilee outside the garden (Jub 3:34).[22] Probably, this kind of Jewish tradition influenced some female Christians of the Corinthian Church. In this regard, although Paul admitted the necessity of marriage, he advocated celibacy for Christians if they could carry it out (1 Cor 7:28, 38, 40). Paul seemed to have the marital relationship between Adam and Eve before the fall in mind when he admonished the husbands of the holy virgins. This interpretation could be supported by Paul's application of the Adam Christology to Jesus for the first time in 1Cor(2), for the text of the holy virgins also belongs to the same letter.

Matthew, who inherited the Adam Christology from Paul through Mark, also received the Adam-typological interpretation of the holy virgins. Thus, Matthew applied the concept of holy virgins to Mary. At the same time, it was also applied to the male disciples, "eunuchs for the kingdom of heaven," so to speak. They were those who voluntarily avoided sexual intercourse with their spouses in order to be pure and holy in front of God, as Adam and Eve were before their fall in the garden of Eden. In other words, the eunuchs for the kingdom of heaven are those who recover the nature of Adam before the fall.

Matthew probably had Joseph in the mind as the model for the eunuchs for the kingdom of heaven. According to the birth narrative, Joseph did not have sexual intercourse with Mary when she was pregnant with Jesus by the Spirit of God (Matt 1:18–19). Scholars have suggested various interpretations. Among them, Dale C. Allison Jr. argues that Joseph, who refrained from sexual intercourse on account of Mary's pregnancy, represents the eunuchs for the kingdom of heaven.[23] For this, Allison introduced the cases of ascetic life in Jewish society and the Greco-Roman world due to a wife's pregnancy. Although I do not agree with the argument for temporary celibacy due to religious instruction about spousal pregnancy, Allison's insight deserves our attention. In my view, Matthew selected Joseph because he was inevitably related to Jesus Christ. According to Matthew, the eunuchs for the kingdom of heaven are those who refrain from sexual intercourse throughout their whole marital life, not just during pregnancy. In this respect, Joseph represents the eunuchs for the kingdom and Mary represents the holy virgins. They are depicted as those who restore the nature of Adam and Eve before their fall in the garden of Eden.

---

sexual life of human beings. Cf. Scroggs, *Last Adam*, 5.

22. On the contrary, Anderson believes that Jubilees implies the sexual relationship between Adam and Eve before they enter the garden of Eden in Jub 3:9–14 (Anderson, "Celibacy," 129, 148).

23. Allison, "Divorce," 5–10.

In conclusion, Matthew applied the Adam typology to the disciples of Jesus and urged them to become eunuchs for the kingdom of heaven. Matthew inherited Paul's instruction about the holy virgins of spiritual marriage and applied it to the male disciples. This is in accordance with the fact that Matthew inherited the Adam Christology from Paul through Mark and applied it to Jesus Christ. Of course, this interpretation is supported by the fact that Matthew graphically identified the kingdom of God or heaven with the garden of Eden.

D. Other Documents

Efforts to connect Jesus Christ to Adam continued through the rest of the Christian Scripture. However, it seems that it was mostly through implication. The Jews frequently used the Adam typology at the time, and the authors of the Christian Scripture were affected by it as well.

John used the Adam typology in different way, applying it to Mary Magdalene's meeting with the resurrected Jesus (John 20:11–18). First, the new tomb where Jesus was buried and resurrected was in the garden (19:41). Used only in John, this description seems to allude to the garden of Eden.[24] Second, the resurrected Jesus appeared as a gardener. However, the tomb and the gardener are contrasted with each other. The gardener who appeared at the place of burial is juxtaposed against Adam, who could not properly guard the garden of Eden where the tree of life was located (Gen 3:22–24). In particular, members of the Qumran community considered their leader a gardener and regarded themselves as trees in the garden (1QH 8:4, 6, 16, 21–23). John probably reflected this Jewish tradition in his description of Jesus as a gardener. As a result, Jesus is minimally connected to Adam. Third, the appearance of the angel also establishes the connection between Jesus and Adam. John wrote that two angels were sitting in the tomb where Jesus' body lay. These angels can be compared to the Cherubim that exiled Adam and Eve by driving them out of the garden of Eden to the land of death (Gen 3:24), whereas the two angels that appeared at the tomb

---

24. In accounting for the Greek words for "garden," scholars give different interpretations. While Genesis uses the term παραδεῖσος for the garden of Eden, John uses κῆπος for the garden where the tomb of Jesus was located. Rejecting the symbolic meaning of the garden, Keener would not accept the relationship between the garden in John and the garden of Eden in Genesis (Keener, *Gospel of John*, 1164). On the contrary, it should be acknowledged that the two Greek words are interchangeable in the fact that παραδεῖσος was usually used for the garden of Eden in heaven at the time of composition of John (2 Cor 12:4; Luke 24:43; Rev 2:7). It seems that the term κῆπος is more suitable for the context of John (Brown, "Creation's Renewal," 281).

of Jesus Christ stayed in place during the resurrection. John contrasted the role of the angels at the most basic level regarding their relationship with Jesus and Adam. John described Jesus as the one who restored the life Adam once lost. Fourth, the meeting of Jesus and Mary Magdalene also refers to the case of Adam and Eve. The resurrected Jesus approached Mary, who was crying; this means that the man Jesus went to meet the woman Mary. In contrast, in the garden of Eden, God led the woman Eve to the man Adam (2:20–23). However, the meeting of a man and woman in a garden is a common element. In this respect, the meeting of Jesus and Mary runs parallel with that of Adam and Eve in the garden of Eden. It seems that John had Adam in mind when he described the resurrected Jesus who appeared to Mary Magdalene in the garden.

John also applied the Adam typology to the event after the resurrection of Jesus. He appeared to the disciples, who were in fear of the Jews, and breathed on them, saying, "Receive the Holy Spirit!" (John 20:19–23). The breath of the resurrected Jesus reminds readers of Adam, into whose nostrils God breathed the breath of life (Gen 2:7).[25] Although a difference is found in the descriptions of the subject (God in Genesis and Jesus in John), it should not be overlooked that John intended to make a theological connection between Adam and Jesus in terms of breath.[26] For the connection between them, John used the term ἐμφυσάω, which was also used in Genesis for Adam (*LXX*). In this respect, John also theologically interpreted that though Adam brought death to people, Jesus brought life to all humankind through resurrection. In this way, John used the Adam typology to describe the status and role of Jesus at the end of his Gospel.

Luke rarely used the Adam typology. To begin with, he only introduced that the genealogy of Jesus goes back to Adam, the first human being created by God (Luke 3:23–38). This is certainly different from that of Matthew, who described that Jesus was the descendant of David and Abraham. While Matthew saw Jesus as a Jew, Luke indicated that even Gentiles could become the people of God by connecting Jesus to the first human, Adam. In this way, Luke taught that the Gentiles were also the objects of salvation under the plan of God and so were the Jews' equals as descendants of Adam. Luke emphasized the salvation of all humanity in the genealogy, for the book was written primarily for the Gentiles, probably in Ephesus of Asia Minor. Second, Luke noted that Jesus mentioned the term "paradise," or the garden of

---

25. For the meaning of the breath that Jesus gave to the disciples, refer to Turner, "Concept," 24–42.

26. Humphrey, "New Creation," 536. On the other hand, Mark made a contrast between the breath of Adam and the spirit descended upon Jesus at the baptism. In this respect, John was different from Mark in his understanding of the breath of Adam.

Eden, on the cross (Luke 23:42–43). He promised paradise to the thief who had repented and asked for his kingdom. His promise indicates the transference from death to life; in this sense, Jesus on the cross reminds readers of the fruit of the tree of life. Luke implicitly applied the same Adam typology to Jesus on the cross that Paul had used first, followed by Mark and Matthew. It is noteworthy that Luke reduced the number of allusions to Adam in the texts inherited from Mark, in spite of the fact that it was primary written for the Gentiles. Though the Adam Christology was weakened in Luke compared to the other Gospels, it was sustained in terms of the typological description of Jesus until the beginning of the second century CE.

[A] E. Conclusion

In consideration of the theological trends of the first century CE, it is possible to apply the Adam typology to Jesus Christ. This was because the Jews at that time used the typology to compare their leaders to Adam. The Adam typology about Jesus started with Paul's declaratory description and was then succeeded by Mark, who applied it to some texts of biographical descriptions of Jesus. Later, Matthew developed the Adam typology by applying it to Jesus and changing it into a historical literary description. Matthew extensively developed and applied the Adam typology, even to the disciples of Jesus. Other documents used the Adam typology through brief descriptions. By using this typology, each writer conveyed that while Adam fell into temptation and went into the path of death, Jesus overcame temptation and opened the path leading to life. Thus, Jesus Christ is described as the Savior of all humanity—namely, the descendants of Adam.

13

The Birth of Jesus Christ

THE STORY ABOUT THE birth of Jesus Christ was developed theologically. It was not mentioned in Q or by the First Christians. On the other hand, Mark simply refers to Jesus' mother, Mary. In addition, John merely mentioned the place where Jesus was raised. Paul himself, then, was the first to introduce the birth of the Son of God, who was born according to the Scriptures. Following Paul, Matthew and Luke developed the theological interpretation about Jesus' birth. Many events relating to the birth of Jesus were created in this process, through which each Gospel conveyed the meaning of Jesus' birth. Although the Gospels described Jesus' birth as a historical event, there is not much outside information available. The authors of the Gospels made their own theological interpretations, showing how the gospel related to the birth of Jesus was formed and developed in the latter part of the first century CE.

A. The Pauline Epistles

Paul did not write much historically about the birth of Jesus Christ, since he probably did not have knowledge of it. However, Paul interpreted the birth of Jesus according to his own understanding in Gal 4:4–5; Rom 1:3; and Phil 2:7. These passages hold significant meaning from a theological perspective, since they base the birth of Jesus, the Son of God, on prophecy. Paul's interpretation was formed as a part of the gospel in connection with Bible prophecies.

Paul's theological understanding has particular significance regarding the birth of Jesus Christ. According to him, "But when the time had fully come, God sent his Son, born of a woman, born under law, to redeem those under law, that we might receive the full rights of sons" (Gal 4:4–5). In the full verse, we find three major proclamations dealing with time, means, and purpose. Each of these elements deserves to be developed.

First, in the fulfillment of time, God sent his Son to the world. This means that God planned a specific moment for sending his Son, referring not just to the nine months spent in his mother's womb but more specifically to the fulfillment of the Bible's prophecies. Since God sent his Son to the world for this purpose, it is necessary to uncover the prophecies that serve as the context for the birth of Jesus Christ, the Son of God, in terms of specific time. This prophecy then becomes part of the gospel about the birth of Jesus according to Paul's perspective. Of course, the interpretation about Jesus' birth was made according to Paul's theological understanding.

Second, Paul wrote that God sent his Son through a woman (referencing physical birth). Obviously, there is no one in the world who was not born of a woman; however, this does not simply speak to Jesus' physical entrance into the world. Rather, it means that the Son of God was the descendant who came to the world through a woman at the proper time. Q includes a statement that there was no one greater than John among those born by women (Q^4 7:28). Although it is not definite whether Paul applied this verse to Jesus, it is noteworthy that he focused on a woman in terms of the specific means of birth. At this time, he seemed to have Gen 3:15 in mind. God gave this prophecy to the serpent that tempted Adam and Eve in the garden of Eden to eat the forbidden fruit. Paul believed that this prophecy was fulfilled when Jesus was born of a woman, although he did not give the woman's identity. Nevertheless, it is possible that Paul interpreted the birth of Jesus in light of this prophecy. As a result, he confessed that the descendant of God who was sent through a woman was Jesus. If this is correct, then Gen 3:15 became part of the gospel about the birth of Jesus according to Paul's perspective.

Third, Paul saw the reason for Jesus' coming from a redemptive perspective. He explained that Jesus was born under the Law in order to redeem those under it. This interpretation resulted from Paul connecting redemption with the birth of Jesus. According to Paul, the Law was the primary object to be destroyed because it had led people to transgressions and death (Gal 3:19–21). As we have shown, Paul took a negative attitude toward the Law after he had been severely challenged by the Gentile Christians sponsored by the Jerusalem apostles. By mentioning the Law in connection with the coming of the Son of God in 4:4, Paul used Gen 3:15 as a theological background, since the offspring of a woman crushing the head of the serpent predicted the fall of evil powers and the salvation of humanity. The head of the serpent could be placed in parallel with the Law, which was regarded as the power of transgressions and death. In this respect, Paul seemed to understand that Jesus had come to this world through a woman, destroyed the Law, and redeemed the people under it according to the Scriptures. Then, Gen 3:15 undoubtedly became part of the gospel for Paul, as it was a prophecy about the birth of Jesus.

Paul interpreted the birth of Jesus from a typological perspective. Jesus was set in parallel with the descendant of a woman, and the Law with the serpent. While Adam and Eve were exiled from the garden of Eden for their sins, Jesus came to the world as the promised descendant of a woman to save their descendants from walking the path of death under sin and the Law. Unlike Adam and Eve, Jesus was implied to be the one who would restore the garden of Eden. In this sense, Paul connected Jesus with Adam at the most basic level. The typological interpretation of the birth of Jesus was possible for Paul because he had already used the Adam typology to describe the role of Christ giving life to the people in 1Cor(2). In this respect, Paul should be credited with a pioneering achievement in his typological approach to the birth of Jesus. He saw Jesus not only as a Jew, since he was a descendent of Abraham (Gal 3:16), but also as a descendent of Adam and Eve, and thus as having a connection to all of humanity (4:4–5). In this way, Paul articulated that Jesus Christ is the Savior for all humankind. Probably, Paul developed this interpretation in response to the challenge of the Galatians, who followed the instruction of the Jerusalem apostles that emphasized keeping the Law, circumcision, and observing rituals as the Jews did. As a result, Paul urged the Galatians to not be like the Jews but to remain as Gentile Christians.

Paul took time to mention the genealogy of Jesus Christ, the Son of God. A new concept about the descendant of David is introduced in Rom(1). Paul states, "regarding his [God's] Son, who as to his human nature was a descendent of David" (Rom 1:3). The description of the genealogy of Jesus includes three elements: filial relationship, Davidic figure, and human nature. Each of these elements deserves to be studied.

To begin, Jesus Christ is identified as the Son of God. Of course, the Son of God is the one about whom Paul received revelation at Damascus around 35 CE (Gal 1:16). As discussed, Paul already defined Jesus Christ as the Son of God when he interpreted the theological meaning of his birth (4:4). His filial relationship with God indicates that Jesus was understood to be a servant designated by God for a particular purpose. Paul preserved this view on the filial relationship of Jesus with God at the time of writing

Rom(1). In this respect, Jesus' filial relationship with God is the key to understanding Paul's theological interpretation about the birth of Jesus.

Second, the title "descendant of David" deserves our attention. It is unclear what is significant about the genealogy in this context. Paul did not explain how Jesus was identified with the descendent of David. Thus, it is difficult to draw out its meaning correctly. As well known figures, the kings of Judah were usually regarded as the sons of David because they were the descendants of King David. Nevertheless, Paul did not seem to apply the genealogic concept to Jesus because he never intended to be a king of the Jews. On the other hand, it could be understood from a political perspective. The descendant(s) of David stood for the political Messiah that would reestablish the kingdom of Judah, starting from the time of the prophets to the intertestamental period (2 Sam 7:11–14; Ps 2:7; 4QFlor. 1.10–11; 4QpsDan A). However, Paul did not say a single word about a political Messiah in his epistles, preferring to refer to the eschatological Messiah. This means that the descendant of David is also to be interpreted from a theological perspective. Although Paul did not give further explanation about the descendant of David, Paul interpreted Jesus as the chosen servant of God who came to this world.

Third, the phrase "as to the human nature [κατὰ σάρκα]" is to be explained in light of the birth of Jesus Christ. If this has a physical meaning, then Jesus was a descendant of David by blood; however, it is doubtful whether this is what Paul intended, since he did not mention here any of Jesus' other ancestors. Yet it is possible that is was Paul's intended meaning, considering how Paul received the tradition about the Son of God and developed it. Based on third redaction of Q, which imposed the role of the Davidic king to Jesus, the Son of God, by the heavenly voice that reminds the reader of Ps 2:7 (Q^3 3:22), Paul could identify the Son of God known to him through revelation with Jesus, the offspring of David in terms of his human nature (Gal 1:15–16; Rom 1:3). As we know, Ps 2:7 is considered to be the divine announcement to King David, the son of God. In this way, Paul seemed to attribute the Davidic linage to Jesus at the time of writing Rom(1). Then, Ps 2:7 becomes part of the gospel because Paul thought of it as a prophecy for the identity of Jesus Christ. Though the birth of Jesus was not different from any other, Paul gave meaning to it through his theological interpretations.

Paul attributed the Davidic linage to Jesus Christ, the Son of God, for specific reasons. As we know, the Roman Church is believed to have been established by the Diaspora Jews, such as Aquila and Priscilla (Rom 16:3). Although there were some converted Gentiles, the majority of the Roman Church was composed of the Diaspora Jews. In order to appeal to the Jewish

Christians, Paul looked for a point of contact by suggesting that Jesus, the Son of God, was the descendant of David according to his human nature. In this way, Paul seemed to encourage the Jewish Christians of the Roman Church to help his mission to Spain so that he could proclaim Jesus, the descendant of David, as the Savior for all humanity. This shows that Paul interpreted the gospel theologically in order to complete his mission under changing circumstances.

Paul also implied the birth of Jesus Christ from a christological perspective. This is implied in a christological hymn to Jesus Christ in Phil(2). Paul wrote that Jesus Christ "being in very nature of God, did not consider equality with God something to be grasped, but made himself nothing, taking the very nature of a servant, being made in human likeness. And being found in appearance as a man" (Phil 2:6–7). Paul displayed his understanding of the birth of Jesus in these verses. In the full verse, we find two major proclamations dealing with nature and means. Each of these elements deserves to be interpreted.

First, the nature of Jesus Christ must be dealt with. What is important is that he was of the very nature of God and then was made into human likeness to appear as a man. This implies similarity, not equality. In other words, Jesus Christ was neither God, nor a human being. It seems that he was a transcendental being. Paul enhanced his christological view on Jesus Christ when he said that Jesus was in very nature of God. This reveals an enhancement beyond Jesus' filial relationship with God. Paul changed the understanding of Jesus' filial relationship to God as written in Galatians and Rom(1) to assert his similarity with God in Phil(2). This modification shows that Paul increasingly exalted Jesus Christ as time passed.

Second, the means of Jesus' becoming a human being merits discussion. Without doubt, Jesus came to the world as a human being. However, Paul did not concretely describe how Jesus came into the world. He simply said that Jesus "made himself nothing," was "made in human likeness," and was "found in appearance as a man." This made Jesus obedient to the will of God even to his death on the cross. It is not, however, certain whether Jesus' metamorphosis from "being in the very nature of God" to human likeness and appearance as a man indicates the incarnation or not. At any rate, Paul thought of Jesus' coming to the world—that is, his birth—as mysterious and transcendental. This shows that Paul greatly emphasized the origin of the Lord Jesus Christ and theologically interpreted his birth at the end of his missionary work.

Paul used the christological hymn to disclose his understanding of the birth of Jesus. In other words, he tried to deliver his instruction to the Philippians, who financially supported him, being in jeopardy of execution. By saying, "Your attitude should be the same as that of Jesus Christ," before the christological hymn, Paul asked the Philippians to imitate Jesus Christ by their obedience to the will of God, even to death. In other words, the christological hymn was used to reveal Paul's self-understanding that he dedicated himself to God. Although we are not sure whether the christological hymn was created by Paul or handed down to him, Paul used it according to his purposes in response to the circumstances.

In conclusion, Paul had little historical knowledge about the birth of Jesus. However, Paul articulated his understanding of the birth of Jesus while applying hermeneutic methods that he had learned as a Pharisee. Instead of abandoning his interest in the second advent in Galatians and afterward, Paul began to be interested in the birth of Jesus after he had been challenged by the Corinthians and the Galatians. Paul interpreted the birth of Jesus theologically in order to introduce him as the divine agent for all humankind. In this way, Paul attempted to turn the eyes of the Gentile Christians from the instruction of the Jewish apostles to his own gospel regarding Jesus Christ, the Son of God. As a result, Paul created the elements of the gospel relating to the birth of Jesus.

B. Mark

Mark did not write about the birth of Jesus Christ. No birth narrative is found in Mark's Gospel. Mark simply contributed to naming Mary as the mother of Jesus. As will be shown, Mark was affected by Paul's theological understanding of the birth of Jesus.

Mark did not write the birth narrative at the beginning of his Gospel. It seems that he did not have knowledge of the birth of Jesus Christ, as Paul did. The only description of Jesus' birth or origin is that he was the son of Mary and that he had brothers and sisters (Mark 3:31–32; 6:3). Mark called Jesus a carpenter but did not mention his father, though it is unclear why. The brothers were James, Joseph, Judas, and Simon, though they had no role except asking Jesus to come out of the house. Among them, James was probably the one Paul called "the Lord's brother" (Gal 1:19). However, it is dubious whether they were actually brothers of Jesus because it is possible that Mark created them on the basis of Paul's mention of the Lord's brothers, including James (1 Cor 9:5). Therefore, it must be concluded that Mark did not actually know about Jesus' birth or family.

Even Mark's introduction of Mary as Jesus' mother resulted from previous traditions. This account came about as Mark changed the theological interpretation of Paul into historical description. Paul wrote that the Son of God was born of a woman (Gal 4:4; Gen 3:15), and Mark introduced Mary as that woman. In fact, nothing is known about the mother of Jesus. Mark probably contributed to the description of Jesus' birth by selecting the name Mary. There are three reasons that Mark chose the name Mary for the mother of Jesus. First, Mary derives from Miriam, the name of Moses' sister. Although the meaning of Miriam is still in dispute, it most likely meant "affection" or "love" in Egyptian.[1] It appears that Mark did not have a problem in choosing Mary as the mother of Jesus because Mary was the woman who gave birth to a son loved by God (Mark 1:11). This resulted from the contemplation of Q; Mark inherited the tradition that Jesus was the son loved by God (Q^3 3:21–22). The reason Mark chose the name Mary was the term "love," which worked as a connecting word so as to imply that God had sent his loving Son, Jesus, to the world through Mary, who herself stood for love. Second, Mary is connected to the Moses/Exodus typology. This typology appeared in the third and fourth redactions of Q; in addition, Paul also used it for the description of Christ in 1Cor(1) and 2Cor(1). Knowing about Q and the Pauline epistles, Mark chose Miriam, who played a prominent role during the Israelites' exodus from Egypt and introduced Mary as the mother of Jesus from a typological perspective. In this vein, Mark could present Moses at the transfiguration of Jesus on a mountain (Mark 9:4). Third, Mark chose Mary because he was incorporating Paul's perspective on the gospel. Mark applied this perspective in choosing the name Miriam or Mary. In this sense, Miriam became part of the Bible prophecy, and Mary fulfilled her function. Therefore, it can be concluded that Mark chose Mary according to his theological interpretation.

Mark described Jesus Christ as the descendant of David, following the tradition of Q and Paul. As discussed above, Jesus is depicted as God's Son at the baptism in the theological context of Ps 2:7 (Q^3 3:22). It is noteworthy that God announced the verse to David. In other words, the third redactor of Q described Jesus as the Son of God in the context of David. Reflecting this tradition, Paul had also proclaimed Jesus as the descendant of David (Rom 1:3). As a result, Mark depicted Jesus as the Son of God at the baptism and showed that he was the son of David since he could cure the blind (Mark 1:10–11; 10:47–48). Mark also emphasized, however, that Jesus was not like the Christ many Jews thought the son of David would be (12:35–37). He was greater than David himself because David would call Jesus "Lord." In

---

1. "The origin and meaning of the name Miriam is unclear, although—as many Levite names are for some reason Egyptian—it may have to do with the Egyptian word for Beloved (see the name Merari). On a Hebrew stage, most scholars derive the name Miriam from the verb מרה (*mara*) meaning to be rebellious or disobedient" (Uittenbogaard, "Etymology and Meaning," lines 1–5).

this way, Mark changed the proclamation of Paul saying that Jesus had come as a descendant of David into a historical description, among further developments. Jesus was not simply a descendant of David by blood, but a son of David who was greater than King David himself. This was the theological interpretation Mark made about the birth of Jesus Christ.

C. Matthew

Theological interpretations about the birth of Jesus Christ are also found in Matthew. He described the event while adding his own sources and theology to those passed down by Paul and Mark. Especially, the conception by the Spirit of God reaches its culmination in the description of the birth of Jesus. As a result, Matthew provided a turning point for its story.

Matthew developed the theology of Paul in connection with the birth of Jesus Christ. Matthew's description about Jesus' birth was fundamentally affected by Paul and can be presented in four parts (Matt 1:18–25). First, like Paul, Matthew explained that the birth of Jesus was an event caused by God. Paul wrote that God had sent his Son into the world (Gal 4:4), and Matthew wrote that God had caused the conception of Jesus through the power of the Holy Spirit. God sent an angel to appear in Joseph's dream and told him that a son would be born and giving specific instructions, including that his name should be "Jesus." In this sense, Matthew, like Paul, interpreted the birth of Jesus as focused on God, showing that Matthew changed Paul's theological statements into narrative descriptions.

Second, the description that Jesus would be born of a woman was also passed on from Paul. Paul wrote that God caused his Son to "be born of a woman" (Gal 4:4), Mark described that woman as Mary (Mark 6:3), and Matthew described her as the Virgin Mary. This change in tradition shows that Paul's theology regarding the birth of Jesus was not only reflected in Matthew as it had been passed down through Mark, but was also extended. While Paul used Gen 3:15 as the origin of the gospel about the birth of Jesus, Matthew added Isa 7:14 as its theological background. So it was that Matthew, in his own way, reinterpreted Paul's theology that the birth of Jesus Christ was the fulfillment of the prophecies of the Bible. This shows how Matthew theologically interpreted the birth of Jesus Christ according to the Scriptures.

Third, Matthew followed the theology of redemption that Paul applied to Jesus Christ. Paul wrote that God sent his Son under the Law to redeem those under the Law (Gal 4:4), and Matthew defined Jesus as the one who would save his people from their sins (Matt 1:21; Exod 3:10). For this purpose, Matthew introduced Jesus as the Savior who would lead people into the heavenly kingdom of God while proclaiming new commandments and laws (Matt 5:1—7:27; especially 5:19-20; 7:21). Thus, Matthew added Exod 3:10 to the theology of redemption established by Paul and Mark using Isa 53:10 as a theological background. This was the result of viewing Jesus as the fulfillment of the Bible's prophecies. This is another example of how Matthew theologically described the birth of Jesus, reflecting Paul's perspective on the gospel.

Fourth, Matthew described Jesus Christ as the descendant of David. While Paul was the first (Rom 1:3) and was followed by Mark, who referred to Jesus as the son of David, Matthew assigned more texts to describe Jesus as the descendent of David. Jesus was born into the family of Joseph a descendant of David. For this purpose, Matthew proclaimed Jesus a descendant of David (Matt 1:1), like Joseph (1:20). Also, he wrote that Jesus was born in Bethlehem in Judea, the hometown of David, his ancestor (2:1–12). Moreover, Matthew called Jesus "the descendant of David" in reference to more events than any of the other Gospels. He added the title in the case of the dispute about Beelzebub, though it had not been used for the same event in Q and Mark (12:23). Matthew used this title when Jesus cured the Canaanite woman's daughter, while Mark did not in the same event (15:22). Matthew also used the title twice to describe the curing of the blind, while Mark used it once (9:27; 20:30–31). Furthermore, Matthew changed the Markan description, "kingdom of David," into "descendant of David" when he described Jesus entering Jerusalem (21:9, 15). In so doing, he proclaimed that the descendant of David was greater than David himself, as Mark had (22:42–45). Therefore, Matthew emphasized that Jesus came to the world as the Christ, the descendant of David. Of course, such a description was the result of the theological interpretation Matthew made and primarily based on the Pauline tradition.

Matthew further developed the description of Mark in relation to Mary, the mother of Jesus. Mark started using Mary as the name of Jesus' mother, but Matthew added that Mary also looked after Jesus as Miriam had done for Moses (Matt 1:18–2:23; Exod 2:4–10). For this purpose, Matthew applied the typology comparing Jesus and Moses' birth and childhood. The event in which King Herod attempted to kill Jesus as a baby by giving orders to kill all the boys in Bethlehem and its vicinity was based on the event in which the Pharaoh of Egypt ordered male Hebrew babies to be killed at birth. Both Jesus and Moses escaped death at the hand of the political rulers of their time. In Exodus, the person who played the crucial role in saving Moses was Miriam. Just as Miriam assisted Moses in this process, Mary looked after baby Jesus. Baby Jesus' escape to Egypt, and later to Galilee, was based on the Israelites entering Canaan after being emancipated from Egypt. In this way, Matthew added more information about Mary, who was selected as the mother of Jesus by Mark.

Matthew added four new elements to the account of Jesus Christ's birth. First, Matthew wrote that Jesus was conceived by the Holy Spirit (Matt 1:18–20). Conception by the Spirit of God was an entirely new concept not mentioned in the Bible. Of course, there is the annunciation in Isaiah about the virgin or young woman giving birth to a son, but this does not mean that the Spirit of God would be involved (Isa 7:14). Nonetheless, Matthew spoke of conception by the Spirit of God and the god-like birth of Jesus. Apart from the Bible, there is another background that sheds light on why Matthew used the Holy Spirit as the means of Jesus' conception. As is already well known, Matthew received the tradition about the Spirit from Q and Mark, which describe that the Spirit of God descended on Jesus when he was baptized (Matt 3:16–17; Q^3 3:21–22; Mark 1:10–11). Moreover, through the Pauline epistles, Matthew knew about the unbreakable relationship between Jesus and the Spirit, since he was the Son of God according to the Spirit (Rom 1:4; Gal 4:4–6). Based on such sources and theology, Matthew wrote that the Holy Spirit of God conceived Jesus, and in so doing, advanced the time of the coming of the Spirit to the conception of Jesus Christ compared to Q and Mark. In addition, the conception of Jesus by the Holy Spirit could fill the theological gap Paul opened when he spoke of a mysterious and transcendental coming to the world in Phil(2). In this way, Matthew's theological interpretation relating to the conception of Jesus by the Spirit of God was formed. Matthew was the first Gospel account that adopted a High Christology.

Second, Matthew taught that Jesus Christ was born as a Savior. By naming him Jesus at the birth, he was introduced as the Savior who would save his people from their sins (Matt 1:21). He lived according to the meaning of his name. For this purpose, Matthew compared Jesus to Moses (Exod 3:10). It is easily demonstrated that the Moses/Exodus typology is used frequently throughout Matthew. Matthew confessed Jesus as the Savior while applying the Moses/Exodus typology he inherited from Q and Paul that compared Jesus to Moses.

Third, Matthew wrote that the Virgin Mary gave birth to Jesus (Matt 1:22–23). Matthew developed the tradition he had inherited from Mark that Mary was Jesus' mother and from Paul's notion of holy virgins. Matthew introduced a new theme in the Virgin Mary. The theological background for this can be seen in Isa 7:14, which Matthew understood and cited as a prophecy about the birth of Jesus. Jesus was born while fulfilling the prophecy of Isaiah. At this moment, some deeper explanation about the Virgin is necessary. As might be known, the word עלמה, meaning "young woman," is used in the Hebrew text. Of course, this meaning would include an unwed virgin. The Septuagint, however, used the Greek word παρθένος, meaning "unwed women" with no sexual experience. This was a reflection of the translator's theology. As a result, Matthew applied this Greek word to the mysterious birth of Jesus. Consequently, God sent his Son, Jesus Christ, to the world by causing the Virgin Mary to conceive through the Holy Spirit. In this way, Jesus was interpreted as the one who fulfilled the prophecy of Isa 7:14. Ultimately, Matthew used it as the origin of the birth of Jesus, which applied Paul's perspective on the gospel. This is how Matthew applied the hermeneutic principle "according to the Scriptures" to the birth of Jesus. In addition, Matthew probably used the Pauline tradition regarding παρθένος, which refers to the holy virgins who married but refused sexual relations with their husbands in order to stay holy before God, as written in 1Cor(2). Matthew seemed to apply the Pauline interpretation to Mary inherited from Mark and reflected in Isa 7:14, saying that Mary did not have a sexual relationship with Joseph while pregnant with Jesus. In this way, Matthew emphasized the holiness of the birth of Jesus. Based on the interpretations above, it can be concluded that Matthew did not hesitate applying the term παρθένος to Mary on the basis of the traditions from Isaiah, Paul, and Mark. This is how the tradition of the birth of Jesus went through the process of theological supplementation.

Fourth, Matthew wrote about Joseph, Mary's husband, in various ways. Above all, although he was her lawful husband, they had not consummated the union for the sake of purity (Matt 1:18–25). As discussed above, Mark introduced only Mary as the mother of Jesus and did not mention his earthly father. With this in mind, Matthew explained how Jesus could be born of a virgin since Mary was engaged to Joseph, the descendant of David, but had not had sexual relations. Ultimately, Matthew described that Jesus was born of the Virgin Mary, who conceived by the power of the Holy Spirit, and added that Jesus' genealogy was connected to David through Joseph, Mary's husband.

Matthew was the first who introduced the father of Jesus and adopted the name of Joseph for him. While Mark called Jesus a carpenter, Matthew assigned this role to Joseph (Matt 13:55). In addition, Matthew expanded the role of Joseph from a typological perspective. For this purpose, he described Joseph based on the Israelites' escape from Egypt. Joseph only appeared when Jesus was born and when they escaped to Egypt and Galilee during Jesus' childhood. This description runs parallel with the Joseph in Genesis who went to Egypt as a slave and eventually brought his family, but requested not to be buried there (Gen 37:25–36; 46:1–7; Exod 13:19). In other words, just as Joseph only acted in connection with the escape of the Israelites from Egypt, the Joseph in Matthew was also involved with the escape of the baby Jesus from Egypt. These two Josephs were connected from a typological perspective. Moreover, Matthew also introduced Joseph as the father of Jesus through the dream motif. Joseph is connected to dreams three times in Genesis. First, as a young boy he dreamed that his parents and brothers bowed down to him (Gen 37:5–11). Second, when in Egyptian prison, he interpreted the dreams of the cupbearer and baker (40:5–43). Third, he interpreted the dream of Pharaoh (41:14–36). Similarly, Matthew wrote that the angel of God appeared in dreams three times to Joseph, giving him instructions each time (Matt 1:20; 2:13, 19). Furthermore, both Josephs endeavored to be sexually pure (Gen 39:7–18; Matt 1:18–21) and were sons of Jacob (Gen 30:22–24; Matt 1:16). Through these descriptions, Matthew used the events of Joseph in Genesis as a type for Joseph, the father of Jesus.

In conclusion, Matthew added his own interpretive perspective to Paul's theological understanding and Mark's historical description in order to depict the birth of Jesus Christ. The most prominent contribution is that the Spirit of God conceived Jesus through the Virgin Mary. In addition, Moses/Exodus typology was applied to Jesus in order to define his status and role. These factors played a role in describing Jesus Christ as the Savior of all humanity. Matthew's theological interpretation about the birth of Jesus shows the origin and process of the gospel's formation according to the Scriptures. In this respect, Matthew was a creative scribe who provided new theological interpretations about the birth of Jesus.

D. Luke

Luke seems to rely heavily on Matthew regarding the birth of Jesus Christ. Although Luke endeavored to describe the events with historical accuracy, like the others, he also conveyed his own theological interpretation. Therefore, Luke shows a significant advance in describing the birth of Jesus.

Luke sought to accurately describe the time when Jesus Christ was born. For this purpose, the author included the historical setting, stating that the event took place when the Roman Emperor Caesar Augustus issued a decree that a census should be taken and when Quirinius was governor of Syria (Luke 2:1–2). This event, which took place around 6 CE, seems to be historically accurate; however, it differs by nearly ten or twelve years from the account of Matthew, who wrote that Jesus was born before King Herod died, around 4 BCE. Some believe that such demonstrable contradictions prove that one of the accounts is not historical, but it could also be that both Matthew and Luke did not describe the event correctly. This also makes it difficult to know much about the actual birth of Jesus. What can be known, however, is that both Luke and Matthew demonstrated their own theological purposes.

There are many similarities between Luke and Matthew's description of the birth of Jesus. First, the Virgin Mary conceived Jesus by the Spirit of God. There are also the descriptions of the annunciation by the angel and the instructions to name the baby Jesus. Both accounts name Bethlehem as the place of his birth and Joseph as his father. This reflects the fact that Luke referred to the description of Matthew; however, this does not mean the descriptions in both Gospels are exactly the same, as different details are included for the same events.

These differences are quite apparent to the casual reader. First, according to Luke, the angel announcing Jesus' conception appeared to Mary instead of Joseph (Luke 1:26–33). This seems to show Luke's special consideration for women. Second, what the angels actually said also differs. Of course, the amount what the angels said is significantly different, but the content demonstrates a different focal point as well. While Matthew emphasized the blood-relationship aspect, calling Joseph the son of David, Luke emphasized that Jesus Christ would play the role of a king, as he himself was the descendant of David (1:30–32). Third, it was written that the angel Gabriel spoke with Mary, who listened and obeyed the will of God (1:27–38). Compared with Matthew, who did not describe this scene, Mary's role in Luke relating to the birth of Jesus stands out. Fourth, Luke described Mary's visit to Elisabeth and introduced a conversation between them (1:39–56). While Elisabeth does not appear in Matthew, she plays the role of Mary's spiritual supporter in Luke. Fifth, the birth of John the Baptist is described prior to that of Jesus in Luke (1:5–25, 57–80), while Matthew is silent about it. Sixth, there is a difference in the descriptions of Jesus' hometown. While Matthew wrote that Jesus' parents originally lived in Bethlehem, Luke states that they moved from Nazareth in Galilee to Bethlehem for the purpose of the census (2:1–7). Seventh, while Matthew emphasized that Jesus was born to fulfill the Bible's prophecies, Luke emphasized the contemporary prophets, Simeon and Anna, who encountered Jesus as a baby (2:22–39). When Mary and Joseph carried Jesus to the temple for dedication according to the Law, they met the prophets and heard prophecies from them. Eighth, Luke did not mention the escape to Egypt that had featured prominently in Matthew. Rather, Mary and Joseph took the baby Jesus straight from the temple to Nazareth in Galilee (2:39). Ninth, Luke wrote extensively about the role of the Virgin Mary, and unlike Matthew, Luke barely mentioned the role of Joseph. As a result, from the beginning, Luke wrote that the angel

Gabriel appeared to Mary and told her that she had conceived by the Spirit of God. Mary asked how this could be since she was a virgin, emphasizing her role rather than Joseph's. Later, Mary's visit to Elizabeth has nothing to do with Joseph. Luke simply records that Joseph took Mary to Bethlehem in Judah from Nazareth in Galilee. Luke clearly maximized the role of the Virgin Mary in connection with the birth of Jesus. Tenth, finally, Luke recorded Jesus' hometown as Nazareth in the region of Galilee, most likely for theological reasons. Nazareth was practically considered a foreign land compared with the region of Judah that included Jerusalem. This was done in order to emphasize the gospel's movement toward the Gentiles. However, because Matthew set the birthplace of Jesus as Bethlehem, Luke said that Joseph and Mary only moved to Bethlehem, his birthplace, because of the census. In this sense, Luke and Matthew show many differences regarding the birth of Jesus.

Considering these points of comparison, it seems that Matthew substantially affected Luke's description of the birth of Jesus Christ. However, Luke showed a different theological position than Matthew. As a result, Luke added and subtracted content from Matthew's description. Luke, however, does not make much use of the hermeneutic principle "according to the Scriptures." Through this, the process of the origin, formation, and development of the gospel relating to the birth of Jesus is revealed.

E. Other Documents

The birth of Jesus Christ is mentioned in other documents as well. However, they differ from each other in focusing more on the theological aspect than the historical aspect at the turn of the first to the second century CE.

John showed a different perspective on the birth of Jesus Christ, proclaiming it declaratively rather than historically. John recorded that Jesus was from Nazareth rather than Bethlehem (John 1:45–46). Coupling this with Mark's statement that Jesus grew up in Nazareth, the theory that Jesus was born there is not entirely impossible since, unlike Matthew and Luke, John does not mention a specific birthplace. On the contrary, John focused his thought on Jesus' origin in heaven (6:38; 51). John also did not speak about the time of Jesus' birth, instead beginning his account with the start of Jesus' public life. In this, John followed the tradition of Mark, which demonstrates that less is known about the birth of Jesus than is commonly thought.

The Deuteropauline epistles proclaimed the birth of Jesus Christ, though not as a historical event. In Colossians, Jesus was the firstborn over all creation (Col 1:15) and was before all things (1:17), emphasizing his preexistence. Second Timothy introduces Jesus as the descendant of David in the admonition to remember Jesus Christ, who was raised from the dead and descended from David (2 Tim 2:8). This is in line with the gospel conveyed by Paul and his account of Jesus as the descendant of David. Although this reference is similar to the son of David mentioned in the Gospels, the point of emphasis is different. With all things considered, the Deuteropauline epistles do not add much to the development of the gospel about the birth of Jesus.

Hebrews described the birth of Jesus Christ from a theological perspective. Quoting 2 Sam 7:14, Hebrews described that God shared a filial relationship with Jesus (Heb 1:5). This is revealed indirectly in that God never said such things to the angels. In addition, it is said that God brings his firstborn into the world again (1:6). This presumes his previous advent—that is, his first birth—but the way Jesus was born is not mentioned at all. Hebrews, rather than making a historical description about the birth of Jesus, simply announced his birth as the Son of God.

The prologue to John showed the most enhanced Christology in the Christian writings. It seems probable that this was a later addition to the Gospel of John in the beginning of the second century CE (John 1:1–18). Jesus is defined as the Word (λόγος) that was God and created the world in the beginning. In this respect, Jesus was proclaimed as the divine and preexistent being. In addition, he came to the world he created as the only Son of God, where he dwelled among people as he became flesh, and his glory was the glory of the one and only Son who came from the Father full of grace and truth. Thus, Jesus' incarnation is described theologically. While Matthew and Luke asserted that Jesus was conceived by the Spirit of God, John went even further theologically. In addition, he went further than Paul, who said Jesus Christ was in the very nature of God in Phil(2). Finally, John confessed the Word, Jesus Christ, as God. This was the most enhanced High Christology in the Christian Scripture to this point and focused on theological meaning more than history. The prologue to John defined Jesus Christ as the Word based on various backgrounds. First, the Word can be connected to the word God used during the creation (Gen 1:3–31). In addition, similarities can be found between the Word and the wisdom that was introduced as the main subject of creation (Prov 8:22–31; cf. Sir 24; Wis 9). Philo of Alexandria considered this in the fact that he applied the *logos* (λόγος) of Platonism to the divination of the Patriarchs of the Jews, such as Moses and Abraham.[2] Contrary to Philo's use of *logos*, however, the

---

2. Brown, *Introduction*, 91–92, 338, 371–72. For the opinion of Philo's influence on John, see Dodd, *Interpretation*, 60–68, 160–68, 222. See also the book by Hamerton-Kelly, *Pre-existence*. As for those who reject the previous opinion, see Brown, *Gospel*,

author of the Johannine prologue applied it to Jesus Christ using Genesis as the background. The author used the words and ideas of the Gentiles while penetrating their culture to reach beyond the range of Judaism. According to Wooil Moon, "the Johannine doctrine of *Logos* is deliberately designed to defend the ontological priority of Jesus and the Johannine community against the Philonic notion of *logos* which defines Israel and several Israelite patriarchs in terms of the divine *logos*."[3]

The prologue to John provides the high point of theological descriptions about the birth of Jesus, since he proclaimed that Jesus is God. The author defined Jesus as the preexistent Word who was with God in order to develop the previous description that he came from heaven (John 6:38, 51). The prologue to John advanced the Christology much more than Paul had in Phil(2). In this respect, the theological interpretation of the birth of Jesus developed further as time passed in the second century CE.

The First Epistle of John also revealed the theological interpretation of the birth of Jesus Christ. Defining Jesus as the Son of God, the author pronounced that through the testimony of the Spirit, Jesus came by water and blood (1 John 5:5–7). This description reminds readers of the dialogue between Jesus and Nicodemus about the need for rebirth (John 3:3, 5) and was the result of his theological interpretation regarding the birth of Jesus. In this way, the gospel about Jesus' birth was developed with advanced Christology in the beginning of the second century CE.

F. Conclusion

There is little concrete historical information about the birth of Jesus Christ. Q did not write about it, and the First Christians did not leave any of their interpretations either. Paul entered into this situation by interpreting the birth of Jesus Christ, the Son of God, based on Gen 3:15 (Gal 4:4), although this also reflects that he did not know about the historical birth of Jesus. Mark left the description that Jesus' mother was Mary, a woman God promised in Gen 3:15, in order to provide at least a fragment of historical fact. Applying the theme of the conception of the Holy Spirit through the Virgin Mary, Matthew provided the turning point of the description of Jesus' birth. Relying upon the traditions from Paul and Mark, Matthew developed the account of his birth further in terms of the fulfillment of the Bible's prophecies, the typological interpretation, the role of Joseph, etc. Matthew is the first Gospel to tell the story of the birth of Jesus from a perspective of High

---

lv–lvi, lviii.

3. Moon, "Philosophical Analysis," 368–69.

Christology. Probably influenced by Matthew and his own theological interpretation, Luke described the birth and background of Jesus with more detail. However, this does not mean that Luke described the birth of Jesus accurately from a historical perspective. John did not describe the birth of Jesus in detail, but later, the author of the prologue to John insisted that he existed before the creation of the world and proclaimed him as God. Other documents do not mention much about the birth of Jesus Christ. Jesus was born as a person and as time passed, he was depicted as the one born as a transcendental figure.

14

The Theology of Redemption

THE THEOLOGY OF REDEMPTION is the acme of the Christian doctrine. It was formed through Jesus Christ upon the hermeneutic principle of "according to the Scriptures." Paul articulated the theology of redemption that Jesus Christ died "for our sins" on the cross according to the Scriptures, and the prophecy about the Suffering Servant of YHWH became part of the gospel of redemption. It can be said that at that moment, Christianity had its foundation. The four Gospels, written later, developed the theology of redemption proclaimed by Paul into historical narrations. At the end of the first century CE, the blood of Christ was focused on as the means of redemption by various authors. Although each author wrote about the redemptive role of Jesus from a different point of view, each described it in terms of his or her own strength. With Paul and the Gospels being followed by the rest of the authors of the Christian Scripture, the theology of redemption became the key instruction of Christianity.

A. The Pauline Epistles

The First Christians were not concerned with the theme of redemption. Although they understood the death of Christ in connection with the prophecy in the Bible, they did not describe the result of the death of Christ. With regard to the redemption, they probably maintained the Jewish instruction. However, having inherited the gospel about the death of Christ from the First Christians, Paul connected it to the concept of redemption when challenged by the Gentile Christians under the sponsorship of the Jerusalem apostles, saying that Christ died "for our sins" on the cross according to the Scriptures.

At the beginning of his missionary endeavors, Paul did not apply the redemptive role to Jesus Christ. Paul did not use the term "sin [ἁμαρτία]" or introduce the concept of forgiveness at all in his first letter, 1Thess(1). Although he mentioned it once, it was not of the Thessalonians but of the Jews (1 Thess 2:16). In investigating the matter of sin, some texts deal with the wrongdoings, such as idolatry, sexual immorality, taking advantage of a brother, or accepting any kind of evil (1:9; 4:3–6). However, Paul does not describe how people can be forgiven for such wrongdoing. Jesus is simply defined as the one "who rescues us from the coming wrath" (1:10). Even if this expression refers to salvation, Paul did not explain how this rescue would come about. It seems that the Thessalonians could be saved by "staying holy" (2:10; 4:3, 7). Otherwise, Paul said nothing about how the Gentile Christians could be saved. Probably, he had living a religiously ethical life according to the teachings of God—that is, the Law—in mind. This implies that Paul was not much different from the apostles of the Jerusalem Church regarding the way of redemption and salvation at the time of writing 1Thess(1).

Paul indirectly dealt with the concept of redemption in 1Cor(1). Only one text is found about the sin of adultery (1 Cor 6:18). However, the concept of redemption can be detected from some texts. Above all, Paul talked about several evil actions, such as sexual immorality, idolatry, adultery, envy, boast, arrogance, rudeness, etc. (1 Cor 6:13–18; 10:7, 8, 14; 13:3–5). Nevertheless, he did not explain how to be forgiven from such evil actions. The Corinthians were simply asked to be holy by the presence of the Spirit because their bodies were the temple of God (3:16–17). In addition, Paul indirectly mentioned the concept of redemption by saying that Christ was bought at a price for them (6:20). However, it is not explained how he was bought at a price for them. Had such an explanation been provided, it could have been the presence of the Spirit, as can be drawn from the context (6:19). On the other hand, from the fact that Paul criticized those who live for their body, the righteous life could be suggested as the way of redemption and salvation (6:13–19). According to Paul, one can be holy and righteous by avoiding unrighteous actions and by the presence of the Spirit. There was no room for the death of Christ to be introduced as a means of redemption in 1Cor(1).

Paul introduced the concept of redemption at the basic level in 1Cor(2). The term "sin" is mentioned several times in the form of the noun (ἁμαρτία) or verb (ἁμαρτάνω); among them, sin is related with the marital life (1 Cor 7:28, 36), while sin against the weak brothers is identified as sin against Christ (8:12), and it is used to describe the religious situation of the Corinthians (15:17). Being guilty of sinning (ἔνοχος) against the body and blood of the Lord is then mentioned (11:27). In addition, Paul mentioned several evil actions, such as division, sexual immorality, greediness, idolatry, insult, drunkenness, etc. (1 Cor 1:10–17; 5:1–5, 11; 11:18–22). However, how to be forgiven from such evil actions had yet to be explained. Different ways of responding were prescribed for each case. Above all, after Paul had introduced the salvation of the spirit on the day of the Lord Jesus (5:5), he insisted that the unrighteous could not inherit the kingdom of God (6:9–10). This implies that the righteous could inherit the kingdom of God—that is, salvation. The righteous were those who lived according to the Law, on which Paul had not yet revealed a negative perspective. This implies that Paul still had the Jewish concept of redemption in mind when writing 1Cor(2). It is, however, noteworthy that Paul introduced the concept of "being cleansed" as well as being holy and righteous in the name of the Lord Jesus Christ and by the Spirit of God (6:11). "Being cleansed" especially implies the status of being forgiven from sins. In other words, this implicitly refers to redemption. The Spirit is involved for the redemption of people for the first time. However, Paul had assigned no redemptive significance to the death of Christ yet in 1Cor(2).

Paul was also silent about redemption in 1Thess(2). Neither the term "sin" nor the concept of forgiveness appears. However, Paul started revealing his belief in the death of Christ in connection with the salvation of Gentile Christians. After mentioning the death of Jesus (1 Thess 4:14), Paul proclaimed that they could be saved by the Lord Jesus Christ, who died "for us" so that, whether awake or asleep, they might live together with him (5:9–10). This is the first case in which the death of Christ "for us" appears in connection with the salvation of Gentiles. Although Paul did not define the way of redemption yet, he was interested in the salvation, which was inseparable from the death of Christ. In other words, considering that salvation is impossible without redemption, the death of Christ is indirectly related with redemption of the Gentiles at the basic level. Although Paul began to show his concern about the death of Christ as the means of salvation, he still emphasized staying holy and blameless until the second coming of Jesus (3:13; 5:23). When he heard that the Thessalonians had refused the instruction of the outsider and recovered from the turmoil, Paul added "staying blameless" to "being holy" in 1Thess(2). However, Paul did not teach how to stay holy and blameless. Probably, they could be holy and blameless by observing the Law.

Paul showed interest in the redemption for the first time in 1Cor(3). The word "sin" was used three times, and the concept of forgiveness definitely appears. First of all, after Paul connected the cross of Christ with the theme of salvation (1 Cor 1:18), he identified Christ as the Passover lamb intended for sacrificial death (5:7) and defined the Corinthians as those bought at a price by him (7:23). Paul connected the death of Christ with the concept of redemption as follows: after proclaiming that whoever believes and keeps what he already proclaimed will be saved (15:2), Paul applied the phrase "for our sins" to the death of Christ (15:3). This indicates that Paul changed the sacrificial death of Christ "for us" into a redemptive death "for our sins" at last. Then, sin is contrasted with righteousness (15:34) and connected with death and the Law (15:56). There was no room for the Law to be the means of redemption and salvation in that Paul took a negative attitude toward it in 1Cor(3). After Paul had faced the serious challenge from the Corinthians, he began to introduce the death of Christ on the cross as a means of redemption instead of the Law. This implies that Paul distinguished himself from the apostles of the Jerusalem Church in terms of the way of redemption and salvation.

Paul continued expanding on the theme of redemption in Galatians. In the beginning, Paul stated that Jesus Christ gave himself "for our sins" to save the people from the present evil generation (Gal 1:4). By repeatedly mentioning the redemptive death of Christ, Paul added the idea of salvation from the present evil generation. Then Paul confessed that he lived by belief in the Son of God, who had given himself for him (2:20). Both of the above texts indicate that Jesus Christ, the Son of God, was not sacrificed compulsorily as a martyr; rather, he died voluntarily for the redemption and salvation of many people, including Paul himself. Finally, Paul taught that Christ was cursed on behalf of "us" by the death on the tree—that is, the wooden cross (3:13). This means that though Christ became a curse for the people, he redeemed them from the curse of the Law (3:13; 4:5; 5:24; 6:14). In other words, he bought them at a price from the curse of the Law—that is, the result of sin. This theological position finds coherency with Paul's negative attitude toward the Law in Galatians (3:19). Rather, Paul emphasized the redemptive death of Christ on the cross, and as a result, brought about a turning point in the gospel about the death of Christ. Paul continued teaching the redemption based on the death of Christ on the cross in Galatians. The serious challenge of the Galatians led Paul to reinforce his instruction that Jesus Christ died for people's sins on the cross.

Paul continued to deliver the theology of redemption later in 2Cor(2). In an attempt to recover the relationship with the Corinthians, he proclaimed that God was reconciling the world to himself in Christ, not counting peoples' sins against them (2 Cor 5:19). Paul connected redemption to reconciliation with God while mentioning sin. He also conveyed his theology of redemption to the Roman Church, emphasizing that sinners were given the grace of redemption in Rom(1) (Rom 4:24–25; 5:6–8), Rome(2) (3:24), and Rom(3) (6:6). The blood of Christ was introduced as the means of justification and salvation in Rom(1) (5:9). These letters are important because they were written near the end of Paul's life to a church that had not challenged him. It shows that Paul articulated his thinking on the redemption of the Gentiles through the death of Christ on the cross until the end of his missionary work.

Redemption was understood in light of the Bible. Paul had a biblical text for the description that Christ "died for our sins according to the Scriptures." In 1Cor(3), Paul for the first time interpreted the death of Jesus in connection with the Passover lamb written of in Exodus, then connected it with the redemptive death of the Suffering Servant of YHWH in Isaiah (1 Cor 5:7; 15:3). As a well-known figure, the Suffering Servant of YHWH is understood as a sacrificial and redemptive offering. Paul conveyed redemption in writing that Christ died "for our sins." Paul's perspective on the voluntary and redemptive death of Christ meant that he took a deeper approach than the First Christians, who saw the death of Christ simply according to the Scriptures. Although Paul neither quoted nor made clear references about Isa 53:10, he used this verse as a theological background in order to explain the redemptive death of Jesus on the cross. This became part of the gospel for Paul because it was regarded as a prophecy about the role of Jesus. Therefore, the death of Jesus Christ was suggested as the way to fulfill redemption.

Paul suggested the redemptive death of Christ on the cross as an alternative to the instruction of the Jerusalem apostles. Paul preferred the teachings of the First Christians over Q when speaking about redemption. When the relationship with the Jerusalem Church became strained, Paul reflected Q's influence less frequently in his writings. He began to teach instead that Jesus was not killed, but rather that he died on the cross "for our sins" in 1Cor(3) and Galatians. In this respect, the Pauline gospel is distinguished from the instruction of the Jerusalem apostles. As a result, contrary to their teaching, Paul taught that the Gentiles did not have to be circumcised nor observe the Law to be redeemed from their sins.

Paul's theology about redemption was his breakthrough. In other words, Paul created Christianity while being completely independent from the Jerusalem apostles. This was a turning point in his missionary work. While Paul made new theological interpretations, his gospel about redemption based on the death of Christ developed and became the core doctrine of Christianity.

B. Mark

Mark changed the declarative statements of Paul into historical descriptions illustrating the redemptive role of Jesus Christ. To this end, Mark created many events emphasizing the need for forgiveness from sin and attributing the redemptive role to Jesus. Mark especially added the Passion Narrative to Jesus' public life in teaching the theology of redemption.

Mark sometimes described the public ministry of Jesus Christ from a redemptive point of view. From the beginning, Mark dealt with the repentance through the mouth of John the Baptist (Mark 1:4). Repentance is necessary because it precedes the forgiveness of sins. Mark then mentioned the authority of Jesus, the Son of Man, to forgive sin (2:10). This is supposed to have been written in the background of Daniel, in which "the one like the Son of Man" was given authority from God (Dan 7:13–14).[1] Having inherited the title "Son of Man" from Q—which ultimately came from "the one like a Son of Man" in Daniel—Mark applied it to Jesus, who had the authority to forgive people of their sins. In addition, Jesus is depicted as the one who came to call the sinners rather than the righteous (Mark 2:17), and in this way, Mark showed the reason that Jesus came to the world. Therefore, it can be said that the forgiveness of sins is an important issue from the beginning of Mark. At the end of his public ministry, Jesus is identified as a guilt offering for many people (10:45) in what has generally been acknowledged as an indirect quotation from Isa 53:10. Mark described Jesus as the Servant of God, who gave himself as a sacrificial and redemptive offering for the people. This was the acme of Mark's description of Jesus' redemptive role during his public ministry.

Mark developed the redemptive role of Jesus Christ further in the Passion Narrative. Above all, according to Mark, at the Lord's Supper held on the Passover—that is, the first day of the Festival of Unleavened Bread—Jesus defined the cup of wine as his blood, which he would shed for many (Mark 14:24). In this respect, Jesus was connected with the Passover lamb that had been sacrificed on behalf of the firstborn sons. At this point, the phrase "for many" connects this saying with 10:45, which introduced Jesus as a guilt offering. In this way, the images of the Passover lamb and the Suffering Servant of YHWH are combined. In addition, Mark reported that Jesus decided to obey the will of God—that is, dying on the cross as a guilt offering—during his prayer at Gethsemane (14:38). Finally, Jesus was depicted as the one who died on the cross, shedding his blood for the redemption of people (15:21–41).

---

1. Marcus, *Mark 1–8*, 222–23.

It is important to observe that Mark described Jesus as a guilt offering for redemption, fulfilling the prophecy about the Suffering Servant of YHWH and Jesus' own prophecy about his death. This observation is further strengthened by the fact that Mark composed the Passion Narrative taking after Isa 52:13—53:12. Mark mostly collected or created the events that comprise the sufferings, including the three notices about the coming suffering, the cleansing of the temple in Jerusalem, the preaching about the end, the arrest and interrogation, and the execution on the cross. Jesus kept silent even though he suffered during his interrogation at the hands of Caiaphas, the high priest, and Pilate, the Roman governor. Jesus walked silently as he carried the cross toward Golgotha, the place of his death. Also, Jesus simply asked God for the reason for his abandonment, saying nothing else even though he was enduring extreme pain during the crucifixion. Eventually, Jesus died on the cross, showing that his death was a sacrificial and redemptive offering. As the story advances in Mark, Jesus is identified as the sacrificial and redemptive offering for many people. All these descriptions seem to have been invented by Mark in order to show that Jesus was fulfilling the prophecies of Isaiah about the Suffering Servant of YHWH. While Paul said that Christ died for our sins according to the Scriptures in 1Cor(3), Galatians, Rom(1), Rome(2), and Rom(3), Mark created the Passion Narrative based on the Pauline tradition. In this way, Mark preserved the perspective of redemption according to the Scriptures.

Mark wrote about how Jesus was handed over in order to emphasize Jesus' role as a ransom and a redemptive offering. For this purpose, he created the story of Judas Iscariot betraying Jesus to the chief priests for thirty pieces of silver (Mark 14:10–11). This seems to be based on the Pauline statement that Christ redeemed (was bought at a price) (1 Cor 6:20; 7:23; Gal 3:13; 4:5) and based on Q, which included Judas, son of James (Q^4 6:13–16). In other words, Mark substituted Judas, son of James, with Judas Iscariot among the twelve apostles and attributed the betrayal to him.[2] In fact, exactly how Jesus was handed over for death is uncertain. This is supported by the fact that it is not mentioned in Q or the Pauline epistles. Mark, however, historically wrote that Jesus was sold in order to redeem the people from their sins on the basis of Paul's declarative statements. In other words, Jesus was handed over by Judas Iscariot like a Passover lamb, and Jesus ultimately died as a redemptive offering on the cross like the Suffering Servant of YHWH. As a result, Mark described Jesus as the man who freed

---

2. The possibility that Mark substituted Judas, the son of James, with Judas Iscariot is supported by the Gospel of John. John introduced a Judas who was not Judas Iscariot (John 14:22). He was probably Judas, the son of James, who is listed in the names of the twelve apostles in Q.

the people from their sins. By these means, Mark confessed the redemption of Jesus as a historical event.

In conclusion, Mark described the death of Jesus Christ from a redemptive point of view. This is revealed in a series of sayings about the guilt offering, the blood of covenant at the Lord's Supper, obedience to the will of God at Gethsemane, and the events of the cross. Ultimately, Jesus became a sacrificial guilt offering when he drank the cup of death on the cross for many people. This is how Mark explained the sacrificial and redemptive role of Jesus as the one who fulfilled the prophecies about the Passover lamb and the Suffering Servant of YHWH.

C. Other Gospels

Matthew and Luke inherited the theology of redemption influenced by Mark. However, they show differences in the intensity of this influence. Moreover, John inherited it in a different way. The theology of redemption, the core of the gospel, was formed and developed according to the author's theological intention.

Matthew also presented Jesus Christ from a redemptive point of view. Above all, Matthew defined Jesus from the beginning as the one who would save his people from their sins (Matt 1:21). The fact that this saying appears only in Matthew implies that Jesus' redemptive role is a very important theme. Second, Matthew also inherited the teaching about Jesus' authority to forgive sin from Mark (9:2–6). It is noteworthy that Matthew assigned the authority of forgiving sins "to men [τοῖς ἀνθρώποις]," namely, the disciples of Jesus (9:8). This is unique to Matthew. Third, and most importantly, Matthew accepted the Markan theology of redemption by quoting Mark 10:45 in Matt 20:28 (Isa 53:10). As shown above, this identifies Jesus as the Suffering Servant of YHWH who played the role of guilt offering. Fourth, Matthew reinforced Jesus' role as the Suffering Servant of YHWH while citing other verses from Isaiah (Matt 8:17; 12:18–21; Isa 42:1–4; 53:4). Fifth, Matthew inherited most of the Passion Narrative written in Mark. Matthew strengthened Jesus' redemptive role by adding the phrase "for the forgiveness of sins" to the bread at the Lord's Supper (Matt 26:28). This treats the Lord's Supper from a redemptive perspective and shows that Jesus came to save his people from their sins. Sixth, Matthew emphasized the redemptive death of Christ through his own accounts. For instance, Christ's the redemptive death is shown in the story of Jesus being handed over to Governor Pilate by the Jews (27:25), who demanded the execution of Jesus and shouted that his blood would be on them and their children. Here, Matthew taught that people who believed in Jesus would be forgiven their sins, and those who did not believe in him would pay for his death. Through this story, Matthew suggests the reason for the destruction of Galilee and Judea—and especially the Jerusalem temple—by the Roman Empire in 65–70 CE, implying that it was because they had handed Jesus over to death. Matthew is the only Gospel that conveys the theology of redemption through such descriptions by adding sources like these to Mark.

John succeeded the theology of redemption at the end of the first century CE. This is shown when John called Jesus the Lamb of God who takes away the sin of the world (John 1:29). The description about the lamb is based on Isa 53:7–8. In other words, the Suffering Servant of YHWH symbolized the lamb as an offering that did not open his mouth in protest even as he was led to slaughter to be punished for the transgressions of the people. This is the image Jesus bore as the lamb, the sacrificial and redemptive offering. John, however, does not quote Mark 10:45 (Isa 53:10). Still, John writes that Jesus was arrested and handed over to death during the Passover Festival (John 13:1; 18:39). This is the result of John inheriting more than just the tradition of Paul, who defined Christ as the Passover lamb and implicitly as the Suffering Servant of YHWH (1 Cor 5:7; 15:3), which was more definitely followed by Mark. In this sense, John also portrayed Jesus as a sacrificial and redemptive offering mixed with the Passover lamb and the Suffering Servant of YHWH. John succeeded Paul and Mark in the perspective of redemption; however, John described it differently. In this way, John used the hermeneutic principle of "according to the Scriptures" based on his own theological interpretation.

The author of the Lucan documents conveyed the teaching on redemption at the beginning of the second century CE. Although he accepted the theology of redemption, he taught it in his own way. For instance, Luke neither quoted Mark 10:45 (Isa 53:10) nor described the death of Jesus as redemptive. Although Luke cited Isa 53:12, it is not relevant to the theme of redemption (Luke 22:37). In addition, Acts quoted Isa 53:7–8 but did not mention Isa 53:10 in the story of the Ethiopian Eunuch (Acts 8:32–35). In this respect, Luke weakened the theology of redemption in the context of the Suffering Servant of YHWH. On the other hand, Luke introduced his own stories about repentance and forgiveness of sins. First of all, the forgiveness of sins is suggested as the precondition for salvation through the mouth of Zechariah, the father of John the Baptist (Luke 1:77). Luke then asked the repentant not to be greedy for material possessions as the fruits worthy of repentance (3:8–14). In addition, confessing that he was a sinner, Peter left everything behind and followed Jesus (5:8–11). Moreover, having inherited the Markan tradition, Luke also mentioned Jesus' authority to forgive sins on earth (5:24). Furthermore, Luke changed the Markan story about a woman who had poured expensive perfume upon the head of Jesus at Bethany into a story about a woman being forgiven her sins (7:36–50). Finally, Zacchaeus was identified as a sinner, and he promised to distribute half of his possessions to the poor (19:1–10). Using material possessions correctly is a sign of repentance and being forgiven, according to Luke. Although Jesus was depicted as a mediator who asked God to forgive people on the cross because they did not know what they had done, his mediatory role is not directly related with their sin (23:34). In this way, Luke identified Jesus as an arbitrator rather than a guilt offering. Significantly, Jesus' redemptive role was weakened by Luke. Instead, Luke emphasized the voluntary distribution of people's material possessions to the poor as the means of repentance and forgiveness at the beginning of the second century CE.

D. Other Documents

The theology of redemption was conveyed through most of the documents of the Christian Scripture written at the end of the first century CE. However, they expressed it in different ways. As a result, the instruction about the theology of redemption developed in diverse ways on the basis of previous traditions.

The Deuteropauline epistles also mention redemption, having inherited Paul's ideas on the subject. In Ephesians, it is written that we are blessed with redemption and the forgiveness of sins through the blood of Christ (Eph 1:7; cf. 1:14; 2:13). This seems to have been passed down from Paul in Rom(1) (Rom 5:9). It is also written that Christ gave himself up for the people as a fragrant offering and sacrifice (Eph 5:2). Through the forgiveness of sins and the sacrificial death of Christ, Ephesians implies the redemptive death of Christ on the cross. Colossians states that people find redemption and forgiveness from sins in the Son of God (Col 1:14). What is unique is that this connects redemption with the resurrection (2:13). This also reminds readers of Paul, who used the resurrection in connection with the people's redemption in 1Cor(1) (1 Cor 6:14, 20). In addition, 1 Timothy also explains that Christ Jesus came into the world to save sinners (1 Tim 1:15). While doing so, he gave himself as a ransom for all people (2:6). Doubtlessly, this inheritance of Paul's theology of redemption started from 1Cor(3) (1 Cor 15:3). Finally, Titus teaches as well that Jesus gave himself for the people to redeem them from lawlessness (Tit 2:14). This also reflects Paul's argument that Jesus came to the world to redeem those who were under the Law in Galatians (Gal 4:4-5). Such descriptions reflect a redemption based on the forgiveness of sins, which Paul tended to emphasize in Christ's blood on the cross.

Hebrews follows the theology of redemption, though it was written from a different perspective than those mentioned above. Jesus is defined as the high priest, and it is written that he had to offer sacrifices for his own sins as well as for the sins of the people (Heb 5:3). Unlike the other high priests, he does not need to offer sacrifices day after day; he sacrificed for their sins once and for all when he offered himself (7:27). He became the blood-shedding offering for redemption by giving himself, unblemished, to God (9:12, 14–15, 26–28). It seems that Hebrews adopted the image of the guilt offerings sacrificed at the temple (Lev 5:6) rather than the Suffering Servant of YHWH. For this reason, people who believe in Christ would be made holy through the sacrifice of his body (Heb 10:10, 12). Moreover, he has made perfect forever those who are being made holy (10:14). This was the joy resulting from Jesus enduring the cross and scorning its shame (12:2). The descriptions written above show that Hebrews declaratively described a view of redemption that sees the death of Christ as a sacrificial offering. However, it also shows a different theological interpretation from Paul and Mark, who made interpretations based on the Suffering Servant of YHWH while connecting his death with the sacrificial, redemptive offering. This is how Hebrews used the principle of "according to the Scriptures" to reveal the meaning of redemption in connection with the death of Christ according to Hebrews' own theological interpretation.

The theology of redemption is also described in 1 Peter, which focuses on the blood of Christ. At the beginning, it mentioned the sparkling of the blood of Jesus Christ (1 Pet 1:2). The sparkling of blood reminds readers of the guilt offering written in Lev 5:9 and 7:2. It is written that the people were redeemed with the precious blood of Christ, a lamb without blemish or defect (1 Pet 1:18–19). The redemptive power of the blood of Christ reminds readers of Rom 5:9, and the lamb seems to reflect the connection with the Johannine document (John 1:29; Rev 5:6–8, etc.). Especially, the blood of the unblemished Christ reminds readers of Hebrews (Heb 9:14–15). Furthermore, it is testified that Christ himself bore the sins of the people on the wood—that is, the cross—so that people might die to sin (1 Pet 2:24). This reminds readers of Paul's statement about the death of Christ on the cross in Galatians, which is the acme of his theology of redemption (Gal 3:13). It is also written that Christ died once for sins, the righteous for the unrighteous, so that the people would be led to God (1 Pet 3:18). It seems to be an expression for the redemption and salvation of the people. In this respect, 1 Peter also seems to inherit both the previous and contemporaneous traditions.

Other Johannine documents also deal with the theology of redemption using various traditions. Revelation described that the blood of Jesus Christ freed the people from their sins (Rev 1:5). Revelation substituted the death of Christ with his blood for the cleansing of sins. The emphasis on the blood of Christ started with Paul in Rom(1) (Rom 5:9), and it was passed down to Ephesians, Hebrews, and 1 Peter. In this respect, as time passed, the blood of Christ gained more attention as the means of redemption. In addition, Revelation described that Jesus Christ bought the people for a price and dedicated them to God by his death (Rev 5:9; 14:3–4). This reminds readers of the Pauline concept of redemption (1 Cor 6:20; 7:23; Gal 3:13; 4:5).[3] In this case, however, Revelation drew on all the traditions used by the contemporaneous authors. First John conveys the theology of redemption from a perspective of atonement. It proclaims, "the blood of Jesus, his Son, purifies us from all sin" and emphasizes repentance from sin (1 John 1:7). The emphasis on the blood of Christ was predominantly used at the turn from the first to the second century CE. Moreover, it is proclaimed in 1 John that Jesus is "the atoning sacrifice [ἱλασμός] for our sins" (2:2). What is more important is the proclamation that God loved the people and sent the Son as an atoning sacrifice for their sins (4:10). The concept of atonement is emphasized in 1 John. This reflects the theology of Paul, which presented Jesus Christ as a sacrifice of atonement (ἱλαστήριον) in Rom(2) (Rom 3:25). The theology of redemption was inherited from Paul and developed until the beginning of the second century CE.

E. Conclusion

The redemptive power of the death of Jesus Christ is a core teaching among Christian doctrine. Even though the death of Jesus is a historical fact, its theological interpretations and meanings are all different. Christians are those who believe the interpretation that Jesus Christ died "for our sins according to the Scriptures." The theology of redemption developed as time passed. First, Q does not mention the redemption of Jesus' death at all. The First Christians then taught the death of Christ in the background of the Scriptures, though they did not do so from a redemptive point of view. Beyond teaching the interpretation that Christ is the Passover lamb as a sacrificial offering, Paul began to imply that Christ died for the sins of the people under the light of the prophecy of Isaiah about the Suffering Servant of YHWH in 1Cor(3) and Galatians. Paul's perspective on redemption resulted from his theological considerations after the challenge by Gentile Christians

---

3. Shin, "Die paulinischen Auswirkungen," 827–28.

sponsored by the apostles of the Jerusalem Church. In this sense, Paul was the first to convey the doctrine of redemption based on the death of Christ. Mark inherited the Pauline theology of redemption and imposed it upon the historical stories of Jesus' suffering and death. Matthew defined the role of Jesus from the beginning as the one who would save his people from their sins, and John taught the theology of redemption using John the Baptist's definition of Jesus as the Lamb of God who takes away the sins of this world. In Hebrews, the theology of redemption was succeeded by the description of the high priest who gave himself for the forgiveness of sins; however, this is totally different from that of the previous documents. At the turn of the first to the second century CE, the blood of Christ was emphasized as the means of redemption in Ephesus, Hebrews, 1 Peter, Revelation, and 1 John. By contrast, Luke weakened the redemptive aspects of Jesus' suffering and death; rather, he emphasized the voluntary distribution of Christans' material possessions as the sign of repentance and forgiveness during his ministry. Through this process, the gospel about the redemptive death of Jesus Christ developed diversely according to the author's theological perspective in the Christian writings during the first hundred years of Christianity.

15

The Lord's Supper

THE LORD'S SUPPER HAS been interpreted differently according to the various authors. Paul alleged that he had received it from the Lord Jesus and interpreted it theologically. The two versions that Paul provided show how he interpreted it in different situations. Later, the authors of the Gospels took the tradition about the Lord's Supper from Paul and applied the theology of redemption to it according to their theological point of view. While Mark tried to impose the meaning of redemption upon the cup of the covenant, Matthew definitely strengthened the meaning of redemption for the Lord's Supper. On the other hand, Luke merely portrayed the Lord's Supper from a festive point of view. On the contrary, John reduced its historical aspect and interpreted it from a metaphoric perspective. The rest of the authors of the Christian Scriptures did not pay attention to it. In this way, each author dealt with it according to their own perspective, and the Lord's Supper finally became an important event in Christianity.

A. The Pauline Epistles

Paul emphasized different meanings in his understanding of the Lord's Supper as situations changed. He mentioned the Lord's Supper twice, each with a different intention. First, Paul dealt with the Lord's Supper in order to build a community around Jesus Christ and avoid idols; later, he used it as a way to resolve conflicts among the Corinthians. Thus, Paul seemed to impose different theological meanings to the Lord's Supper in response to the changed circumstances.

Paul covered the Lord's Supper as a ceremony in order to avoid idolatry and to solidify the Christian community in 1Cor(1). The idolatry was a critical issue at the beginning of Paul's missionary journey, for it is also reflected in 1Thess(1) (1 Thess 1:9). Paul forbade idolatry because the Christians were participating in the blood and body of Christ by partaking of the bread and cup at the Lord's Supper—that is, the Lord's Table in 1Cor(1) (1 Cor 10:14–21). If they were also to eat sacrifices made to idols, they would be participants with demons. In this, Paul emphasized becoming one with Christ through the bread and cup in order to build a community of faith around Christ. Paul interpreted the participation in the cup and bread, which symbolized the blood and body of Christ, from a socio-religious perspective. It seems that Paul intended a specific supper when he mentioned the bread and cup. In other words, it appears there was a supper Paul used as a model. However, he did not mention when and where that supper was held. He simply mentioned the body and blood of Christ and emphasized the theological meaning more than the historical event. Although Paul did not clarify the status of the Lord, it seems that it stood for Christ (10:16). In this way, Paul focused on the lordship of Christ at the Supper.

Paul added the Lord's Supper to the gospel in 1Cor(1) by describing the cup and bread in relation to the event when the Israelites ate the spiritual food and drank the spiritual drink in the wilderness (1 Cor 10:3–6). Paul especially interpreted that the rock they drank from was Christ. As a result, the spiritual food and drink became the model for the bread and cup symbolizing the body and blood of Christ. In this sense, the wilderness event became part of the gospel for Paul, as it was a prophecy about the Lord's Supper. Of course, such connections were the result of Paul's theological interpretation. In this respect, Paul taught the Corinthians to avoid idolatry on account of the gospel.

Paul mentioned the Lord's Supper for a second time in 1Cor(2). He introduced it to resolve conflict among the Corinthians by reminding them of the Lord's death (1 Cor 11:18–29). First, Paul asserted that he received the tradition about the bread and cup from the Lord Jesus (11:23). However, he did not explain in detail how it was passed down to him from Jesus. Moreover, considering that the Supper was not mentioned in Q, it seems that Paul did not hear about this directly from Jesus. In spite of the fact that Paul was not able to meet the historical Jesus, he faced certain circumstances requiring the emphasis of his relationship with Jesus more than the Christ when he wrote about the Lord's Supper in 1Cor(2). It can be deduced from the description that Cephas Peter had visited the Corinthian Church and baptized some members during his stay there; however, his visit and baptisms only left division and quarrels among the Corinthians. Paul also mentioned the division and conflict among the parties that resulted from the table fellowship. In this circumstance, Paul needed to show the Corinthians that his intimacy with the historical Jesus was not less than Peter's. Thus, it was likely that Paul suggested the Lord's Supper as a means of resolving the division and conflict, emphasizing that he had received it from the Lord Jesus. In 1Cor(1), the Lord's Supper was described as a way of avoiding idolatry in the eyes of people outside the church; on the other hand, in 1Cor(2), it was used as a way of resolving conflict within the church.

Second, Paul mentioned the time the Supper was held. It was on the night the Lord Jesus was arrested (1 Cor 11:23). Thus, it can be termed the Lord's Supper. However, Paul did not mention the exact time. Moreover, it should be noted that the mutton, essential to the Passover supper, was not mentioned. The Passover lamb was the symbol of sacrifice on behalf of the first-born sons in Egypt (Exod 12:1–14). Therefore, it seems that the Lord's Supper was the dinner of the night Jesus expected to be arrested. It could also have been a regular dinner, but as he was suddenly arrested that night, the person who passed the story on to others might have said it was the supper the Lord held on the night he was arrested. As a result, Paul interpreted the supper as the Lord's Supper—not of Christ but of the Lord Jesus—without mentioning the exact time when it was held.

Third, Paul taught that Jesus gave special meaning to the elements while taking charge of the supper (1 Cor 11:24–25). According to Paul, after breaking the bread and giving it to his disciples, Jesus said, "This is my body, which is for you; do this in remembrance of me." Paul probably added the phrase "for you" to the primitive tradition. This is supported by the fact that the phrase does not appear in the first description of the bread in 1Cor(1).[1] By adding it, Paul tried to connect the tradition of the Lord's Supper with the story of Christ's death passed down from the First Christians. In this way, Paul once again emphasized the sacrificial death of the Lord Jesus.[2] In addition, Paul wrote that Jesus gave a special meaning to the cup when he said, "This cup is the new covenant in my blood; do this." This reminds readers of Jeremiah's prophecy about the new covenant (Jer 31:31–34). At the same time, it has to be noted that the declaration appears after the wine is mentioned (31:29–30). Thus, Paul thought of this prophetic declaration as part of the gospel about the cup of the new covenant. Then, Christians'

---

1. Barrett, *Commentary*, 267. It is a possibility that Jesus said the bread was his body during the Supper.

2. Cf. Mack, *Who Wrote*, 87–91.

participation in the cup of the new covenant means that they became the people of God.[3] Paul applied the ritual service, the Lord's Supper, to the Gentiles, so that they could be the people of God as Jeremiah had prophesied. In this way, Paul connected the Lord's Supper with the gospel in terms of the new covenant. This is somewhat different from Paul's previous interpretation in that the Lord's Supper was understood in the background of the spiritual food, drink, and the rock in 1Cor(1). Paul's theological interpretation changed and developed as time passed and circumstance changed.

Fourth, Paul added an interpretation about the Lord's Supper that is unique to him: the participants in the Lord's Supper must proclaim the death of Jesus until he comes (1 Cor 11:26). In detail, since the Lord Jesus attributed the phrase "my body for you" to the bread and "the new covenant in my blood" to the cup, Paul understood them to refer to the sacrificial death of Jesus. In addition, Paul encouraged the Corinthians who participated in the Lord's Supper to proclaim his sacrificial death on behalf of humanity and practice the sacrificial life in order to be called the people of God. Paul taught the Corinthians to sacrifice themselves as the Lord Jesus had so that they could reconcile with each other and restore unity as the people of God, rising above the conflict among them. In interpreting that the Lord Jesus died for the Corinthians on the cross in his description of the Lord's Supper, Paul tried to remedy the tension among them. In this way, Paul added a new theological interpretation to a previous tradition in terms of sacrifice and the people of God. This is substantially different from Paul's previous teaching that the Lord's Supper cannot coincide with the idolatry in 1Cor(1).

Fifth, Paul explained how to participate in the Lord's Supper. He wrote that everyone ought to examine his or her conscience before eating the bread and drinking from the cup (1 Cor 11:27–29). Paul said, "Whoever eats the bread or drinks the cup of the Lord in an unworthy manner will be guilty of sinning against the body and blood of the Lord." This statement is significant due to its relationship to guilt, though Paul had not yet shown the theology of redemption regarding the death of Christ embedded in the Lord's Supper. Since the Lord's Supper is not a method of cleansing sin, Paul urged the Corinthians not to be guilty by allowing division among themselves before they participated in the Lord's Supper. This is how Paul added a fresh interpretation to the Lord's Supper in 1Cor(2), adjusting its relationship with the gospel according to the changing situation.

In conclusion, Paul used the Lord's Supper in two different ways in 1Cor(1) and 1Cor(2). While the former described the Lord's Supper as a way of avoiding idolatry, the latter applied it to resolving conflict within the

---

3. Barrett, *Commentary*, 269.

Corinthian Church. While the Exodus event served as background for the former, the prophecy of Jeremiah was the context for the latter. Both became part of the gospel according to Paul's view. This shows that Paul used the Lord's Supper to cope with changing situations.

B. Mark

Mark inherited the tradition about the Lord's Supper from Paul, and yet he conveyed his own theology by changing many elements. In doing so, Mark described the Supper as a historical event. Most importantly, Mark indirectly explained the redemptive death of Jesus Christ in connection with the cup of covenant.

Mark uniquely connected the Lord's Supper to the Passover after receiving Paul's tradition. Mark combined the tradition that the Lord Jesus gave bread and a cup to his disciples at the supper on the night of arrest in 1Cor(2) with the tradition that Jesus Christ is the Passover lamb in 1Cor(3). Although Paul taught that the Lord's Supper was held on the night the Lord Jesus was arrested, he did not mention the time in detail. This supper could have been a common meal held at anytime because mutton, the most important food of the Passover meal, did not appear. There also does not seem to be any connection between Jesus saying that the bread was his body and describing Christ as the Passover lamb. However, Mark combined both traditions and wrote that Jesus was arrested on the night of the Passover, the first day of the Festival of Unleavened Bread (Mark 14:12–26). In this way, Jesus was identified as the Passover lamb. As a result, the day of Jesus' arrest was described as the day the Passover began, and the Lord's Supper was explained as a Passover dinner. Mark should be credited with a unique achievement in combining the Lord's Supper and the Passover.

Mark connected the Lord's Supper to the death of Jesus Christ, just as Paul had. While Paul connected the Lord's Supper with the proclamation of his death in 1Cor(2), Mark revealed the relationship through a series of stories. Having mentioned the cup of death that Jesus would drink from and identified him as a guilt offering for many people, Mark defined the cup of wine as the blood that he would shed for the people (Mark 10:38–39, 45; 14:24). Mark explained that Jesus mentioned the cup of death again in the prayer at Gethsemane and died on the cross shedding blood as the guilt offering (14:34–36; 15:21–41). Thus, the wine (the cup of covenant) was connected to the blood Jesus shed on the cross as the guilt offering for many people. In conclusion, Mark taught that the Lord's Supper was a symbolic ritual leading Jesus to the sacrificial and redemptive death on the cross.

Mark further developed Paul's tradition about various elements of the Lord's Supper. This is revealed by the differences in the descriptions between 1Cor(2) and Mark. First, the descriptions about the role of the bread and cup are different. While Paul proclaimed, "This is my body, which is for you," in reference to the bread, Mark simply wrote, "This is my body." Also, while Paul emphasized that the cup was the new covenant in his blood, Mark's account emphasized, "This is my blood of the covenant, which is poured out for many." What is important here is the fact that the term "for" was applied differently. Paul applied this to the bread symbolizing the body of Jesus, while Mark applied it to the cup symbolizing the blood of Jesus. Mark focused on the death of Jesus and the shedding of blood as a means of redemption for many people. As a result, while Paul conveyed the sacrificial death of Jesus through the interpretation "for you" in 1Cor(2) and showed Jesus' redemptive death through the interpretation "for our sins" in 1Cor(3) and Galatians, Mark later inherited both of Paul's interpretations and applied them to the cup of covenant to describe the death of Jesus as a guilt offering. In this manner, Mark interpreted Jesus' death as redemptive, beyond the meaning of sacrifice. In conclusion, Mark changed Paul's interpretation of the Lord's Supper from a perspective of sacrificial offering to one that showed Jesus' death as the means of redemption.

Second, Mark's understanding of the covenant was different. While Paul emphasized the blood of the new covenant, Mark simply mentioned the blood of the covenant. Paul referenced Jer 31:29–33 as part of the gospel about the new covenant and connected this to the wine cup, which symbolized the blood in 1Cor(2). Mark, on the other hand, excluded the reference to the new covenant, choosing simply to talk about the covenant: "Jesus Christ truly said, 'I will not drink again of the fruit of the vine until that day when I drink it anew in the kingdom of God'" (Mark 14:25). Drinking from the cup of the covenant referred to the disciples of Jesus' decision not to drink of it any more on earth until they drink anew in the kingdom. In other words, the disciples are those who are willing to participate in death along with Jesus and who expect to drink at the Messianic feast in the kingdom of God. Although Jesus would not be with them in the world anymore, they were promised to partake in the Messianic feast in future.[4] While Paul put an emphasis on becoming God's people with the term "new covenant," Mark focused on participation in the death of Jesus with the term "covenant" and reunion at the Messianic feast. According to Mark, participation in Jesus' death is the key to believing the gospel that is the teaching from

---

4. Cf. Robbins, "Last Meal," 37.

Jesus Christ's life. As a result, it is important to observe that Jesus Christ is described as the Son of God who gave his own covenant to the disciples.

Third, the beneficiary of the Lord's Supper also changed. While Paul referred to specific people using the expression "for you" in 1Cor(2), Mark referred to random people through the expression "for many" (Mark 14:24). Paul portrayed the Lord's Supper as a secret ceremony Jesus conducted for only a limited number of people, but Mark expanded it into a typical ceremony that was held for many people. Therefore, Mark connected this to the description of "as a ransom for many" (10:45). In doing so, Mark enthroned Jesus as the Savior of all people, not only the disciples who were at the Lord's Supper. In this way, Mark made the Lord's Supper a part of the life of Jesus that carried its own instruction; thus, the Lord's Supper became a part of the gospel.

Fourth, Mark and Paul had different perspectives on the time for commemorating the Lord's Supper. According to Paul, it should be conducted continuously, as people proclaimed the Lord's death until he comes. Mark, on the other hand, wrote that the Lord's Supper was a singular event, describing it as if it would not be conducted again in this world until Christians drank the wine anew in the kingdom of God. In this sense, Mark omitted the expression of Paul, who wrote "in remembrance of me." Mark presented the meaning of the Lord's Supper as a historical event given as a model for many people. In other words, Mark taught that the disciples should participate in the sacrificial death of Jesus by taking the Lord's Supper only once in their lives. Considering that laying down one's life for Jesus is related to the gospel (Mark 8:35; 10:29), participating in the Lord's Supper (laying one's life down with Jesus) is also related to the gospel. In this respect, the Lord's Supper, as part of the life of Jesus, became a part of the gospel in Mark. In this way, Mark enhanced the meaning of the gospel about the Lord's Supper.

C. Other Gospels

Matthew, Luke, and John portrayed the Lord's Supper using Mark's descriptions as a source. While Matthew reflected redemption according to the description of Mark, Luke weakened this aspect of the Lord's Supper. On the contrary, John only delivered the metaphoric meaning. Such differences were the result of each author's theological interpretations.

Matthew conveyed the theology of redemption more directly than Mark when describing the Lord's Supper. This is revealed through the phrase "This is my blood of the covenant, which is poured out for many for the forgiveness of sins" (Matt 26:26–29). The phrase "for the forgiveness of sins" does not appear in Mark. Matthew reflected more of the sacrificial meaning Paul had given to the cup as the blood of the new covenant, and Matthew further developed the indirect meaning of redemption given by Mark. Matthew also defined Jesus as the Savior through the Lord's Supper. This was revealed in Matthew's discussion of the theology of redemption, which gave the wine cup the meaning of forgiveness of sin. Therefore, Matthew referred to the proclamation that Jesus came to the world to save his people from their sins (1:21). Matthew taught that not only the disciples of the community but also the Gentiles who would become the objects of their missionary work could participate in the Lord's Supper and enjoy redemption. Following Mark, Matthew understood the cup of wine in the context of the kingdom of God the Father. In this respect, Matthew seems to have regarded the Lord's Supper as part of the gospel. This was Matthew's own theological interpretation and showed the gradual adoption of the Lord's Supper as an element of the gospel.

Luke described the Lord's Supper from a different perspective than both Mark and Matthew did (Luke 22:14-20). First, Luke emphasized the Lord's Supper in relation to the Passover in his description of Jesus saying he eagerly desired to eat the Passover and that he would not eat it again until it found fulfillment in the kingdom of God. Luke compared the Passover coming to this world to the coming of the kingdom of God. The reason he emphasized the Passover was because it symbolized liberation and salvation. Luke emphasized that Lord's Supper would be held on the Passover in the kingdom. Luke's author taught people to yearn for the spiritual liberation and salvation they would earn in the kingdom of God. In this way, the Lord's Supper is related to the gospel about the kingdom of God according to Luke. Second, Luke conveyed the meaning of sacrifice through the bread and the cup. Luke followed the description of Paul when he wrote, "This is my body given for you; do this in remembrance of me," and combined Paul and Mark's descriptions when he wrote, "This cup is the new covenant in my blood, which is poured out for you." Luke emphasized that both the bread and the cup were "for you," making the sacrifice of Jesus prominent. However, the author did not think that Jesus fulfilled the image of the Suffering Servant of YHWH, the redemptive offering. Third, Luke gave a festive meaning to the Lord's Supper, which is seen in the double description of the cup of wine, unlike in Mark and Matthew. This is connected to the frequent mention of feasts in Luke. The author described that Jesus often spoke about food and drink while giving feasts (7:34; 14:15; 15:3-10; 22:29-30, etc.). In this sense, Luke saw the Lord's Supper from the perspective of the feast enjoyed in the kingdom of God while emphasizing food and drink. Luke gave the Lord's

Supper as an example of the festive table. This was Luke's interpretation in connection with the Lord's Supper, developed in his own way.

John describes the Lord's Supper in a completely different way from the Synoptic Gospels, removing the liturgical aspect and emphasizing its metaphoric meaning (John 6:52–59). According to John, Jesus compared his flesh to the bread of life, and then the Jews quarreled about his teaching. Responding to their debate, Jesus identified himself with the Son of God and asked them to take his flesh and blood so that they might receive eternal life in the end of the world. In addition, Jesus said that his flesh was true food and his blood was true drink, promising that he would be among those who eat and that they would be with him. John removed the liturgical elements of the Supper but strengthened the metaphoric teaching about Jesus' flesh and blood.

D. Conclusion

The Lord's Supper has been interpreted in various ways. As time passed, each author understood it differently. The many interpretations about the Lord's Supper also show that the contents of the gospel developed in different ways within Christianity during the first century CE. Above all, Paul thought of the Lord's Supper as important. He considered even the smallest tradition about the Supper as essential even though he had inherited almost nothing from the Lord Jesus. Consequently, Paul made different interpretations about the meaning of the Lord's Supper according to the time and situation. While Paul presented the Lord's Supper in order to build a community based on Christ and to teach rejection of idolatry, he later presented it as a ceremony that fulfilled the new covenant and the sacrifice of Jesus. Mark showed Jesus Christ as the guilt offering for many people and connected the Lord's Supper to the Passover meal. Mark presented the cup, which stood for the blood of the covenant in the Lord's Supper, for this purpose. In this way, Mark connected the blood Jesus shed when he died with redemption. Matthew reinforced the meaning of redemption in connection with sin. Later, Luke weakened it, reinforcing instead the Supper's festive significance, while John emphasized its metaphoric elements. Various meanings can be found for the Lord's Supper as the result of each author's theological interpretation. Such changes show how the content of the Lord's Supper was formed and developed according to each author's theological purpose in response to changing circumstances.

Epilogue

THE GOSPEL BEGAN WITH God. The good news God spread to his people through the prophets is part of the gospel. Jesus himself proclaimed the gospel around the late twenties or early thirties CE. In this sense, Jesus was understood to be a prophet. Later, in the beginning of the forties, the twelve apostles, or those under their supervision, put what Jesus had said and done in writing. This document, known as Q, is believed to be a record of the words and actions of Jesus that the disciples wanted to leave to the coming generations. Jesus became one of those who spread the wisdom and prophecies of God as a wise teacher and prophet.

Paul inherited the gospel about Christ from the First Christians after receiving a revelation of the Son of God around the mid-thirties CE. This was based on four aspects of Christ: his death, burial, resurrection, and epiphany. Then Paul visited Cephas Peter, from whom he learned about the teachings of Jesus and from whom he probably heard about the first three redactions of Q. However, Paul did not embrace these teachings completely in his later epistles. Instead, Paul selectively combined the two traditions about Jesus and Christ.

Paul developed these perspectives on the gospel based on the principle "according to the Scriptures," an idea he inherited from the First Christians. As a result, he saw the prophecies about Jesus Christ as part of the gospel, explicitly stated in Rom 1:2–3 in the late fifties CE. This is why Paul connected many verses of the Bible with Christ. While doing so, he expanded the range of the gospel after the event at Antioch, at which point he turned his back on the apostles of the Jerusalem Church. The core of that gospel was the redemptive death of Jesus Christ on the cross (1 Cor 15:3; Gal 3:13), which he confessed based on Isa 53:10. In this sense, Paul was the theologian who creatively reinterpreted the sacrificial death of Jesus Christ as redemptive.

After 70 CE, the Gospel writers understood the gospel in connection with previous traditions. Mark saw the life of Jesus Christ itself as the gospel and made theological interpretations by describing it accordingly. Consequently, the declaratory confessions changed into descriptive ones, and Jesus Christ's life was proclaimed as the gospel. For this purpose, following Paul's theology of redemption, Mark described the life of Jesus Christ using the Suffering Servant of YHWH prophesied by Isaiah as a model. Mark completed the life of Jesus Christ by adding the Passion Narrative—based on the four elements conveyed by the First Christians—to the biographic descriptions of Jesus presented in Q. At that time, Mark added the redemption taught by Paul and wrote a Gospel. As a result, Jesus Christ was confessed as the one who died as a sacrificial and redemptive offering for the salvation of many. In this sense, the romantic descriptions about Jesus Christ became a unique form of literature known as "Gospel" that taught redemption. Later, Matthew, Luke, John, and many others continued to describe Jesus Christ based on their own theological interpretations. The Gospels were developed up to the second century CE, including not only those in the Christian Scripture, but also those that were excluded (e.g., *The Gospel of Thomas*). The authors saw Jesus Christ's words about the kingdom of God as part of the gospel. In this respect, I have argued that the Christian gospel is composed of historical events from Jesus' life and his followers' theological interpretations of Christ.

The Spirit worked within the writers who confessed Jesus, the Son of God, as Christ the Savior, whether declaratively or descriptively. This is the movement of the Holy Spirit and revelation as it is commonly understood. This was fulfilled not only through the prophets of the biblical era, but also through Paul and the twelve apostles of the Christian Scripture. In the same way, God, who is eternal, causes us to know his will as we meet and relate with him. This is the revelation and movement of the Holy Spirit today.

The revelation of God and the movement of the Holy Spirit do not simply fall from the sky. God worked by developing the sources and theology of previous times. Jesus' words and actions were recorded in Q, and the First Christians left the gospel about Christ while interpreting the Bible. Paul, who learned about Jesus and inherited faith in Christ from the First Christians, did not remain at that level of understanding but also confessed Jesus as the Christ. This was done through the inspiration of the Spirit of God. This process also occurred in the case of Mark, Matthew, and Luke. All the writers of the first century CE, in their own way, made theological interpretations according to inspiration from previous sources. As a result, different descriptions have been written about the same events. These differences are not wrong; rather, they are theological interpretations and spiritual confessions about Jesus Christ from different perspectives.

True Christians are those who make theological interpretations and spiritual confessions about the work of God, particularly judging their own lives in view of Jesus Christ's example. This was shown by the disciples of the first century CE. In that process, the Spirit of God has worked and continues to work. The Spirit has worked through many priests, monks, and theologians over the past two thousand years. They have made theological interpretations according to the movement of the Holy Spirit and the revelation of God. The Trinitarian doctrine that was formed throughout the second and fourth century is a typical example. This was a theological interpretation by Latin theologians who understood God, Jesus, and the Holy Spirit based on their own philosophy. Such interpretation and confession should be continued even today, so that at last we can say we have living faith. Throughout this process, Christianity has developed.

I would like to emphasize an important proposition that faith is confidence in what we heard from Christ and/or God (Rom 10:17). This was what the writers of the first century CE had in mind when they made theological interpretations about Jesus Christ, and Christians today must also make theological interpretation as well as spiritual confession. Christians are those who testify about what they hope and see with their spiritual eyes beyond the level of historical fact. Of course, they should do so under the guidance of the Spirit of God, rather than simply their own will.

Those who live by the revelation of God must make theological interpretations and confessions about the God they meet in their lives. Those confessions must not simply be made with the words in the Bible, but instead should be their own based on the Bible—confessions that should be made today, in view of the Jesus Christ confessed in the Christian Scripture. This is the special grace and blessing of God given to those who relate to him. When a person can make such theological interpretations and spiritual confessions, then he or she is a true believer in God and a person who truly confesses Jesus as Christ the Savior. When that spiritual confession is written down, it becomes the word of God to that person.

Many people should make spiritual confessions. The work of God will become prosperous as many more people come to sympathize with it following such confessions. In this way, God is understood anew by the confession of the spiritually living community. People can find and confess God since he has special plans for each person and community. This kind of work should also be left in writing, and as it becomes the Word of God, we can proclaim that God is with us and live in joy.

The gospel lives even today, and Christians who believe in the gospel should also be alive in faith. The Spirit of God helps us see his work and make confessions about it even today. Only then can churches be spiritually alive and give life to society. If churches lose this power, they have no reason to exist. For this purpose, spiritual confessions must be kept alive. I sincerely hope that our spiritual lives continue.

Bibliography

Aalders, G. Charles. *Genesis*. Vol. 1. The Bible Student's Commentary 311S. Grand Rapids: Zondervan, 1981.

Allison, Dale C., Jr. "Divorce, Celibacy and Joseph (Matthew 1:18-25 and 19:1-12)." *JSNT* 49 (1993) 3-10.

———. "Eunuchs Because of the Kingdom of Heaven (Matt 19:12)." *TSF Bulletin* 8 (1984) 2-5.

———. *The Intertextual Jesus: Scripture in Q*. Harrisburg, PA: Trinity Press International, 2000.

———. *The Jesus Tradition in Q*. Harrisburg, PA: Trinity Press International, 1997.

Anderson, Gary A. "Celibacy or Consummation in the Garden? Reflection on Early Jewish and Christian Interpretations of the Garden of Eden." *HTR* 82 (1989) 121-48.

Arnal, William E. *Jesus and the Village Scribes: Galilean Conflicts and the Setting of Q*. Minneapolis: Fortress, 2001.

Barker, Margaret. *The Lost Paradise: The Book of Enoch and Its Influence on Christianity*. Nashville, TN: Abingdon, 1988.

Barrett, C. K. *A Commentary on the First Letter to the Corinthians*. Peabody: Hendrickson, 1987.

Beare, F. W. *A Commentary on the Epistle to the Philippians*. London: Adam & Charles Black, 1959.

Beker, Johan Christiaan. *Paul and the Apostle: The Triumph of God in Life and Thought*. Philadelphia: Fortress, 1980.

Best, Ernest. *The Temptation and the Passion: The Markan Soteriology*. 2nd ed. Society for New Testament Studies Manuscript Series 2. Cambridge: Cambridge University Press, 1990.

Brown, Jennie K. "Creation's Renewal in the Gospel of John." *CBQ* 72 (2010) 275-90.

Brown, Raymond Edward. *An Introduction to the New Testament*. New Haven: Yale University Press, 2010.

———. *The Gospel According to John I-XII: Introduction, Translation, and Notes*. Vol. 1. Garden City, NY: Doubleday, 1966.

Charlesworth, James H. *Jesus and the Dead Sea Scrolls*. Anchor Bible Reference Library. New York: Doubleday, 1992.

———, ed. *The Messiah: Development in Earliest Judaism and Christianity*. Minneapolis: Fortress, 1992.

Collins, John J. *The Apocalyptic Imagination*. New York: Crossroad, 1987.
———. "The Kingdom of God in Apocrypha and Pseudepigrapha." In *The Kingdom of God in Twentieth-century Interpretation*, edited by Wendell Willis, 81–95. Peabody: Hendrickson, 1987.
Conzelmann, Hans Dieter. *I Corinthians: A Commentary on the First Epistle to the Corinthians*. Hermeneia: A Critical and Historical Commentary on the Bible. Philadelphia: Fortress, 1975.
———. "On the Analysis of the Confessional Formula in I Corinthians 15:3–5." *Interpretation* 20 (1966) 15–25.
Crossan, John Dominic. *The Cross That Spoke: the Origins of the Passion Narrative*. San Francisco: Harper & Row, 1988.
Cullmann, Oscar. *Die Christologie des Neuen Testaments*. Tübingen, Germany: J. C. B. Mohr, 1957.
Dodd, C. H. *The Interpretation of the Fourth Gospel*. Cambridge: Cambridge University Press, 1953.
Dunn, James D. G. *Christology in the Making: A New Testament Inquiry into the Origins of the Doctrine of the Incarnation*. 2nd ed. London: SCM, 1989.
Eliade, Mircea. *From Gautama Buddha to the Triumph of Christianity*. Vol. 2 of *A History of Religious Ideas*. Translated by Willard R. Trask. Chicago: University of Chicago Press, 1982.
Fawcett, Thomas. *Hebrew Myth and Christian Gospel*. London: SCM, 1973.
Fleddermann, Harry T. "Mark's Use of Q: The Beelzebul Controversy and the Cross Saying." In *Jesus, Mark and Q: The Teaching of Jesus and Its Earliest Records*, edited by Micahel Labahn and Andreas Schmidt, 17–33. JSNTS 214. Sheffield: Sheffield Academic, 2001.
Furnish, Victor Paul. *II Corinthians: Translated with Introduction, Notes, and Commentary*. Anchor Bible 32A. Garden City, NY: Doubleday, 1984.
Garland, D. "The Composition and Unity of Philippians." *NovT* 27 (1985) 141–73.
Gnilka, Joachim. *Das Matthäusevangelium*. Vol. 1. HTKNT. Freiburg im Breisgau, Germany: Herder, 1988.
Hahn, Ferdinand. *Christologische Hoheitstitel: ihre Geschichte im frühen Christentum*. Forschungen zur Religion und Literatur des Alten und Neuen Testaments 83. Göttingen, Germany: Vandenhoech & Ruprecht, 1964.
Hamerton-Kelly, R. G. *Pre-existence, Wisdom, and the Son of Man: A Study of the Idea of Pre-existence in the New Testament*. SNTSMS 21. Cambridge: Cambridge University Press, 1973.
Hawthorne, Gerald F. *Philippians*. Revised by Ralph P. Martin. Rev. ed. WBC 43. Nashville, TN: Nelson, 2004.
Himmelfarb, Martha. *Ascent to Heaven in Jewish and Christian Apocalypses*. New York: Oxford University Press, 1993.
Hofius, Otfried. *Der Christushymnus Philipper 2,6–11*. Tübingen, Germany: J. C. B. Mohr, 1976.
Hooker, Morna Dorothy. *Jesus and the Servant: The Influence of the Servant Concept of Deutero Isaiah in the New Testament*. London: SPCK, 1959.
Humphrey, Edith M. "New Creation." *Dictionary for Theological Interpretation of the Bible*, 536–37. Grand Rapids: Baker, 2005.
Hurd, John C., Jr. *The Origin of I Corinthians*. London: SPCK, 1965.

Hurst, L. D. "Re-enter the Pre-existent Christ in Philippians 2.5–11?" *NTS* 32 (1986) 449–57.
Isaac, E. "1 Enoch." In vol. 1 of *Old Testament Pseudepigrapha*, edited by J. H. Charlesworth, 5–89. Garden City, NY: Doubleday, 1983.
Jacobson, Arland Dean. *The First Gospel: An Introduction to Q*. Sonoma, CA: Polebridge, 1992.
Jeremias, Joachim. *The Eucharistic Words of Jesus*. Translated by N. Perrin. New York: Scribner's, 1966.
———. *The Proclamation of Jesus*. Vol. 1 of *New Testament Theology*. London: SCM, 1971.
Keener, Craig S. *The Gospel of John: A Commentary*. 2 Vols. Peabody: Hendrickson, 2003.
Kim, Seyoon. *The Origin of Paul's Gospel*. Tübingen, Germany: J. B. C. Mohr, 1981.
Kloppenborg, John S. *The Formation of Q: Trajectories in Ancient Wisdom Collections*. Philadelphia: Fortress, 1987.
———. *Q, the Earliest Gospel: An Introduction to the Original Stories and Sayings of Jesus*. Louisville: Westminster John Knox, 1987.
Knibb, Michael A. "1 Enoch." In *The Apocryphal Old Testament*, edited by H. F. D. Sparks, 169–320. Oxford: Clarendon, 1984.
Koester, Helmut, and James M. Robinson. *Entwicklungslinien durch die Welt des Frühchristentums*. Tübingen, Germany: Mohr-Siebeck, 1971.
Lambrecht, J. "John the Baptist and Jesus in Mark 1.1–15: Markan Redaction of Q?" *NTS* 38 (1992) 357–84.
Lohr, C. H. "Oral Techniques in the Gospel of Matthew." *CBQ* 23 (1961) 403–35.
Luck, William F. *Divorce and Remarriage: Rediscovering the Biblical Law*. San Francisco: Harper & Row, 1987.
Lührmann, Dieter. *Redaktion der Logienquelle*. Neukirchen-Vluyn, Germany: Neukirchen, 1969.
Luz, Ulrich. *Das Evangelium nach Matthäus*. EKK. Zürich: Neukirchen, 1990.
Mack, Burton L. *The Lost Gospel: The Book of Q and Christian Origin*. San Francisco: HarperSanFrancisco, 1993.
———. *Who Wrote the New Testament? The Making of the Christian Myth*. San Francisco: HarperSanFrancisco, 1995.
Marcus, Joel. *Mark 1–8: A New Translation with Introduction and Commentary*. Anchor Bible 27. New York: Doubleday, 2000.
Martin, Ralph P. *Carmen Christ: Philippians 2:5–11 in Recent Interpretation and in the Setting of Early Christian Worship*. 2nd ed. Society for New Testament Studies Monograph Series 4. Grand Rapids: Eerdmans, 1983.
Mearns, Christopher L. "Dating the Similitudes of Enoch." *NTS* 25 (1979) 360–69.
Meeks, Wayne A. "The Image of the Androgyne: Some Uses of a Symbol in Earliest Christianity." *History of Religions* 13 (1974) 165–208.
Moon, Wooil. "A Philosophical Analysis of the Concept of Logos in the Fourth Gospel." *KNTS* 20 (2013) 339–69.
Neirynck, F. "The First Synoptic Pericope: The Appearance of John the Baptist in Q?" *ETL* 72 (1996) 41–74.
Osiek, Carolyn. *Philippians, Philemon*. Abingdon New Testament Commentaries. Nashville, TN: Abingdon, 2000.

Owen, Paul, and David Shepherd. "Speaking Up for Qumran, Dalman and the Son of Man: Was *Bar Enasha* A Common Term for 'Man' in the Time of Jesus?" *JSNT* 81 (2001) 81–122.

Pokony, Petr. "The Temptation Stories and Their Intention." *NTS* 20 (1973–1974) 115–27.

Ra, Yoseop. "Return to the Garden of Eden: The Adamic Jesus and the Gardenic Kingdom of Heaven in Matthew's Gospel." PhD diss., Iliff School of Theology and University of Denver, 1997.

———. *Paul the Founder of Christianity*. Daegu, South Korea: My Lord, 2011.

———. *Q: The First Writing about Jesus*. Daegu, South Korea: My Lord, 2002.

Reuman, John Henry Paul. *Philippians: A New Translation with Introduction and Commentary*. Anchor Yale Bible 33B. New Haven: Yale University Press, 2008.

Robbins, Vernon K. "Last Meal: Preparation, Betrayal, and Absence (Mark 14:12–25)." In *The Passion in Mark. Studies on Mark 14–16*, edited by Werner H. Kelber, 21–40. Philadelphia: Fortress, 1976.

Robinson, James McConkey, et al., eds. *The Critical Edition of Q: Synopsis Including the Gospels of Matthew and Luke, Mark and Thomas*. Hermeneia: A Critical and Historical Commentary on the Bible. Minneapolis: Fortress, 2000.

Rowley, H. H. *Jewish Apocalyptic and the Dead Sea Scrolls*. London: Athlone, 1957.

Sand, Alexander. *Reich Gottes und Eheverzicht im Evangelium nach Matthäus*. Stuttgart, Germany: Katholisches Bibelwerk, 1983.

Sato, Migaku. *Q und Prophetie: Studien zur Gattungs-und Traditionsgeschichte der Quelle Q*. WUNT 29. Tübingen, Germany: Mohr-Siebeck, 1971.

Schnelle, Udo. *History and Theology of the New Testament Writing*. Translated by M. Eugene Boring. Minneapolis: Fortress, 1998.

Schulz, Siegfried. *Q: Die Spruchquelle der Evangelisten*. Zürich: Theologischer, 1972.

Scroggs, Robin. *The Last Adam: A Study in Pauline Anthropology*. Philadelphia: Fortress, 1966.

Seeley, David. "The Background of the Philippians Hymn (2:6–11)." *The Journal of Higher Criticism* 1 (1994) 49–72.

Senior, Donald. *The Passion of Jesus in the Gospel of Mark*. Collegeville, MN: Liturgical, 1984.

Seo, Dong Soo. "Der historische Jesus: Eine kleine Untersuchung ueber die Relation der theologischen Bedeutungen von Gottes Sohn in Roem 1,3–4 und Gottes Gestalt in Phil 2,6–11." *KNTS* 12 (2005) 461–95.

Shin, Dong-Ook. "Die paulinischen Auswirkungen auf die Apokalypse des Johannes." *KNTS* 20 (2013) 817–54.

Standhartinger, Angela. "'Join in Imitating Me' (Philippians 3:17)." *NTS* 54 (2008) 418–26.

Steck, Odil Hannes. *Israel und das gewaltsame Geschick der Propheten: Untersuchung zur Überlieferung des deuteronomistischen Geschichtsbildes im Alten Testament, Spätjudentum und Urchristentum*. WMANT 23. Neukirchen-Vluyn, Germany: Neukirchen Verlag, 1967.

Theissen, Gerd. *The Gospels in Context: Social and Political History in the Synoptic Tradition*. Translated by L. M. Malony. Minneapolis: Fortress, 1991.

Tuckett, Christopher M. *Q and the History of Early Christianity: Studies on Q*. Edinburgh: Hendrickson, 1996.

Turner, M. M. B. "The Concept of Receiving the Spirit in John's Gospel." *VoxEv* 10 (1977) 24–42.
Uittenbogaard, Aire. "Etymology and Meaning of the Name Miriam." *Abarim Publications*, http://www.abarim-publications.com/Meaning/Miriam.html.
Vermes, Geza. *The Dead Sea Scrolls in English*. 3rd ed. London: Penguin, 1987.
Verseput, Donald J. *The Rejection of the Humble Messianic Kingdom*. Frankfurt: Peter Lang, 1986.
Vielhauer, Philipp. "Paul and the Cephas Party in Corinth." *The Journal of Higher Criticism* 1 (1994) 129–42.
Waetjen, Herman C. *A Reordering of Power. A Sociopolitical Reading of Mark's Gospel*. Philadelphia: Fortress, 1989.
Weber, Hans-Ruedi. *Kreuz: Uberlieferung und Deutung der Kreuzigung Jesu im Neutestamentlichen Kulturraum*. Stuttgart, Germany: Kreuz, 1975.
Westermann, Claus. *Genesis 1–11: A Continental Commentary*. Translated by J. Scullion. Minneapolis: Fortress, 1984.
Wright, N. T. "Adam in Pauline Christology." In *1983 SBLSP*, edited by K. H. Richards, 359–89. Chico, CA: Scholars, 1983.

Ancient Document Index

Genesis

1:2	147
1:3–31	176
2:7	140, 142, 160
2:8	155
2:9	155
2:16–17	155
2:17	144
2:18	155
2:18—3:24	106
2:19	143
2:20–23	160
2:21–23	155
2:24	157
2:24–25	155
3:1–6	144, 149
3:4	150, 155
3:6	64, 150, 151
3:6–7	154
3:6–10	155
3:8–10	148
3:11–14	155
3:11–21	154
3:15	106, 143, 144, 163, 164, 168, 169, 177
3:17–18	143
3:19	140, 144
3:22–24	144, 148, 159
3:24	143, 153, 159
4:1	155
4:1–7	154
5:24	126
11:31–32	4
12:1–5	4
12:3	34
30:22–24	173
37:5–11	173
37:25–36	172
39:7–18	173
40:5–43	173
41:14–36	173
46:1–7	172

Exodus

2:4–10	170
3:10	29, 49, 169, 171
12:1–14	63, 194
12:46	65
13:19	172
14:21–25	46
20:18	128
23:20	43
34:29–35	47

Leviticus

5:6	189
5:9	189
7:2	189

Numbers

9:12	65
20:10–13	34, 46

Deuteronomy

6:13	44, 151
6:16	44, 151
8:3	44, 151
21:23	20
34:6	85
34:1–8	92

Judges

8:23	99n2

2 Samuel

7:11–14	19n16, 165, 176

1 Kings

17:8–16	27
17:17–24	27

2 Kings

2:11	85
4:1–7	27
4:17–37	27
4:42–44	27

Psalms

2:7	14, 19n16, 147, 165, 168
22:1	62
22:7	62
22:8	64, 150
22:18	62, 65
69:21	62, 65
91:11–12	149
110:1	119, 122
145:13	99n2
146:10	100n2

Proverbs

8:22–31	176

Isaiah

1–39	13n5
7:14	169, 171, 172
29:18–19	32, 77
35:5–6	32, 77
40–55	13n5
40:3	43
42:1	14, 147
42:1–4	28, 186
45	141n4
52:13—53:12	20, 20n17, 27, 47, 185
53:4	28, 49, 186
53:6	67
53:7	30, 65, 67
53:7–8	187
53:7–9	48
53:9	63, 71, 73
53:10	26, 28, 35, 36, 49, 67, 170, 183, 184, 186, 187, 201
53:12	28, 187
56–66	13n5
60:2	89
61:1	32, 77

Jeremiah

31:29–30	194
31:29–33	197
31:31–34	194

Ezekiel

1:24	128
40–47	107
40:1–2	153
40:2	107, 144, 152
47:6–12	107, 144
47:12	148, 152, 153

Daniel

7:13–14	14, 118, 122, 123, 126, 130, 131, 132, 135, 184

Hosea

6:1–2	78, 79, 87

Jonah

1:17	78n2

Malachi

3:1	43

Wisdoms

2:16–18	150
9	176

Sirach

24	176

Jubilees

2:5–7	111
3:9	143, 152
3:9–14	158n22
3:15	143
3:17	149
3:18	150
3:19	152
3:34	158
4:25–26	144, 153
4:26	107
8:19	144, 153

1 Enoch

1–36	101n4
18:6–8	107
18:8	152
18:14	101
24:3—25:5	148
24:4–6	107, 152
24:4—25:6	144, 153
25:5–6	107, 152
32:1–3	107
32:4	107
37:5	104
39:3–4	104, 109
39:8	104
46:2–6	118
48:3	118
48:6	118
58:3	112
60:23	104, 109
61:8	104
62:7	118

Testament of Twelve Patriarchs

T Levi 18:11	148

Apocalypse of Moses

7:2–3	149
16:1	149
17:1	149
17:5	150
29:10–11	152
37:5–6	109
40:1	109

Ascension of Moses

10:11	85

2 Enoch

8:1	110
8:6	107
31:1–2	111
31:3–6	149
42:3	110
42:3–4	112
72:1	152

4 Ezra

3:6	111
8:11	148

Jewish Antiquities

15:395	107, 152

Jewish War

5:210–211	107, 152

Q

3:2–4	9
3:2b–4	26
3:4	43
3:7–8a	9
3:7–9	26
3:8bc	9, 13n6
3:9	9
3:16–17	9, 26
3:21–22	9, 14, 19, 26, 44, 142, 147, 168, 171
3:22	142, 165, 168
4:1–13	9, 13, 14, 26, 44, 54, 117n3, 143, 152
4:4	44
4:8	44
4:9–12	54
4:12	44
6:12–16	9
6:13–16	13, 14, 16, 26, 44, 185
6:20a	9
6:20b	9, 33, 100, 100n3
6:21	9, 100n3
6:22	117
6:22–23b	9, 19, 100n3
6:23c	9, 33, 54, 100n3, 101
6:27–38	9
6:39–42	10
6:43–45	10
6:46	129
6:46–49	10
7:1–10	10
7:6–7	129
7:18–27	10
7:22	32, 33, 37, 76, 77, 78
7:24–26	33
7:27	26, 43
7:28	10, 101, 163
7:29–30	10
7:31–34	10
7:34	117
7:35	10
9:57–58	10
9:58	117
9:59–60	10, 54
10:2	10, 129
10:3	10, 54
10:4–11	26
10:4–12	10
10:9	100, 108
10:13–16	10, 19
10:21–22	14, 19
10:21–24	10, 44
10:24	33
11:2	100, 109, 145
11:2–4	10
11:4	145
11:9–10	10
11:11–13	10
11:14–15	10, 26
11:16	11, 26
11:17–20	10, 26
11:20	100, 103, 104
11:21–23	10
11:24–26	10
11:29–30	11, 26
11:30	117, 147
11:31	77, 78
11:31–32	11, 77, 128
11:32	33, 77, 78, 80, 147
11:33	26, 107n11
11:33–35	11
11:39–46	11, 19
11:47	33
11:47–51	11, 54, 56n2, 101
11:52	11, 19
12:2–3	11, 26, 129
12:4–5	11, 54
12:6–7	11
12:8–9	11, 14, 116, 117, 129
12:10	117, 117n3
12:10–12	11
12:22–31	11
12:31	100
12:33–34	11
12:39	129

12:39–40	11, 100, 117, 125, 129, 134
12:40	14, 131
12:42–46	11, 100, 129
12:49	11
12:49–53	54
12:51–53	11
12:54–56	11
12:58–59	11
13:18–19	26, 107
13:18–20	126
13:18–21	11, 100
13:20–21	107
13:24–27	11, 100, 101
13:25	129
13:28	104
13:28–30	11, 101
13:34	33
13:34–35	11, 54, 101
14:5	12, 12n4, 13
14:8	11
14:11	11
14:16–24	11, 111, 111n19
14:26–27	11, 26, 53
14:34–35	11
15:4–7	11
16:13	11
16:16	10, 12n4, 101
16:16–18	13
16:17–18	12, 12n4
17:1–2	12, 54
17:3–4	11
17:6	10
17:23–24	12, 100, 117, 129
17:24	14, 117, 131, 134
17:26	117
17:26–27	12, 100, 117, 126, 129, 131
17:30	14, 100, 117, 126, 129, 131
17:33	11, 26, 54, 72
17:34–35	12, 100, 126, 128, 129
17:37	54
17:37c	12
19:12–26	12
22:30	12, 14, 44, 109, 131

Matthew

1:1	170
1:16	173
1:18–19	158
1:18–20	171
1:18–21	173
1:18–25	169, 172
1:18—2:23	170
1:20	170, 173
1:21	29, 49, 169, 171, 186, 199
1:22	37
1:22–23	49, 171
1:23	84, 121
2:1–12	28, 170
2:5	48
2:13	173
2:13–23	29, 49
2:15	37, 49
2:17–18	37, 49
2:19	173
2:23	37, 49
3:1–3	9
3:2	108
3:3	49
3:5–6	9
3:7–9a	9
3:9bc	9
3:10	9
3:11–12	9
3:13–17	29, 146
3:16	146, 147
3:16–17	9, 49, 171
3:17	148
4:1	149
4:1–11	9, 28, 29, 49, 149
4:3	64, 149, 150
4:3–4	150
4:4	48, 151, 153
4:5	149, 152
4:5–7	150
4:6	48, 64, 149
4:7	44, 48, 151, 153
4:8	149
4:8–10	150
4:9	64
4:10	48, 149, 151, 153

Matthew (continued)

Reference	Page
4:11	153
4:14	37
4:14–16	49
4:17	108
4:23	37
5–7	29
5:1a	9
5:1b	9
5:1—7:27	28, 29, 49, 170
5:2b–3	9
5:4	9
5:6	9
5:11–12b	9
5:12c	9
5:13	11
5:15	11
5:18	12
5:19–20	170
5:20	109
5:21	49
5:21–22	154
5:21–48	154
5:25–26	11
5:27	49, 155
5:31	49, 155
5:32	12
5:33	49, 155
5:37	155
5:38	49
5:38–39a	155
5:39–40	9
5:39b–42	155
5:42	9
5:43	49, 155
5:44	9
5:45	155
5:45–48	9
6:9–13	10
6:10	109
6:19–21	11
6:22–23	11
6:24	11
6:25–33	11
7:1–2	9
7:3–5	10
7:7–8	10
7:9–11	10
7:12	9
7:13–14	11
7:16	10
7:18	10
7:21	10, 170
7:21–23	109
7:22–23	11
7:24–27	10
8:1—9:34	29, 49
8:5–10	10
8:11–12	11
8:13	10
8:17	28, 37, 49, 186
8:17–18	49
8:19–20	10
8:21–22	10
9:2–6	186
9:8	186
9:13	49
9:27	170
9:35	37
9:37–38	10
10	29
10:2–4	9, 29, 49
10:7	108
10:7–15	10
10:16	147
10:16a	10
10:18–19	11
10:24–25	10
10:26–27	11
10:28	11
10:29–31	11
10:32–33	11, 120
10:34–36	11
10:37–38	11
10:39	11
10:40	10
11:2–10	10
11:5	37
11:10	48
11:11	10
11:12	109
11:12–13	10
11:16–19a	10
11:19c	10
11:21–23	10

11:24	10	20:16	11
11:25–27	10	20:28	28, 49
12:7	49	20:30–31	170
12:11–12	12	21:1—27:66	49
12:17–21	37, 49	21:4	37
12:18–21	28, 186	21:4–5	49
12:22–28	10	21:9	170
12:23	170	21:12–17	29
12:29–30	10	21:13	48
12:32	11	21:15	170
12:33–35	10	21:16	49
12:38–40	11	21:31	109
12:39–40	78n2	21:31–32	10
12:41–42	11	21:33–41	110
12:43–45	10	21:42	49
13	29	22:1–10	11, 111
13:11	110	22:24	49
13:14–15	49	22:32	49
13:16–17	10	22:37	49
13:24–30	110	22:39	49
13:31–32	110	22:42–45	170
13:31–33	11	22:44	49
13:35	37, 49	23:4	11
13:44	110	23:6	11
13:44–46	111	23:6–7	11
13:47–50	110	23:12	11
13:55	172	23:13	11, 111
15:4	49	23:23	11
15:8–9	49	23:25–26	11
15:14	10	23:27–28	11
15:22	170	23:29–31	11
16:2–3	11	23:34–36	11
16:27–17:8	109	23:37–39	11
17:1–8	29, 49	24:14	37
17:20	10	24:15	49
18:6–7	12	24:26–27	12
18:12–14	11	24:27	131
18:15	11	24:28	12
18:20	84, 121	24:29–31	120
18:21–22	11	24:31	131
18:21–35	110	24:37–39	12, 131
19:5	49	24:40–41	12, 120
19:7	49	24:43–44	11
19:10–12	156n16	24:44	131
19:12	156	24:45–51	11
19:18–19	49	25–27	29
19:28	12, 109	25:1–13	111
20:1–16	110	25:10–12	11

Matthew (continued)

25:14–30	12, 110
25:31	131
25:31–46	110
25:34	111
26:6–16	73
26:26–29	198
26:28	64, 186
26:31	48
26:36–46	153
26:54	49
26:64	121, 131
27:9	37, 49
27:25	186
27:32–44	149
27:33–34	150
27:34	64
27:40	64, 149, 152
27:40–42	149, 150
27:41	149
27:42	151
27:42–43	64
27:43	64, 149, 150
27:44	149
27:45–57	146
27:46	49
27:50	146, 153
27:52	147
27:52–53	147
27:54	148
27:57	73
28:1–10	83
28:2	153
28:11–15	84
28:16–20	28, 29, 49, 92
28:20	84, 121

Mark

1:1	26, 35
1:2	47
1:2–5	26
1:4	184
1:7–8	26
1:9–11	26, 142
1:10	142
1:10–11	168, 171
1:11	142, 168
1:12–13	26, 106, 143, 152
1:12–15	143
1:14	108, 153
1:14–15	35
1:15	105, 106
1:16–20	27
2:1–12	27
2:10	184
2:17	184
2:23—3:6	27
3:16–19	26
3:22–29	26
3:31–32	167
4:1–20	27
4:3–9	106
4:11	106
4:12	47
4:14–20	106
4:21–22	26, 107n11
4:26–29	106
4:30–32	26, 107
5:22–24	27
5:35–43	29
6:3	167, 169
6:7–11	26
6:35–44	27
7:6	47
7:10	47
8:1–10	27
8:11–12	26
8:31	48, 62, 71, 82
8:34–35	26
8:35	35, 62, 72, 198
9:1–8	107, 109
9:2–13	27
9:4	168
9:31	48, 62, 71, 82
10:2–12	157
10:4	47
10:19	47
10:29	35, 198
10:29–30	62
10:33–34	48, 62, 71, 82
10:35–40	71
10:38–39	62, 196
10:45	26, 28, 36, 49, 62, 184, 186, 187, 196, 19

10:47–48	168	15:34	47, 62
11:1—15:47	47	15:36	62, 107
11:15–18	29	15:38	142
11:17	47	15:39	63
12:1–12	108n14, 110	15:42–47	70
12:10–11	47	15:42—16:4	71
12:19	47	15:47—16:2	72
12:26	47	16:1–8	27, 82
12:29–31	47	16:5	72
12:35–37	168	16:7	82, 91
12:36	47	16:8	73, 82n3
13:26	130		
13:26–27	134	Luke	
14:3–9	35, 71		
14:8–9	62	1:5–25	174
14:10–11	185	1:26–33	174
14:12–26	196	1:27–38	174
14:24	36, 62, 63, 64, 184, 196, 198	1:30–32	174
		1:39–56	174
14:25	107, 197	1:57–80	174
14:27	47	1:77	187
14:27–31	48	2:1–2	173
14:28	82, 91	2:1–7	174
14:32–42	27, 144	2:1–21	28
14:34–36	196	2:22–39	174
14:36	36, 62	2:23	50
14:38	184	2:24	50
14:49	47	2:39	174
14:50	48	3:2–4	9
14:51–52	72	3:4	50
14:53–65	27	3:7–8a	9
14:60	48	3:8bc	9
14:60–65	119	3:8–14	187
14:62	121, 131, 134	3:9	9
14:66–72	48	3:16–17	9
15:4	48	3:21–22	9
15:6–16	27	3:23–38	115, 160
15:20	48	4:1–13	9, 28
15:21–32	27	4:4	50
15:21–39	62	4:8	50
15:21–41	36, 145, 184, 196	4:10	50
15:23	107	4:12	50
15:24	47, 62	4:16–30	29
15:27	63	4:17	50
15:29	62	4:21	37, 50
15:30	63	4:43	37
15:31	47	5:8–11	187
15:31–32	63	5:24	188

Luke (continued)

6:3	50
6:12–16	9
6:20	114
6:20a	9
6:20b	9
6:20–49	28
6:21	9
6:22–23b	9
6:23c	9
6:27–38	9
6:39–42	10
6:43–45	10
6:46–49	10
7:1–10	10
7:16	29
7:18–27	10
7:22	37
7:27	50
7:28	10
7:29–30	10
7:31–34	10
7:34	199
7:35	10
7:36–50	73, 188
8:1	37
9:2	114
9:27–36	114
9:29–30	123
9:30	85
9:57–58	10
9:59–60	10
10:2	10
10:3	10
10:4–12	10
10:9	114
10:13–16	10
10:21–24	10
10:27	50
11:2–4	10
11:9–10	10
11:11–13	10
11:14–15	10
11:16	11
11:17–20	10
11:20	114
11:21–23	10
11:24–26	10
11:29–30	11
11:31–32	11
11:33–35	11
11:39–46	11
11:47–51	11
11:52	11
12:2–3	11
12:4–5	11
12:6–7	11
12:8–9	11
12:10–12	11
12:22–31	11
12:33–34	11
12:39–40	11, 134
12:42–46	11
12:49	11
12:51–53	11
12:54–56	11
12:58–59	11
13:18–21	11, 114
13:24–27	11
13:28–30	11, 114
13:29–30	114
13:34–35	11
14:5	12
14:8	11
14:11	11
14:15	114, 199
14:16–24	11, 111n19
14:26–27	11
14:34–35	11
15:3–10	199
15:4–7	11
16:13	11
16:16	10, 37
16:17–18	12
17:1–2	12
17:3–4	11
17:6	10
17:21	114
17:23–24	12
17:24	134
17:26–27	12
17:30	12
17:33	11
17:34–35	12
17:37c	12

18:16–17	114	3:5	112, 177
18:20	50	3:13	121, 132
18:31	50	5:39	50
18:31–33	67	6:31	50
19:1–10	18	6:35	30
19:11	114	6:38	175, 177
19:12–26	12	6:45	50
19:45–48	29	6:51	175, 177
19:46	50	6:52–59	200
20:17	50	6:62	121, 132
20:28	50	7:42	50
20:37	50	8:2	50
20:42	50	8:2–11	29n28
21:27	134	8:12	30
21:31	114	10:9	30
22:14–20	199	10:11	30
22:16–18	114	11:25	30
22:20	114	12:1–8	74
22:29–30	199	12:15	50
22:30	12	12:38	50
22:37	28, 50, 187	12:40	50
22:69	134	13:1	187
23:34	67, 188	13:18	50
23:39–43	67	13:34–35	30
23:42–43	115, 161	14:2–3	132
23:47	67	14:6	30
23:51	114	14:22	185n2
24:1–12	84	14:28	132
24:4	123	15:1	30
24:12–35	93	15:25	50
24:13–35	28	16:7	121
24:26–27	37	16:17	122
24:27	50	16:28	122
24:36–49	93	17:11	122
24:43	159n24	17:12	50
24:44–45	37, 50	18:36	112
24:50–51	123	18:38	65
		18:39	187

John

1:1–18	29n28, 30, 176	19:4	65
1:3	112	19:6	65
1:23	50	19:7–11	65
1:29	30, 65, 187, 189	19:12–16	65
1:45–46	175	19:20–22	65
2:13–22	29	19:24	50, 65
2:17	50	19:25–27	65
3:3	112, 177	19:28	50, 65
		19:30	65
		19:31–37	65

John (continued)

19:34	132
19:36	50, 65
19:36–41	74
19:37	50
19:41	159
20:1–13	84
20:11–18	159
20:11–29	92
20:19–23	160

Acts

1:3–5	93
1:6–11	93, 123
1:11	134
1:16	50
1:21–22	94
1:22	85
2:24	85
2:31	85
3:15	85
3:18	37
3:18–26	50
3:20–21	134
3:20–26	37
4:10	85
5:30	85
8:32–33	28
8:32–35	187
9:1–9	19, 93
9:20–22	15n11
9:23–25	15
10:40	85
13:27	50
13:29	50
13:37	85
15:1–21	16n13
15:36–41	26
17:3	85
17:31	85
22:5–16	94
26:12–18	94
26:23	85

Romans

1:1–17	24
1:2–3	34, 201
1:3	162, 164, 165, 168, 170
1:4	59, 81, 103n6, 171
1:17	46
1:18—3:31	24
2:17–29	61
2:24	46
3:4	46
3:10	46
3:22	104, 109
3:24	183
3:25	190
4:1—5:11	24
4:3	46
4:6–8	46
4:13–15	24, 61
4:17	46
4:18	46
4:23	46
4:24	59, 81
4:24–25	183
5:6–8	183
5:6–10	59
5:9	66, 183, 188, 189, 190
5:12—8:30	24
5:14	47
5:14–15	140
5:17–18	140
5:20	61
6:3–4	69
6:3–11	59
6:4	81
6:6	183
6:6–7	60
6:9	81
7:4	81
7:4–6	60, 61
8:3	61
8:11	60, 81
8:15	144
8:31–39	24
8:34	60, 81, 119, 121
8:36	46
9–11	24n25

9:1—12:2	24	1:18—3:15	23
9:13	46	1:19	46
9:15	46	1:31	46
9:25–26	46	2:4	103
9:27–28	46	2:6–16	61
9:29	46	2:9	46
9:31	61	3:16	127
9:33	46	3:16–17	22, 180
10:5	46	3:18–23	23
10:7–9	60	3:19	46
10:9	81	4:1–21	23
10:11	46	4:5	129
10:15	46	4:20	103
10:17	203	5:1–5	23, 181
10:19	46	5:5	181
10:20	46	5:6–8	23
11:8	46	5:7	182, 183, 187
11:9	46	5:9–13	23
11:26	46	5:11	181
12:3–13	24	6:1–11	23
12:14—13:7	24	6:9–10	102, 106n10, 181
12:19	46	6:9–11	109
13:8–14	24	6:11	103, 104, 181
14:1—16:16	24	6:12–20	23
14:7	59	6:13–18	180
14:9	59, 81	6:13–19	180
14:11	46	6:14	80, 188
14:15	59	6:14–15	56
14:17	104	6:15	102
15:3	46	6:16	46
15:9	46	6:18	102, 180
15:10	46	6:19	180
15:12	46	6:20	180, 185, 188, 190
15:21	46	7:1–17	23
16:3	165	7:18–24	23
16:17–20	24	7:23	182, 185, 190
16:21–27	24	7:25–40	23, 157
		7:28	158, 180
		7:36	180
1 Corinthians		7:38	158
1:1–9	22	7:40	158
1:7	127	8:1–13	23
1:8	127	8:11	57, 60n4,
1:10–17	23, 56, 181	8:12	181
1:18	182	9:1–2	91
1:18–25	62	9:1–27	23
1:18—2:9	19	9:4–7	23
1:18—2:16	25, 58	9:5	167

1 Corinthians (continued)

9:8–9	61
9:9	46
9:10	46
9:20–21	61
10:1–2	46
10:1–22	23
10:3–6	193
10:4	34, 46
10:7	46, 180
10:8	180
10:14	180
10:14–21	193
10:16	193
10:23—11:1	23
11:2	61, 127
11:2–16	23
11:17–29	23
11:18–22	181
11:18–29	193
11:23	193, 194
11:23–26	18, 57
11:24–25	194
11:24–26	60n4
11:26	128, 195
11:27	181
11:27–29	195
11:30–32	23
11:33–34	23
12:1	23
12:1–3	61
12:2–3	23
12:4–12	23
12:13	23
12:14–31a	23
12:31b—14:1a	22, 23
13:3–5	180
14:1b–19	23
14:20–22	22, 23
14:21	46, 61, 127
14:23–25	22
14:23–33a	23
14:33b–38	23
14:34	61, 127
14:39–40	23
15:1–2	89
15:1–8	14
15:1–11	22, 23
15:2	182
15:3	4, 19, 20n17, 25, 26, 35, 58, 182, 183, 188, 201
15:3–5	14, 16n12, 27n27
15:3–8	15
15:3b–5a	16, 18, 41
15:3b–5	15
15:3b–7	15
15:4	16n12, 68, 69, 77, 79, 80
15:5	13, 16n12, 89, 90n1
15:5–8	90
15:8	15
15:12–26	80
15:12–28	22, 23, 139
15:17	181
15:20	84
15:21	140
15:21–22	47
15:22	140
15:23–24	128
15:24–25	102n5
15:29–34	23
15:34	182
15:35–49	23, 139
15:44	140
15:45	46, 47, 140
15:46	140
15:50	103
15:50–58	23
15:54	46
15:56	61, 182
16:1–4	23
16:5–6	23
16:7–9	23
16:10–11	23
16:12	23
16:13–14	23
16:15–18	23
16: 19–24	23
16:22	129

2 Corinthians

1:1—2:13	23
2:4	23

2:13	22	2:1–14	25
2:14—6:13	23	2:16	104, 109
2:14—7:4	22	2:18–19	61
3:2–18	47	2:20	59, 60n4, 182
4:13	46	3:1	25, 59, 145
4:14	80	3:1–5	61
5:17–19	66	3:3	103
5:19	182	3:5	103n6
6:2	46	3:8	34
6:11–13	22	3:10	46, 61
6:14—7:1	22	3:13	20, 25, 46, 59, 145, 182, 185, 189, 201
6:16–18	46		
7:2–4	22, 23	3:16	164
7:5	22	3:19	61, 182
7:5–16	23	3:19–21	163
7:8	23	3:27	70, 72
8:1–24	23	3:27–28	70n2
8:12	22	4:4	105, 164, 168, 169, 177
8:15	46		
9:1–15	23	4:4–5	162, 163, 164, 188
9:6	22	4:4–6	143, 144, 163, 171
9:9	46	4:5	182, 185, 190
10:1—13:10	23	4:21	61
11:5	59	4:22	46
11:12–15	23	4:25	15
11:13–15	59	4:27	46
11:21–27	23	4:29	103
11:32–33	15	5:3	61
12:1–4	104, 109	5:11	59
12:4	159n24	5:14	46
12:21	106n10	5:16–17	103
13:4	59, 80	5:19–21	103, 109
13:11–13	23	5:21–22	104
		5:24	59, 182
		6:8	103

Galatians

		6:12	59
1:1	59, 80	6:13	61
1:4	20, 26, 59, 182	6:14	59, 182
1:13	18		
1:15–16	18, 165	## Ephesians	
1:15–17	15, 16, 19		
1:15–18	16n13	1:7	188
1:16	164	1:13	38
1:17	18	1:14	188
1:18–19	16, 18, 19	1:20	85
1:19	167	1:20–21	122
1:22–23	18	2:5	85
2:1–10	16n13	2:13	188

Ephesians (continued)

2:16	66
3:6-7	38
4:9-10	122
5:2	188
5:5	113

Philippians

1:1	21
1:1—3:1a	21
2:5-11	60, 60n3, 141, 141n4
2:6-7	166
2:7	162
2:9	81
2:25—3:1a	21
3:1a	21
3:1b	21n21
3:1b-6	58
3:1b—4:3	21
3:5-6	18
3:9	61
3:10	58, 80
3:18	58
3:19-20	58
3:20	129
4:3	21
4:4-7	21
4:8	21
4:8-9	21
4:10-23	21

Colossians

1:13	113
1:14	188
1:15	175
1:17	175
1:18	84, 85
1:20-22	66
2:12	74, 85
2:13	188
2:14-15	66
3:1	122
3:4	133
4:11	113

1 Thessalonians

1:1—2:16	20
1:9	180, 193
1:10	19, 26, 56, 80, 127, 180
2:7	90
2:10	180
2:12	102
2:14	18
2:14-16	56n2
2:15	56
2:16	180
2:17—3:13	20, 21
3:13	128, 181
4:1	20
4:1-8	20
4:1-28	20
4:3	180
4:3-6	102, 180
4:7	102, 180
4:9—5:28	21
4:13-17	118-9, 128
4:14	58, 80, 181
4:15	129
4:16	131
4:16-17	121
4:17	128
5:4	129, 131
5:9-10	58, 60n4, 181
5:10	19
5:23	128, 181

2 Thessalonians

1:5	113
1:7	133
1:10	133
2:1	133
2:8	133

1 Timothy

1:15	188
2:6	188
6:14	133

2 Timothy

2:8	66, 85, 176
4:1	113, 133
4:8	133
4:11	26

Titus

2:4	188

Hebrews

1:2–4	51
1:3	122
1:5	176
1:5–14	51
1:6	133, 176
1:8	114
2:6–8	51, 114
2:12–13	51
3:1	51
3:7–11	51
3:15	50
4:1	38
4:2	38
4:3	51
4:4–5	51
4:6	38
4:7	51
4:14	122
5:3	189
5:5–6	51
6:6	66
6:14	51
7:17	51
7:21	51
7:27	189
8:1	122
8:5	51
8:8	51
9:12	189
9:14–15	189
9:20	51
9:26–28	189
9:28	134
10:5–7	51
10:8	51
10:10	189
10:12	122, 189
10:14	189
10:15	51
10:30	51
10:37–38	51
12:2	66, 122, 189
12:5–6	51
12:20–21	51
12:28	114
13:5–6	51
13:20	86

James

2:5	114

1 Peter

1:2	189
1:3	66, 86
1:7	134
1:12	38
1:13	134
1:18–19	189
1:21	66, 86
1:25	38
2:22–25	66
2:23	67
2:24	189
2:24–25	67
3:18	66, 189
3:21	86
4:6	38
4:17	38

2 Peter

1:11	114

1 John

1:7	190
2:2	190
2:28	133
4:10	190
5:5–7	177

Revelation

1:5	84, 190
1:7	132
2:7	148, 159n24
5:6–8	189
5:9	190
10:7	38
11:15	112
12:10	112
14:3–4	190
14:6	39
20:1–15	102n5
21:1–2	113
21:1—22:5	110, 112
21:10	153
21:12–21	112
22:1–2	112, 113
22:1–5	113
22:2–4	153
22:3	112
22:5	112
22:20	132

Hymns of Thanksgiving (1QH)

8:4	108, 141, 159
8:6	108, 141, 159
8:16	108, 141, 159
8:21–23	108, 141, 159

www.ingramcontent.com/pod-product-compliance
Lightning Source LLC
Chambersburg PA
CBHW062019220426
43662CB00010B/1389